PROJECT DISCLOSURE: REVEALING GOVERNMENT SECRETS AND BREAKING THE TRUTH EMBARGO

CONSPIRACIES AND COVER-UPS

PROJECT DISCLOSURE: REVEALING GOVERNMENT SECRETS AND BREAKING THE TRUTH EMBARGO

RICHARD M. DOLAN
AND BRYCE ZABEL

ROSEN
PUBLISHING®
New York

This edition published in 2015 by:
The Rosen Publishing Group, Inc.
29 East 21st Street
New York, NY 10010

Library of Congress Cataloging-in-Publication Data

Dolan, Richard M., author.
[A.D., after disclosure]
Project disclosure: revealing government secrets and breaking the truth embargo /Richard M. Dolan and Bryce Zabel.
pages cm. — (Conspiracies and cover-ups)
Originally published as A.D., after disclosure. Pompton Plains, N.J. : New Page Books, ©2012.
Includes bibliographical references and index.
ISBN 978-1-4777-8155-5 (library bound)
1. Unidentified flying objects—Sightings and encounters. 2. Unidentified flying objects—Social aspects. 3. Government information—United States. 4. Conspiracies—United States. I. Zabel, Bryce, author. II. Title.
TL789.D65 2015
001.942—dc23

2014029490

Manufactured in the United States

Acknowledgments

From Richard

In the course of my research, there have been many individuals who have helped me in my journey on the difficult road of envisioning a world in which the truth of UFOs is openly known. Among them all, two friends stand out.

One of them is Vince White. Through the years, Vince has described his vision of a post-disclosure world, of its inevitability, of the dramatic changes it will bring in its wake. I don't know of anyone who has thought this through with as much detail, or as much courage.

The other is Stephen Bassett. Anyone who has met Stephen knows the energy and focus he brings to the issue of Disclosure. Along the way he has made many admirers, and a few critics, too, who feel that "disclosure" and "exopolitics" are wrong-headed and premature in a world that will not even acknowledge the reality of UFOs themselves. Most of these criticisms are misguided, in my view. Future generations will remember Stephen as one of the key figures who helped to bring the world to an open acceptance of the truth: that "Others" are here on Earth, observing and interacting with humanity.

Other people have helped with their conversation and insights. Among them I wish to acknowledge Thomas Darling, PhD, Edgar Mitchell, ScD, Jim Marrs (who graciously wrote the Foreword to this book), and two of my U.K. friends: Nick Pope and Anthony Beckett. To these and the many others—most of whom know who they are—I offer my lasting thanks.

Finally, I would like to thank the support and patience of my family: Karyn, Michael, and Elaine. Through the thick and through the thin, they have been there to support me.

From Bryce

My journey of consciousness-raising began with my mother, Lucile Zabel, who got a copy of *The Interrupted Journey* when I was a kid and couldn't put it down.

Finding friends who will discuss UFOs without prejudice or ridicule is not always easy and, in particular, I note the many hours I've spent with my "two Dons," Don Most and Don Clark. My other open-minded friends through the years have included Roger Clark, Eric Close, Manny Coto, Matt Gross, John Landgraf, Stan Lee, Coleman Luck, Brad Markowitz, Dave Ransil, Jeff Sagansky, Fred Saxon, Whitley Strieber, Peter Telep, Tracy Torme, Jeff Wachtel, Megan Ward, Rich Whitley, and Alan Zabel. Along with my gifted coauthor Richard Dolan, the two researchers who have taught me the most are Stanton Friedman and Donald Schmitt. And the people who helped make this specific book possible include Cherish Alexander, Alex Asher Sears, Rob Kirk, and especially Nancy Tokos.

My *Dark Skies* co-creator Brent V. Friedman will be one of my very first calls when Disclosure happens. Also, David E. Kelly, who hired me to work on *L.A. Law*, because he thought a script I wrote about alien abductions felt real to him.

Thanks also go to my father, Harvey Zabel, who taught high school American history and, shortly before he died, finally talked about his Army buddy's experience at Roswell, knowing that it would mean all the textbooks from which he had taught would be re-written. And to my children —Jared, Lauren, and Jonathan—whose own children will read those new books in school.

Finally, to my wife, Jackie, who abducted my heart and always believes in me.

Contents

Foreword
by Jim Marrs

How do you—meaning you reading these words—deal with the idea of Unidentified Flying Objects?

Do you simply ignore the issue, like the majority of your fellow citizens? Do you disdain any serious discussion of the topic because it may cause discomfort to your cherished beliefs and worldview? Or, like a small minority, do you consider with an open mind the possibility that life may exist outside of our conventional three-dimensional material reality? Or perhaps you wait impatiently for a meeting with "our space brothers," as does an even smaller minority?

Regardless of your viewpoint, we—all humans on Earth—are in for a real awakening…and probably sooner rather than later.

For some, this awakening to the reality of visitation by "Others," the designation used by the authors of this book, will be a confirmation of long-held beliefs. For many more it will be a shattering of their worldview, leaving them in psychological shock and confusion…and most probably more than a little angry with the "experts" who have lied and dissembled for so long.

After all, haven't our authority figures—military officers, prominent scientists, mass media pundits—for many years told us that UFOs simply do not exist? Haven't the people who said such things are real been denigrated as publicity seekers and nuts wearing aluminum hats? Haven't all UFO sightings been explained as mere illusions, secret government test craft, or misinterpreted natural phenomena? And haven't we all been schooled and conditioned to respect and trust our authorities?

In the case of UFOs, such trust and respect has been misplaced.

Since the 1940's or earlier, the Freedom of Information Act lawsuits have produced a mountain of documentary evidence that instituted a program of denial and ridicule within the highest levels of our military and government regarding UFOs. The message was, "You didn't see anything and if you persist in saying you did, then you probably need mental health care."

And it worked admirably.

Until most recently, the prospect of derision and ridicule coupled with a patriotic impulse to assist the government in hiding secrets resulted in thousands of citizens keeping mum about their personal experiences with UFOs. This resulted in a distorted view of our world and events and created a dysfunctional and hypocritical society.

After all, no matter how smart you are, if you are operating from incomplete or erroneous information, you will never have a correct understanding of any issue. Those who dismiss the idea of non-human intelligent life and UFOs will never begin to truly comprehend the full picture of our world, as they have discarded a large piece of the puzzle.

But such denial and secrecy has begun to crack in recent years with the advent of the personal camcorder and the camera-bearing cell phone. Prior to this technology, only occasionally did a person obtain a photograph of a UFO, and even then it was just a blurry spot of light in the dark sky, hardly satisfying proof to anyone.

But today, not a day goes by that someone, somewhere in the world does not get a reasonably clear picture of something unusual in the air. Naturally, this does not impinge on those whose worldview is either locked into denial or supporting some hidden agenda.

Although a good many photos are creations of Photoshop, a hubcap soaring over the backyard, or a shot of Venus on a clear night, enough are unexplainable to convince any thoughtful person that something is happening in the skies above.

The reality of UFO visitation becomes even more obvious when these photos and government documents are placed into context with physical evidence such as radar contacts, the innumerable personal accounts of sightings, and physical abduction.

So, to the open-minded, the controversy is settled—UFOs exist. Although it remains unclear whether they represent travelers from another solar or star system, another dimension, or another time line, they most certainly represent yet another part of our reality. And the sooner the human race comes to deal with this fact, the better.

The question now becomes, "Who occupies UFOs and why are they here?" And even more importantly, "What are we going to do about this new reality?"

It is this question that is addressed in this book and one that deserves serious consideration because, sooner or later, we will all have to answer this for ourselves.

Jim Marrs
Ft. Worth, Texas

Preface
by Stephen Bassett

Disclosure, the formal acknowledgment by the world's governments of an extraterrestrial presence engaging the human race, is inevitable. So was this book.

To my knowledge it is the first work to specifically and comprehensively address the concept of "big D" Disclosure from an exopolitical perspective, which is to say it attempts to bring the concept into focus for the mass of people who may have no inkling of what is headed their way.

If *The Hitchhiker's Guide to the Galaxy* is a how-to book about what to do when the world ends, this is a how-to book on what to do when a new world begins.

To this purpose Richard Dolan and Bryce Zabel are well suited. Richard is a grounded historian whose developing trilogy, *UFOs and the National Security State*, is building a chronological backbone to the history of the UFO/ET issue from 1947 onward. Bryce has written and produced for television, and thus understands how to communicate to the larger audience beyond the realms of research and academia.

Given that most parents generally have nine months to prepare for the birth of a new human being, it is somewhat unnerving that human beings will be lucky if they have 90 seconds to prepare for the birth of a new reality. This is because the United States Government has no intention of providing a user manual or early warning concerning Disclosure—the most profound event in human history. One evening you are eating Chinese take-out in front of the television. Five minutes later you are in a new paradigm, the world has changed in a billion ways and you haven't even finished the kung pao chicken.

The truth embargo (what some call the UFO cover-up) is in its seventh decade. According to Richard and Bryce, it will end soon. Pay close attention; you need to know that. All of the old paradigm assertions: "You don't have a need to know," "You can't handle the truth," and "don't ask, don't tell," will get tossed out the window. A little preparation will help ensure you don't jump out the window with them.

Many thousands of books will be written on the subject of Disclosure before the sun cools, expands, and swallows up the solar system. You'll want to read them all, but this book is a very good beginning.

But permit me to suggest that there is one group of people who desperately need to read this book ASAP. They are the elected members of Congress, the commanding officers in the military, the managers of the intelligence agencies, and most assuredly the President of the United States.

You see, there is an implicit irony in this book that may escape your notice. One of the key assumptions of this book is that governments will be forced to reveal the truth regarding an extraterrestrial presence by a dramatic event that forces their hand. This is strategically unwise. The sight of members of Congress being chased down the halls of their office buildings by packs of screaming reporters with cameras and pens clicking away will not inspire confidence in that August body, which recently hit an all time low.

Should they bother to read this book, it is quite possible they might see the wisdom of actually doing their job and effectuating a proactive, orderly Disclosure event that gets the job done without unnecessary, self-destructive melodrama.

If this happens the government would feel good about itself, the people would be more assured, and even the extraterrestrials might take comfort in the rare display of maturity on the part of human institutions.

So do yourself and your nation a favor and send a copy to your elected representatives. I'm sure they'll thank you for it in a nicely worded form letter.

Stephen Bassett
Washington, D.C.

Introduction

Thousands of books, all debating whether UFOs are real or just figments of our imaginations, have been published.

This book is not one of them.

More than six decades into this quiet revolution, we can now see the outlines of a reality that has been sneaking up on us, one step at a time.

The issue that was hushed up by one generation, then turned into an object of derision by another, now demands to be heard straight in ours.

Since the first major wave of UFO sightings in 1947, the number of people who believe that UFOs are of extraterrestrial origin has steadily risen. Today, a majority of Americans, as well as other global citizens, believe this is so, and at least five percent claim to have seen a UFO.

The evidence that something strange has been happening is voluminous and convincing. All you have to do is look for it. Through the years, determined researchers have forced the release of classified reports prepared by the U.S. government and other nations. These accounts tell a story of contact through the eyes of thousands of professional witnesses, such as law enforcement, military pilots, and even astronauts. Most people now reject the theory that all sightings can be explained away as weather balloons, swamp gas flares, ball lighting, or mass hallucination. Instead, they have settled on one conclusion: Some UFOs appear to be intelligently controlled physical craft of some kind from some place that is not here.

Accepting that as our starting point makes our book different.

This book is the first project to focus on what might happen after an announcement that UFOs are real.

Even if you are skeptical about UFOs, or (if you believe in them) doubt that the secrecy will end any time soon, this book should still engage you. Consider it a fascinating "What if?"

What if UFO secrecy were to end? How would that change our world?

No secret can last forever. Our society is changing so fast, so completely, that we will be unrecognizable a mere century from now. In such a world, with intelligent computers, advanced quantum computing, and nearly unforeseeable developments in global communication, can we really believe that a secret such as the presence of an alien intelligence on Earth can continue to remain hidden and undisclosed? At what point between now and then do we cross the threshold of knowing the truth about UFOs, and having an open acknowledgment of them in our world? It might be as soon as next week, or as long as several more generations, but it won't be forever. It will happen. The wall of official denial that has been in place for more than half a century is now crumbling.

And yet, an acknowledgment that "UFOs are real and some of them are *not us*" will not end the debate. It will only lead to more questions, and mark a new phase of the mystery.

Will Disclosure lead to social panic? Undermine religion? Destroy the stock market? Or will it lead to revolutionary new technologies, extended life spans, and world peace?

If alien civilizations have sent their own explorers across the universe to visit us, who are they? What do they want? And why would some of our people keep the news of their arrival from the rest of us? What will unmasking a truth of this magnitude do to our reality, our way of life, our culture, our society? Could it be that these beings are not "visitors" from another part of our universe, but full-time residents of our world already? Are even stranger physics involved, such as dimensions or time travel?

Any such revelation will be a game-changer of monumental proportions. Unlike 9/11 when we said everything changed, in this case it really will. Full Disclosure could usher in an age of human unity or one of greater global conflict. It could lead to paradise or hell.

Those are the questions that have kept us up at nights; because we wanted answers, we have written this book. Both of us feel that our previous research has led us inexorably to this project. We may now be believers in UFO reality, but we did not start out that way. We followed the facts where they led.

Richard Dolan has a graduate degree in history from the University of Rochester, where he studied U.S. Cold War strategy, Soviet history, and international diplomacy. He was writing a book about U.S. national security policy during the early Cold War when he became fixated on the issue of UFOs. His research evolved into *UFOs and the National Security State*, a multi-volume historical study of the attitudes and policies toward UFOs by the military and intelligence community, and the fascinating development of citizen movements to end UFO secrecy.

Bryce Zabel grew up near McMinnville, Oregon, just a few miles from the spot where two of the most famous UFO photographs in history were taken. Even so, as a TV network correspondent and investigative reporter, he started as a skeptic. Yet, he found his mind opening when his research for several high-profile film and TV projects suggested to him that UFOs were not science fiction, but science fact. He created the NBC TV series, *Dark Skies*, wrote the SyFy Channel's first original film *Official Denial*, and worked with Steven Spielberg on *Taken*.

Throughout both our careers, we have each sifted through the evidence, listened to the believers and deniers and, frankly, done the homework that investigative journalists and university scholars should have done, but which few have tried. And while the work has been rewarding, it has never been easy, and has often been troubling.

A detached review of the proven evidence, much of which is freely available in once-classified documents released through the Freedom of Information Act, tells us that militaries from around the world have been plagued by UFOs. There is no other way to characterize these events.

Time after time, sensitive and restricted air space has been the scene of violations by objects tracked on radar and seen visually by base personnel. Attempts to intercept have often been made, typically ending in failure. The documents describe these unknown objects as performing maneuvers that would have destroyed our best fighter aircraft. UFOs could hover indefinitely, and then accelerate instantaneously. Witnesses often described them as roundish or disk-shaped, giving rise to the term *flying saucer*.

To read one or two such reports, we might well be inclined to dismiss them as mistakes: unknown natural phenomena, equipment malfunctions, or some other error in perception. But hundreds of such reports have come down to us. Their tone is serious. Higher level military and intelligence personnel discussed them and were left perplexed and sometimes distressed.

The general scenario is clear. Advanced technology has been traversing the Earth. Regardless of who it belongs to, it is technology that is not supposed to exist—and yet it does. Moreover, those individuals in strategic positions of power were able to create and maintain a system of secrecy designed to keep the rest of the world in the dark.

Was it right to keep this secret from the people since the 1940s? To laugh at people who saw what they saw, to make them feel small and ridiculous for speaking out? To transform the most important information of our time into fodder for stand-up comedy?

No, it was not. Perhaps, after the truth is known, there will be efforts to bring some of these secret-keepers to justice. More likely, however, many people will shrug their shoulders and reflect that they might have done the same thing had they been confronted with the problem of UFOs. They will also find, as we have in the course of our research, that the problem of UFOs has seldom been clear, and never simple.

And yet, whatever the reasons for keeping us in the dark, we deserve to hear the full story now. We deserve to make our own plans. The truth may be wonderful, or it may be disturbing, but whatever it is, people have the capacity, and more importantly the right, to learn it and act upon it.

In any case, we as a society *will* learn it. The structure of secrecy, when it falls apart in the months or years ahead, could disappear with astonishing speed. One day it will be there and the next it will not.

Those who have held this secret for so long need to understand that the river of time cannot stop, and that truth cannot indefinitely be denied. The day is coming when they will be forced to come clean, and it is best for them, as well as for humanity, that they do this sooner rather than later. We will need all the wisdom, foresight, and time possible to make a smooth transition to the new reality, After Disclosure, or A.D.

To the group of beings we have come to call the "Others"—whoever and whatever they are—we want to remind them that, whatever their attitude about the human race, our scientific trajectory may soon enable us to leap into their world. It may well be that, at some point in the future, they will be forced to answer to us for past transgressions, or we may be thanking them for past services rendered. Either way, the human race is poised to advance to the next level of civilization.

If there is a final thought to the journey of this book, it is a couple words of advice: no fear. That means: Do not be afraid to express your views regarding the reality of other intelligences interacting with humanity, for the truth is that more people believe this than you realize. Do not fear the secret-keepers, for they are people, too, who have generally done what they have out of the belief that it was best. Also, do not fear their power, as they are not infallible, and time is against them. You have your own resources to marshal the truth. Do not fear the Others, either, no matter what that truth may be. Whether they are angels, demons, good, bad, or indifferent to our fate, do not fear them. You lived well enough up until now, and you will survive well enough after the Great Change. Above all, believe in humankind, in our ability to face unexpected challenges, in the strength and wisdom that reside within us, waiting for the moment to manifest.

Although the nature of this book is speculative we have worked hard to keep such speculations informed and supported by solid research. You will notice, however, that some of the sources we refer to are listed as "confidential," rather than by name. Although we wish this were not so, there are many people who have been touched by this cover-up who do not feel comfortable speaking openly, either because of past oaths of secrecy, fear of personal jeopardy, or ridicule. We want our readers to know that, through our professional training in the fields of history and investigative journalism, we have applied standards of credibility to such comments. Only those individuals who cross a threshold of reliability have been included. Hopefully, the day is not so far away when all people can speak openly on this subject.

Because we are seeking, in a sense, to paint a picture of how we believe the future will look, we have added a series of vignettes, and have placed them between the chapters of this book. These fictional depictions are meant to convey some of the ideas we are expressing, and we hope that they help the reader form a concrete idea as to how Disclosure might affect our world. Better still would be to help the reader form his or her own ideas more clearly.

A final observation about this unique study: After assessing the probable transformations that will affect our society and ourselves following Disclosure, we have gained a deeper appreciation for why UFO secrecy has been maintained for so long. In that sense, even if Disclosure were never to happen, or at least never to happen as we think it will, we feel this book is of value by demonstrating the multifaceted, revolutionary nature of the UFO phenomenon. You may not agree with all of our examples, scenarios, or conclusions, but we welcome the debate.

We are, however, confident that the truth will come out. We are not alone. And the Others are not light years away, some kind of cosmic pen-pals chatting by radio telescope. They are here, now.

The day will come when humanity reviews its history and divides it between everything before the truth was spoken outloud and everything *A.D.*, or *After Disclosure*. Soon enough, we will all be living in the brave new world of life after contact.

Richard M. Dolan
Rochester, New York

Bryce Zabel
Los Angeles, California

Chapter 1

Day One: The Day Everything Changes

However long the night,
the dawn will break.

—African Proverb

White House correspondents are in an uproar. A few hours earlier, the press secretary told them that the president would appear in the late afternoon to make a "major announcement" on a topic of "global importance." This brought howls of protest concerning the lateness of it all, a bit of unfortunate timing that guaranteed missed deadlines and high-stress "live" shots.

Even while jammed into their windowless, cramped cubicles and spartan offices in the basement of the West Wing, these elite journalists from around the world had known for days that something was going on upstairs. They had reported about the late-night comings-and-goings around other power centers of Washington, D.C., but no reporter broke a story about what it meant. Instead, they tried to draw out the truth from each other without revealing any of their own suspicions.

Now, in the James S. Brady Press Briefing Room, the anxiety is palpable. Each of the lucky occupants of the 49 assigned seats claimed their space early to avoid poaching. Meanwhile, the rest of the room is packed, with nearly as many reporters standing on the sidelines. This is not the first time they have been told of an inconvenient forthcoming announcement, but no one can remember one coming this late on a Friday. The reporter for the Associated Press, now seated front-row center, scribbles potential first questions. He stops, however, when the correspondent for National Public Radio, seated in the row immediately behind, wonders half-jokingly to no one in particular if it matters that the stock market just closed.

The news reaches them that the president is on the way. The informal betting pool, run by the photographers, is closed to new wagers. The short odds now tilt toward military action against a terrorist training camp, followed by a radical new trade deal with China. The acknowledgment of a classified U.S. defense technology remains a long-shot that could pay off nicely. And while no one has placed a bet on it, a few wonder if this has something to do with that inexplicable "event" from last week. Clearly, there has to be a rational explanation for it, but *what if....*

The president enters. With him are key members of the U.S. Congress, the Secretary of Defense, the Director of Central Intelligence, and the Chairman of the Joint Chiefs of Staff. This assembly of power seems to favor the military angle. Then someone notices that the Secretary of Commerce is also, inexplicably, standing with the group.

The Commander-in-Chief of the United States of America checks his watch and steps up to the familiar podium.

"After consultation with key members of our defense and intelligence community," the president begins, "including the officials accompanying me here at this podium, it has been made clear to me that there is persuasive evidence that the Earth has been, and is currently being, interacted with by one or more intelligent non-human species."

He pauses and surveys the room, allowing time for his statement to settle into the minds of those listening.

Within a single minute, the world has changed.

The president preaches calm, although deep inside he is a bit panicked, too. He has only last week learned the details of this reality himself. He explains that recent highly visible sightings of UFOs, including a mass sighting that had been well-documented, caused him to demand a full investigation into what the United States government knew on the subject.

Witnessing A.D.1: The world changes instantly and forever. Presidential News Conference, East Room. Photo courtesy of The Associated Press/ Susan Walsh.

"Despite the issues that disclosure of this fact now obviously raises, I do believe that the people of the United States, and the people of Earth, have a right to know," the president continues. "Because of the need for calm debate, I have taken the precautionary move of making the National Guard available to any state governor who feels that its use is necessary to maintain public safety. Additionally, to protect our nation's economic security, through my executive authority, I am closing the nation's banks for a period of one week, and ordering the closure of the stock market until further notice."

From here, the press conference becomes decidedly more challenging. Under questioning, the president promises an on-going, "transparent" review of all classified files dealing with the UFO phenomenon and the ET presence. This will be supervised by members of Senate and House intelligence committees. He even announces the formation of an Office of Contact Affairs. Meanwhile, foreign leaders worldwide have begun to make similar announcements, part of a coordinated effort at Disclosure that rolls across the time zones of the Earth. Even the Pope will speak to thousands from his balcony at the Vatican Sunday at noon.

The president does not take all the heat alone. This is why he has brought the Secretary of Commerce and the Secretary of Defense to answer some of the pointed questions in the news conference that will follow. That news conference will be the most eventful one that the world has ever seen, creating more headlines, spinning off more "live" shots, and generating more demand for follow-up than anything we have ever seen before, or ever will.

✧

This Disclosure scenario only serves purposes of illustration. It is possible that the lifting of the veil will not originate in the United States, or even involve its elected leader. It could even come courtesy of insiders within the secrecy group itself who force the issue into the open and take the world by surprise. There are many roads that can be taken on the journey to truth.

Whatever specific actions precede the announcement, however, the first 24 hours will be like none that have ever existed before. The world has never experienced a planetary event of this magnitude. Not even the existential shock of the Kennedy assassination, the dark impact of 9/11, or the reverent awe of the Moon landing.

The day will become the "Where Were You?" moment for all people who live through it. For the rest of their lives, they will talk about what they were doing when they first heard the news. History will have a new dividing line, one that heralds the first day of a new world, the end of an old one.

Originally, the term *A.D.* came from the Latin phrase *Anno Domini*, and referred to the time after the birth of Christ in the Gregorian calendar. It will still continue as the unofficial global standard and as the basis of scholarly dating.

Now the phrase "A.D." will be appropriated by the world culture as the reference for the time *After Disclosure*. There will be surprising global acceptance of this re-interpretation, given that more than two-thirds of the world isn't even Christian. Even *B.C.* will come to stand for something else: *Before Confirmation*.

The younger generation will embrace the change most enthusiastically. This new reference point will be more relevant to their lives. It can be easily texted and still carry full meaning. Two keystrokes and a number, no spaces. AD1.

First Reactions

The first second After Disclosure—when someone in authority acknowledges that intelligent non-human life is a fact—you will know instantly that the world has changed completely and forever.

The first minute After Disclosure, you will be concerned for the safety of your friends and family, but the reassurances will make you feel better for the moment.

The first hour After Disclosure will be full of cell phone calls, e-mails, and texts to those same people, as we all collectively watch television and surf the Internet, hungry for new information.

The first 24 hours After Disclosure will see the serious questions start. People will wonder how this could have happened, and ask what it really means.

At the very beginning, as the citizens of the world play catch-up to this breaking story, their questions will fall into five main categories:

1. **Intelligent Non-Humans.** How long have these beings been here? Where do they come from? What do they look like? Do they walk among us now? Is there more than one type?

2. **Their Agenda.** How much do we know about their activities? Are these beings benign in intent, or malevolent? Have we had meetings with them? Are we in communication with them now?
3. **Safety.** Has our military been chasing after UFOs, as some have claimed? Have we lost aircraft as a result? Is it true that UFOs have been interested in our nuclear weapons sites? Will we now share technical data with other nations in order to create a military system capable of defending against potentially hostile beings?
4. **Secrecy.** Why was this information kept from the public for so long? How was that even accomplished? Are we going to learn the full story now, or just some of it?
5. **Disclosure.** Going forward, how will we even know if what is being said is the truth? Will all classified records be released, or only some? Will amnesty be granted so those involved in the cover-up can speak freely?

Unfortunately, there will not be complete and honest answers to some of them for years, if ever.

On the first day, however, everyone in the world will be asking everyone else these questions and more. The jolt from these initial conversations will be unprecedented because it will be an experience shared by billions.

Our curious minds will not be at a loss for words. Thirsting for clarity, we will plug them into search engines in record numbers. When we cannot find the right word or phrase, we will invent new ones.

In Other Words

Because we live in a wired world, there will be a sudden creation of new terms, and fresh definitions of old words and phrases. Along with the embrace of A.D. for *After Disclosure*, the new nomenclature will gain traction because it conveys a shorthand concept that spreads virally. Here, we propose a start-up glossary of ways that words might change in order to convey new ideas. We will use them in this book to do just that.

Day One

Among the ongoing redefinitions in the new world will be "Day One," instantly appropriated to refer to this tumultuous first day. This designation is less-hysterical than 9/11, and more forward-looking. "9/11" invokes emergency calls and sudden terror, but Day One solidifies the obvious: no matter what comes next, whatever came before is over. Day One is when the calendars start again in our instantaneous reboot of consciousness.

Disclosure

At the same time, the word *disclosure* will be changed. As a lower-case word, it will carry all the usual meanings. But there will be a new meaning for big "D" disclosure. That "Disclosure" will be used, as it is used in this book, to refer to the overall process of acknowledging humanity's contact with other intelligent beings. It covers all aspects, all the moving pieces, all the complexity, of the event's impact. You can disclose a fact about UFOs, but Disclosure is the event and the process. It encompasses all that happens when we say, "We are not alone."

The Others

The biggest re-definition will be how we come to refer to the "intelligent non-humans" that have been in contact with us. It is possible that when Disclosure comes, these beings may be referred to by the name that they call themselves, or it may be a name used by the intelligence groups that have monitored them. For this book, we will call them "The Others."

The other common terms have too much baggage. Most are too specific, and many could be wrong. Terms such as *extraterrestrial*, *ET*, *EBE*, or *Eben* (the last two for "extraterrestrial biological entity" commonly invoke outer space. Calling them *visitors* sounds like the reptoids from the television series, *V*. Besides, it may turn out that they are not visiting at all. The word *aliens* has a certain accuracy, in that these beings are probably alien to humanity in key ways. But then again, maybe not. The word is also emotionally charged—it predisposes us to see them as enemies, and even has been politicized by current immigration debates.

What we do know about them is that they are not us. This means, by definition, that they are Others.

The Breakaway Group

In the 1950s, retired Marine Corps Major Donald Keyhoe called the secret-keepers the "Silence Group." If certain documents leaked in the 1980s are to be believed, the group had the name of Majestic-12 or MJ-12. These days there is no direct evidence that name is still. "The Breakaway Group" is our name for them. We believe they are still at work today, having become a quasi-private, quasi-public group. To a large extent, these people have their own rules, their own secrecy protocols, their own technology. As the following pages will suggest, they have probably developed their own society, separate from the one that spawned it, yet still interacting with it. The existence of The "Breakaway Group" is nearly as important a secret as that of the non-human intelligences themselves.

Ground Zero

"Ground Zero" once referred to a nuclear blast contact point. Then, following 9/11, it referred to the hole where the World Trade Center once stood. If the cover-up begins to unravel with a mass sighting, the term will be re-defined yet again as the location where the slide toward Disclosure gained traction. For example, let us assume for illustration purposes that a mass sighting occurs in Montreal, Canada. If that is the event that begins the final disintegration of the secret, the city will be referred to as Ground Zero—even though, as pedants will point out, the event never took place on the ground, but in the sky above.

Trigger Event

Something will start the process toward Disclosure. As we already suggested, it could be an undeniable mass sighting of a UFO. But it might also be a compelling revelation from Wikileaks or some other citizen-based group that hacks into classified records. It may be the appearance of physical evidence discovered in the attic of a Roswell witness. Or perhaps a deathbed confession by an ex-president or prominent general who sees a chance for immortality by speaking the truth. It could be a foreign government, such as China, Russia, or Brazil, acting unilaterally. It could also be the Others themselves, although they have apparently declined every previous opportunity throughout the years to announce themselves. But whatever the trigger event is, it will be a tipping point that shifts the momentum from secrecy to openness.

Avalanche

After the trigger event comes the avalanche. They often start slowly, then gather momentum. Finally, they become unstoppable. In the rapid downhill fall of UFO secrecy, one event leads to another, then to another. Finally, their cumulative weight makes the process unstoppable and overwhelming. An avalanche can bury the past, which can be a good thing, but it also has great potential for destruction.

Shock and Awe

"Shock and Awe" will no longer refer to the 2003 aerial bombing blitz of Baghdad. After Disclosure, it will convey the intense emotional impact people feel at first hearing the news. In the first month A.D., among youth, it will be the answer to "How are you?" The answer is a simple, "Shock and awe, dude, shock and awe."

Nomenclature aside, it may feel to many that the announcement of the Others came out of nowhere. The truth, however, is that it will have been visible on the horizon for days, weeks, or even months before.

The Gathering Storm

The most gripping and contentious issue in ufology today is this singular issue of Disclosure. Across the Internet, especially on podcasts focusing on the paranormal, perhaps the most common question asked of guests is, "When?" This has many levels and complexities, but there is an answer.

In their wildest dreams, the secret-keepers could never have thought the secret would last this long. Now that it has, however, they do not intend to change the status quo unless they must.

Disclosure waits until it can wait no longer. And then it happens.

After generations of silence and denial, the Breakaway Group will not change course voluntarily. Although a contingency plan of slow gradual revelation may exist (as some speculate in the form of mass media indoctrination), there is no evidence it will be voluntarily deployed. Only something unexpected and overwhelming will force the secret-keepers to make some sort of public acknowledgment. This could 20 years from now, or it could be tomorrow. Those who believe the secret will last forever, however, will find that human society will be the thing that surprises them. It is our collective selves that will prove to be the great agent of change, the unstoppable force that ultimately ends the secret. As we will argue, it is most likely to happen within the next generation or sooner.

Whatever and whenever the trigger event happens to be, it will be followed by a period of a week to 10 days where calls for answers grow louder from increasingly authoritative voices. The events leading from the trigger event to Day One will not be random. Instead, they will follow an undeniable logic.

Behind the scenes, several key players, probably including the U.S. President and other world leaders, will receive their first authentic, but limited, briefing on the topic. They will be told that, after seven decades of study, UFOs are perceived as a threat, though not necessarily an imminent one. If they represented an imminent physical attack, there would probably have been a more noticeable military mobilization than what has occurred, and of a different type and scale. On the other hand, if there was no threat whatsoever, the system would have had no need to maintain the secrecy apparatus.

This will unleash a tsunami of classified e-mail, encrypted texts, video conferences, secure calls, and ever-growing anticipation. The world media will be hysterical with speculation and will even receive a few tips about UFOs. Yet, media outlets will be too timid and compromised to publish them, even though they will know something big is about to happen. Even in the event of a spectacular mass sighting, there will be those who expect a prosaic explanation, possibly the announcement that we have built our own flying saucers, or that the object seen in the skies was a military-developed hologram. Others will not be so sure this time.

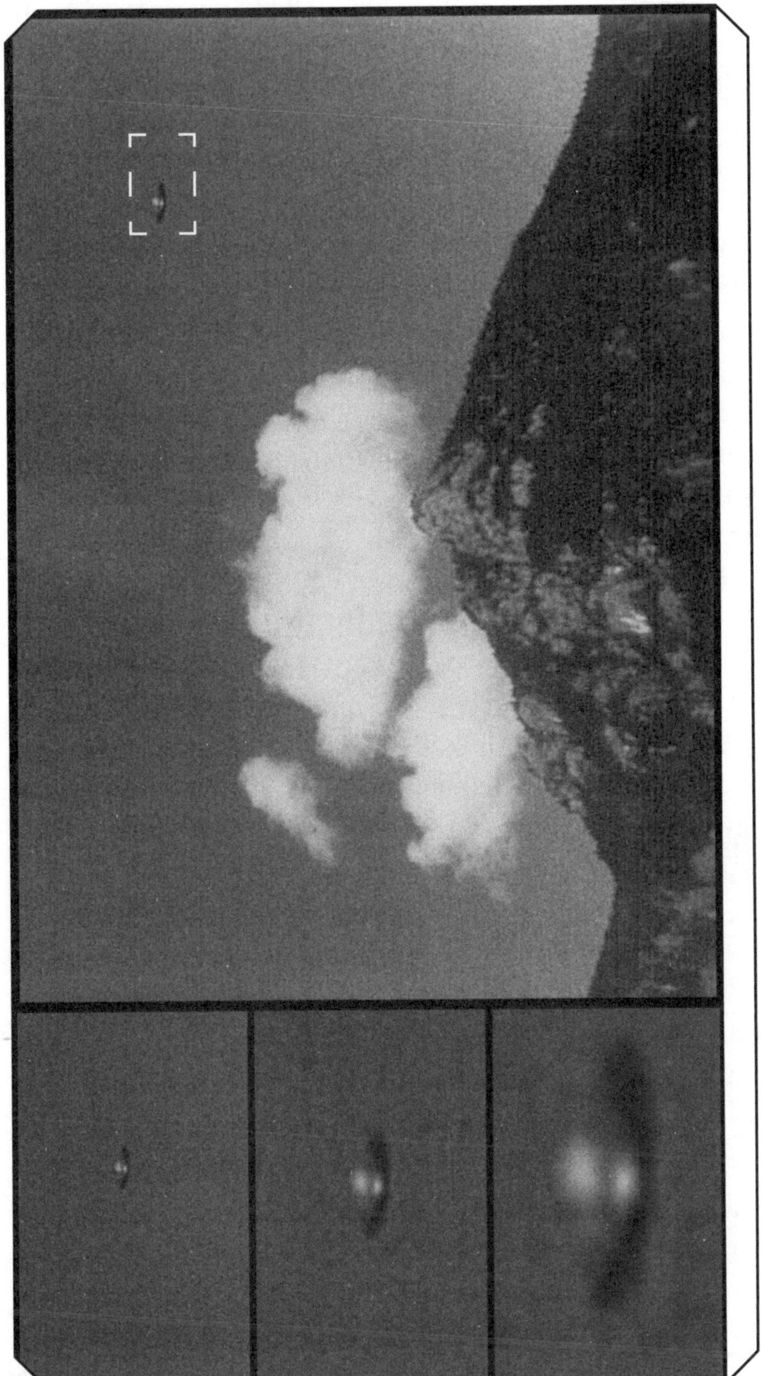

Facing the facts in the air. Previously ignored accounts of unknown craft become key evidence overnight. Vancouver, B.C., October 8th, 1981. Photo courtesy of Hannah McRoberts.

During this shadow period, world capitals will be in a state of excitement and anxiety, as officials consult each other formally and through back-channels. In the United States, preparatory meetings will take place to coordinate across the three branches of government, as well as the military and intelligence communities. All of this will be aimed at synchronizing, containing, and managing. The major agencies and institutions will need guidelines in order to provide a unified message. This will create leaks that will be firmly and categorically denied until they are confirmed and it happens.

The announcement will not come from any sense of patriotism or altruism. The decision to change the world, to *let* the world change, will simply be a matter of damage control. It is only at the point where the thing that has always seemed impossible—Disclosure—will now become inevitable.

Full [Radical] Disclosure

When the leadership of the Breakaway Group makes a decision to disclose, they must decide what to say. This is a complex secret, full of nuance, with the potential to rend the fabric of the status quo. They will have several options in deciding what to tell, how to tell it, and how truthful—or deceptive—they will be.

The government might disclose as much as it can as fast as it can. Although it would take weeks or months to fill in the full mosaic of contact, the idea is to let it all hang out from the finest moments of joining the brotherhood of the universe to the darkest hours of feeling under threat by malevolent forces.

This is a risky throw of the dice. Some argue for it and even romanticize it, knowing that they will never have to make the decision. All voices on the inside, however, are apt to look at this option with fear and dread.

What they would have to onsider is a scenario where the government immediately dumps massive amounts of evidence, hoping that this one single *mea culpa* allows its leaders to put the controversy behind them. This involves the release of an avalanche of supporting evidence—DVDs, decrypted files, or secure download sites full of video and photos (including corpses and wreckage)—and would involve the posting of tens of thousands of pages of documents to the Internet. The next edition of the *New York Times* would perhaps read alarmingly like many previous issues of the *National Enquirer*.

By releasing it all at once, much like President Nixon did when he released all of the Watergate tape transcripts at the same time, the hope would be that there will be so much to process that the public reaction would initially be enormous, and then die down. Nixon, however, provides his own cautionary tale. Rather than releasing the actual tapes and forcing the reporters and the Supreme Court clerks to sift through them, he released redacted transcripts. People, fed up with his lying, rejected that. Nor will they accept a Disclosure that is stripped of its full content. If the idea coming from the Breakaway Group is to deliver the so-called UFO truth *Full Monty*, style then they will have to do just that.

The technical obstacles alone would be overwhelming. First, simply assembling the films, videos, and photos would increase the likelihood that they would leak prematurely and create a *War of the Worlds*-type panic. More important, posting everything to the Internet would be impossible without a proper declassification review, unless the government wanted to offer the conspiracy theorists a first opportunity to interpret them.

There is another reason why full Disclosure may be an unattractive option. It may well be that, during the period leading to the great announcement, the president is briefed by intelligence experts who describe truly disturbing elements of the UFO phenomenon. After all, we can presume that the other intelligences here on Earth are very likely to be more advanced than we are. And the fact that they, too, have been rather secretive about their presence may not bode well. Simply because they are demonstrably smart does not mean that their intentions are "good" from the limited point of view of the humans that happen to inhabit Earth.

Partial (Controlled) Disclosure

A partial, or limited, Disclosure confirms the basic fact that "we are not alone," and tries to manage the tidal wave of questions and accusations on a case-by-case basis. Essentially, this is a stall for time. One motivation for this strategy comes from the top: to conceal crimes that have been committed while preserving the secret. Also, the secret-keepers can reassure themselves that they are giving the public a chance to absorb this new information in a calm manner, preventing a panic and societal implosion.

Even so, simply announcing that "they're here" will break like a tidal wave over the public's consciousness. The "go slow" approach would be an attempt by governments to appear forthcoming, but also evaluating the evidence in a deliberate, responsible manner.

This will still be a death by a thousand cuts. Here, the information is dribbled out piecemeal; much of it is protected and released unwillingly. It is not a pleasant strategy, yet it will be the favored one. It is the only way for those erstwhile secret-keepers (now forced to be secret-givers) to try to maintain some semblance of control over the situation. This has been their obsession and a mission for a long time, and will not cease because of a forced announcement. They, and their representatives, will still face a set of difficult questions where "no comment" will not satisfy.

It is not just that all of the information released at once would be unsettling. It is that any part of *all* of the information will be unsettling and potentially explosive. For instance, how might Disclosure affect the financial markets, given that there will be technologies from UFOs that may be introduced? How might these same technologies affect international relations? What if the Others have substantial underground bases here on Earth—does one come out and just say so? What if some of *them* look like *us*—would it be a good idea to mention this? How does one talk about abductions? What if there had been some measure of collaboration between them and certain intelligence groups? How bad might public panic be?

Because of these concerns, even if there is a mass sighting those in charge of maintaining the secret may only confirm the existence of one species, possibly the common "Grays," providing the information that they are from Zeti-Reticuli, if that is the case (and assuming this information is known), or naming where they do come from, if it is not. This will be a significant bombshell, of course. Yet, it would only be a very limited disclosure if the truth turns out to be that there are dozens of other species observing us from other worlds, dimensions, or times.

This means that the "big picture" spills out first, while the media—asleep at the switch all these years—tries to repair its damaged reputation by leaping on the story. It will usher in a true battle royale over what we "need-to-know." Even though the public will eventually answer that question with a definitive *everything*, that will come later, as the days turn to weeks, then to months, then to years.

False [Deceptive] Disclosure

Nothing is a certainty in the world of trillion-dollar secrets, security classifications that are levels above the president, and lies and deception going back for more than half a century. It is possible to imagine a situation where the true holders of the secret know they have to say something important in order to appease a demanding population. They would then offer up a form of Disclosure that is only a bigger lie.

In the event of a widely recorded mass sighting, for instance, the strategy would be to admit that, yes, something unusual was flying in the sky, and was actually classified human military technology. In other words, they confirm that the hardware exists, but insist it is entirely human. They then fall back on national security, and refuse to answer any more questions.

It is elegant in its simplicity. By acknowledging the truth of the sighting, the greatest act of debunking is primed. It is also, if practiced by a superpower like the United States, Russia, or China, a dodge against a potential enemy, saying in effect that "my weapons are so impressive you thought they had to be extraterrestrial."

Whatever country uses that strategy has turned its competitors into reluctant co-conspirators. Other nations may well choose not to challenge such a statement publicly, as this would force them into the position of claiming that UFOs are real. This form of False Disclosure, then, is a double-down. It allows one country to bluff the rest of the world, co-opt its enemies, and maintain the status quo for another few years at minimum.

As attractive as this might seem, it is a risky course that would probably backfire. At some point, it would be necessary to demonstrate the technology to aviation and aerospace experts. The public could be skeptical of such a claim, and credibility could become a serious issue.

Another form of False Disclosure would be to admit that whatever the sighting event was, it was certainly unusual, and that the government is just as curious as its citizens. In this scenario, a president or other foreign leader would try to put him- or herself and the country on the side of the people, and would probably create a commission to deliver a report on UFOs within a certain period of time. This is stonewalling of the highest order, of course. Yet, while the commission is busy at its business of determining what is behind the UFO phenomenon, the government, the Breakaway Group, and other secret-keepers have more time to assess the damage and determine their next step.

Yet another form of False Disclosure would be something that has been widely discussed on countless Internet blogs and social network sites: announcing that a hostile ET race threatens humanity. This would be a type of "false flag" operation, in which a secret agency carries out an operation to make it appear that other groups or entities are responsible. False Flag operations have occurred at various times throughout the history of warfare, but also in modern history as covert operations designed to confuse and manipulate the public, the most notorious example being the Reichstag Fire of 1933, an event carried out by the Nazis but blamed on Communists, and which served as the foundation for Hitler's dictatorship.

It has been claimed that an alien false flag invasion has been planned for many years under the code name "Blue Beam." The idea would be to fake an ET invasion through advanced holography and other technologies, and then terrorize the public into acquiescing to the creation of a global police state. Could this happen?

Nothing can be ruled out in the 21st century, in which people are manipulated and pacified daily via an entertainment complex that often works hand-in-glove with the state apparatuses around the world. Also, there are technologies available to covert groups that now exceed the wildest imaginations of prior generations. We must say, why not, indeed?

However, claims require evidence, and here Blue Beam has always fallen short. So, too, in the logic of its implementation. The logistics alone would be a planner's worst nightmare. Moreover, does faking an alien invasion mean there really are no aliens? Many Blue Beam proponents appear to believe this. If, however, Others of some sort are here, then the perpetrators of a Blue Beam event would seem to be taking a huge risk, assuming that the Others go along with everything without a hitch. Perhaps there would be reason to think so, and perhaps there could be collaboration between the human elites and "them" to make it happen. But the problem is that there is no evidence to support any of this conjecture. It's easy to make claims, but much harder to make a case.

Considering all factors involved, it is more likely that the decision-makers behind Disclosure would rather play matters down. Bold lies always bring great danger, but this particular bold lie would be a powder keg beyond all others.

But if Blue Beam lacks evidence and logic, it remains possible that Disclosure could be used as an attempt to spread fear of the Others and enforce docility among the public. At all events, we must assume that those people who have managed the secret all these years will not simply walk away from the table after Disclosure.

Spin City

Day One starts with confirmation. No matter what form Disclosure takes, the public will be subjected to what military public relations experts call "information shaping." From the perspective of any government, this will be necessary. Any chief executive forced to discuss this with the world will be in a tough position, especially if there is any bad news to report.

National leaders will do everything possible to control public discourse as it unfolds. Whether or not they succeed will be of great significance. Most certainly, the leaders of the key UFO secrecy nations will have a general plan that was previously worked out in preparation to Disclosure.

These leaders will need to decide how frightened they want the world to be. A certain amount of fear is useful to someone who is out front on a major issue. Fear causes people to look for leadership to calm the social order. Too much fear, however, can devolve into something that cannot be controlled.

If hostile intent of any kind is hinted at or acknowledged, the world will look toward the United States, the most powerful military power, for reassurance. In that case, the talking points of the U.S. President will be as follows:

- ✧ "To the extent that the Earth is under threat, we have the capability to respond. Our military has a plan and significant capabilities to implement it, if necessary."
- ✧ "World leaders are in constant communication on this issue. All nations have individual plans of action that are being coordinated with all the global powers, aimed at providing security to the citizens of the world."

If hostile intent is not assumed, the decision may be to minimize as much as possible, even making it seem as though it was all known already. This "*So what's the big deal?* thinking will be front and center among many who have denied the reality for years, people who now suddenly must get with the program. Strong deniers will shrug and say they never doubted the existence of aliens, just that they were here.

The logic we hear will be simple. The universe is a very, very big place—as many as 200 billion galaxies, each one containing billions of stars with a fair amount of those stars supporting planets. Some of them should have spawned intelligent life. Said paleontologist Stephen Jay Gould, "The most important scientific revolutions all include, as their only common feature, the dethronement of human arrogance from one pedestal after another of previous convictions about our centrality in the cosmos."

It is even possible that governments will downplay the UFO phenomenon by continuing a strategy employed by the CIA since the 1990s that states many of the UFO reports throughout the years were of classified aircraft. This strategy would have the double advantage of minimizing what the Others may have at their disposal, while maximizing what "we" may have. It is conceivable that in the unveiling, the only UFO produced by the government will be pictures from a crash and fragments and pieces. The photo-op will go instead to some newly de-classified and deadly hardware, possibly made by the United States.

All this will be possible because government and major media on Day One will still be working hand-in-glove, still finding mutual self-interest in propping each other up.

But governments will fail to manage public discourse on the Internet. This is where the real divide will take place, where the difficult questions will be asked immediately. Starting on Day One, a popular movement will spring to life, seeking to force more rapid disclosures and more meaningful information from governments and secret cabals.

For this reason, any attempt at deception (as opposed to mere withholding of the truth) by governments on the nature of UFOs and the Others will carry great risks. Researchers from around the world, who have spent years investigating the reality of this topic, are unlikely to allow government lies to stand unopposed. And this time, people will be listening to those researchers.

The ultimate question concerns the Others themselves. This will be especially difficult for governments, as there are some people in the world who already have answers about them. They do not need to speculate about "the possible nature of aliens." They have seen them and, whether classified or not, some of these ideas and experiences will be shared with the world.

This allows us to make another assumption. If the powers-that-be decide Disclosure must happen, they will know that they must "show us the aliens." This means that all those UFO photos that people thought were Photoshopped (many were) or too unclear and out-of-focus (the saucer would not hold still) will be replaced by "the good stuff." Let us define that as, at the least, a photo that is crystal clear and could not possibly be anything other than what it is purported to be: a craft from another planet, another dimension, or another reality altogether. The proof might be gun camera footage from an Air Force jet, or photos taken from the recovery of a crashed saucer.

Still, given the quality of modern cinematic special effects, film and photos will not suffice. At some point, people will need to see wreckage, bodies, or something else that is tangible and clearly authentic. The idea of taking a collection of reporters from top media outlets to a secret location where they can see for themselves, record photos and videos for their audiences and readers, and go on a tour, should not be ruled out.

Even then, for some people this will not be enough. There will be those who see any government admission of cover-up as just another cover-up in itself. They will think that something else, something even bigger and more nefarious is in the wind if the government has to blame it on aliens. Given a lifetime of lies and secrecy by their government, such an attitude is understandable.

A Moment in Time

Despite the uniqueness of this moment, much of what will follow is reasonably clear, based on past experience. We can even take an educated guess as to the day of the week it will happen and the time of day it will be scheduled.

The President will probably shut down the stock market and close the banks, just as President Franklin D. Roosevelt did during the Great Depression. Also, remember, that the media will be unleashed on this story as it has never been on anything before. This means that, unless the Motherships actually do show up hovering above the world's cities, Day One will start on a Friday, probably between 4:00 p.m. and 5:00 p.m. EST.

The reason is that the stock market will have already closed, and the banks in every town will be shutting down. Everyone will have a full weekend to consider the news and its implications before they panic and try to pull their money out of their savings accounts or sell all their stocks. It also avoids media images of an empty New York Stock Exchange and citizens protesting outside banks.

This need coincides with a separate desire to keep the media off-balance and more-or-less compliant. The ideal time for most briefings is early in the day Eastern Standard Time, so that the establishment reporters can file their stories for the evening news. On this day, however, the insiders will not want them to have all day to work the story. They will instead want the weekend to observe how the story is being received, in order to adjust their plans accordingly when Monday arrives. There will be plenty to observe, because every network will pre-empt its programming for this story, and every cable news outlet will throw all their resources into it.

If Disclosure does happen on a Friday, expect journalists to travel under a government escort to a previously secret location such as Nevada's Area 51, or U.S. Air Force Headquarters at Wright-Patterson Air Force Base over the weekend.

Some of the first day's tremors are public; some are concealed. Many workers are sent home from the office. "Essential" personnel, however, are on-the-job in a big way.

The media trots out experts, charts, and polls. It wags fingers at the government. Public employees scramble for answers, just like everyone else. It is like a Richter 13 magnitude earthquake, and no one is escaping collateral damage. The military pivots to DEFCON 2 (just short of imminent nuclear war), science turns upside down, religion scrambles to dress up old sermons for new realities, and corporate leaders text each other about profit potentials and risks. And this is on Day One. The world is just getting started.

The shock of this news will not exist in a vacuum. It will instead be multiplied by the feeling that the truth has been withheld, and the people who are briefing everyone are the same people who have either behaved stupidly or just plain lied. There will eventually be blowback on a huge scale. Yet on Day One, the feeling of having been lied to for generations will not have had time to form completely. The first 24 hours will be about understanding that the news is real and adapting to this knowledge in the most basic way possible.

Most people, including the self-described "skeptics," have refused to read anything about UFOs. They have avoided thinking about the subject in any way other than as story fodder for science fiction films. They will be the most shocked; their belief spectrum will shift radically, all at once. Others less dogmatic, or especially those who have taken some time to acquaint themselves of the facts as they can be known, will have less distance to travel.

Preparation to hear and accept this news may be more important than you think. You can do the world a great deal of good if you are one of a critical mass of people who can react with calm rationality on Day One. This early consideration of what is coming is important because, as historians routinely advise us, whenever contact between two civilizations occurs, it is the less-advanced one (at least technologically) that collapses. There are many analogous situations—Cortez and the Aztecs, Pizarro and the Incas. Indeed, in the film *Apocalypto*, the arrival of the Spaniards at the Yucatan in 1502 is portrayed as the fulfillment of an Oracle's prophecy that these strangers would come to "scratch out the Earth. Scratch you out. And end your world."

Consider the shock those civilizations may have felt. Now consider how our overcrowded, technologically sophisticated world, in which news travels instantaneously and news cycles are measured in hours, will shape and distort our perceptions of threat. Consider, too, how it will affect our collective, societal self-esteem. Collapse in ancient times may have taken decades. For us, it could be instantaneous.

If there is one silver lining to this fear for the collapse of civilization, it is that a threat from the Others might serve to drive humanity together. In *Apocalypto*, for example, the two killers from the dominant native culture stop the pursuit of their intended victim, and instead gaze with him at the arrival of Europeans wading ashore from their huge, unfathomable sailing ships. May this perhaps be a metaphor for our contemporary national strivings and hatreds that seemed so important the minute before Disclosure, now transformed into uncomprehending awe at the ships and visitors who have come here for unknown reasons?

In the days and weeks after Day One, there will be a second wave of revelations, a second wave of events. They will affect every aspect of our world. Although the financial industry stands down, for instance, the military will stand up. There will be a worldwide military alert, and questions will arise as to human capabilities of meeting a potential ET threat. Martial law will also be declared at various places around the world. Looting will be widespread, even if it is nothing more than an instinctive reaction from panic. The media will still jump into the fray 24/7, ignoring its own culpability in the cover-up. For those working in the news business, this will be the biggest shot of adrenaline ever. Reporters the world over will be working the story for months, if not years. Headlines will read, "We Are Not Alone," "World Leaders Say UFOs Real," "Aliens Here Now."

Cellphone towers and Internet relays will be stretched beyond their capabilities. People everywhere will pray, and the world's religions will not all agree on what we are dealing with. This will be a matter of great potential strife. Almost certainly, some shrewd minister, priest, rabbi, imam, or some other religious leader will exploit this change with a new message, creating a new faith.

Us and Them

The overriding factor in this equation—the great unknown—will be the Others. Everyone will want to know three things immediately:

1. Who are they?
2. What do they want?
3. Are we safe?

Much depends on the answers to these questions, especially whether these beings are friendly or hostile. But maybe they are neither. Or perhaps there are multiple types of them.

There is another question worth asking. It may not be asked immediately, but it ought to be: What will the Others do when they realize we all know about their existence?

They have had a free ride here in our world for years, perhaps eons. They have invaded our military airspace, abducted our citizens, and even crashed in our deserts—all while the public was assured they did not exist.

If we all learn this at once, will they react to our knowledge? Those who have been studying this issue and asking these questions for years might have an answer. Still, whatever agenda the Others have it is probable that secrecy was a part of it, and that Disclosure will complicate matters for us and them.

Looking back at his brother's assassination, Senator Robert Kennedy lived through the kind of sea change of perspective we will be experiencing. "I found out something I never knew," said RFK. "I found out that my world was not the real world." If political assassination could generate that kind of reaction from a hardened politico like Kennedy, imagine what a revelation of non-human intelligences being here, now, can do to society.

Vignette #1

Remarks by The President on the Reality of Extraterrestrial Life

✧✦✧

The White House

Office of the Press Secretary

For Immediate Release May 14, 2021

Remarks by The President on the Reality of Extraterrestrial Life

Friday, 5/14/21

4:15 P.M. EDT

THE PRESIDENT:

Thank you, everybody.

I'll be making a brief announcement, followed by a statement from the Secretary of Defense, and the Secretary of Commerce. After all of us have spoken, we'll take your questions.

In cities across the world—a total of 103 countries, I believe—the same basic announcement is being made, some simultaneously, others later, depending on the time zone.

After consultation with key members of our defense and intelligence community, it has been made clear to me that *there is persuasive evidence that Earth is currently interacting with one or more intelligent non-human species.*

Despite the issues that disclosure of this fact now obviously raises, I do believe that the people of the United States and the people of Earth, have a right to know. In my consultations with our allies and with other countries around the world, a consensus was reached that, while some of us might have preferred to have more time, events have overtaken us, and we can wait no longer.

I want to emphasize two things immediately: First, there is virtually no evidence at this time that we are under attack. In fact, the opposite seems to be true. To say that we are under some kind of observation seems more accurate. The Secretary of Defense will speak in a moment and he can address directly the steps that are being taken as we speak to secure the nation—and the world. Second, I am—through a separate Executive

Order—creating an Office of Contact Affairs, which will be staffed and funded as a part of our Department of Homeland Security. It has been given the mandate of reporting directly to me about the scope of this current visitation. I have, concurrently, directed the Attorney General to begin her own investigation into the nature and content of apparent secrecy with which some of these facts have long been held.

Because of the need for calm debate, I have taken the precautionary move of making the National Guard available to any state governor who feels that it is needed to keep the public order. Additionally, to protect our nation's economic security, through my executive authority, I am closing the nation's banks for a period of one week, and ordering the closure of the stock market until further notice.

Now, before I provide the details on this, let me speak directly to our nation's children and young people. It is quite clear that the facts I have confirmed today are disturbing. Like your parents, I'm sure you have many, many questions and that some of you are scared. Throughout the weekend, we will be addressing as many of those questions as possible. But I want you to know that you are safe. Your homes are safe. Our nation is safe. We are entering a new era, that much is clear, but we do so with strength and confidence and an abiding belief that humanity has much to give to other life-forms that may exist in the vast universe we live in, and that we also can learn much from these visitors.

To the media, the press secretary assures me that you will find full information packets and hard drives with a selection of photos, videos, and reports that I have unclassified through presidential order. The Attorney General will begin a thorough review of other material, in consultation with Congress and the chairs of the House and Senate Intelligence committees, as to what can be released in the future and in what time frame. I ask for your patience. The process will be difficult, yet today we begin it together.

So thank you all very much. The Secretary of Defense will speak now.

END

4:21 P.M. EDT

Chapter 2

Breakaway:

How Secrets Created a World Within a World

Secrecy is the first essential in affairs of the State.

—Cardinal De Richelieu

In 1960, the U.S. government tasked the Brookings Institute with analyzing the implications of the fledgling U.S. space program. The report, completed in December 1960, included an examination of the possibility that the space program might find evidence of intelligent alien life, such as artifacts on the moon or Mars.

The implications were taken seriously by the authors, who feared social disintegration if humanity came in contact with an extraterrestrial life form. "Anthropological files contain many examples of societies sure of their place in the universe," stated the Brookings Institute writers, "which have disintegrated when they had to associate with previously unfamiliar societies...espousing different ideas and different life ways."[1] The authors suggested that if the U.S. space program found evidence of alien life or technology, it might be advisable to withhold this information from the public.

The Brookings Report reinforced a longstanding U.S. government policy. No less an authority than the former Director of Central Intelligence,

Admiral Roscoe Hillenkoetter admitted to a cover-up in a letter to the *New York Times* in 1960, shortly before publication of the report. "Behind the scenes, high-ranking Air Force officers are soberly concerned about UFOs," said Hillenkoetter. "But through official secrecy and ridicule, citizens are led to believe the unknown flying objects are nonsense. To hide the facts, the Air Force has silenced its personnel."[2]

The World of 1947

In an ideal world, something as reality-shattering as the presence of another intelligent civilization interacting with our own would prompt the political system to act in a coherent manner. In such a world, governments everywhere would speak for the people, work on their behalf, and answer to them. But we have to live in the real world.

Despite the provocative nature of the phenomenon (or, more likely, because of it), the political structure of the United States immediately began debunking it. Other governments of the world followed suit. That policy has now evolved into the most successful cover-up of all time. Despite the continuous sightings, books, and statements by prominent public figures, it remains in place.

It is not hard to see why the world's top power brokers would want to conceal the reality of something as monumental as UFOs.

The world of 1947 was in the midst of tremendous change. Fresh from the most destructive war of all time, millions of people in Europe, Africa, and Asia were homeless refugees. Millions more were rebuilding their nations from piles of rubble, and many others were on the brink of starvation. A new weapon of terrifying power had recently been unleashed on the world, and the United States was now engaged in a struggle with the Soviet Union for world dominance. President Harry S. Truman signed the National Security Act, all at once creating the CIA, the National Security Council, an independent Air Force, and the Department of Defense.

At the same time, the problem of UFOs with extraordinary capabilities forced its way into the public consciousness. Reports of unusual, unknown aerial phenomena ("foo fighters") had been made by military pilots during the war. Then, in 1946, so-called "ghost rockets" were reported over Europe. In 1947, Americans began seeing them. By late June, they had a name: "flying saucers."

Then, in early July, if scores of witnesses are to be believed, one of these objects crashed near America's only nuclear base in Roswell, New Mexico.[3] Soon after, the news reached the desk of President Truman. On that very desk sat a draft copy of the National Security Act Truman was about to sign. On it was also the famous sign that said, "The Buck Stops Here."

Creating the cover-up. Roswell witnesses testify strongly that the weather balloon was a staged lie. Major Jesse Marcel said a spacecraft and bodies were found.
Photo courtesy of *The Fort Worth Star Telegram*, photograph collection, special collections. The University of Texas at Arlington Library, Arlington, Texas.

Truman's instinct might have supported a public announcement that intelligent beings from elsewhere were here on Earth. Yet, there can be little doubt that, following his briefing from the military, he discounted such an action. After all, the United States was unwilling to share its atomic technology with the Soviets, or even with the United Nations—a major political issue at the time. Telling the world about something as advanced as alien technology? Not in 1947.

Frankie Rowe

Consider the story of Frankie Rowe, one of many people connected to the Roswell event. A woman with impeccable credibility and decency, she spoke to the authors in 2010. In 1947, Frankie was 12 years old when her father, the town fire captain, led the first team to a wreckage site. He came home that night talking about bodies and saucers. The next day, the police officer who accompanied the firefighters showed up at the station where Frankie was recovering from tonsil surgery. He showed them a piece of the craft he had taken. Frankie played with it for 15 minutes and described it, as so many other witnesses have, as "memory metal." It could not be burned, broken, or torn. It would unfold instantly into complete flatness.

She also described how, the following day, a military policeman from the base came to her house. In front of her mother, he told Frankie never to speak of what "didn't happen." If she did, she and her parents might end up in the Japanese internment camp south of town, or in a desert grave where "nobody will ever find your bones."[4]

Something happened at Roswell that was so extreme, so strange, and so important that a man in uniform made a house call to threaten a 12-year-old with death.

A Nuclear "What If?"

Skeptics of Roswell as a UFO story say it would be impossible to hide something as significant as the crash of an alien craft. History says otherwise.

The Manhattan Project, in which the United States secretly developed and tested the atomic bomb, was the godfather of modern government secrecy. The project was so extraordinary, so revolutionary, that secrecy was paramount. Yet, it was so expensive and so vast that developing an appropriate structure of secrecy was no mean task.

"Compartmentation" became widely practiced. Each person involved in the project knew only what he or she "needed to know." Very few had all the information, fewer still were in a position to tell anything to the public. Within Congress, just a handful of men had any idea.

The secrecy was so well executed that when, on July 16, 1945, at exactly 5:30 a.m., the United States detonated the world's first atomic bomb in White Sands, New Mexico, no one else knew about it. The explosion was seen from 100 miles away, and many citizens contacted local police about it. Several days later, a news story stated that an ammunition dump had exploded.

It was one of the most momentous events in the history of science, and not a word of it was breathed to the rest of the world.

Now, consider a hypothetical scenario in which Japan might have surrendered before the atomic bomb had been used against its cities. Would President Truman have told the world of the incredible new weapon the United States had developed? Probably not. After all, once you inform the world of what you have, your allies would want you to share your research and your enemies would try to steal it.

If the United States had decided that the world must never know that an atomic bomb had ever been used, how long could the secret have been kept? If all the participants had been forced to a lifetime of secrecy, if all rumors were met by official denial, if the press and academic world became allies to squash rumors, and the cover story about an ammo dump explosion was supported by alleged witnesses, what would be left? Only the rumors themselves, forever unconfirmed, leaving widespread suspicion but little more.

There might be deathbed confessions from old soldiers, leaked documents dismissed as forgeries, desperate researchers trying to prove the existence of something like the "Manhattan Project," and TV reporters chasing the story of the "White Sands Myth" in the desert.

Following the recovery of exotic technology at Roswell (technology not from our civilization), logic would dictate that the president organize an elite team, charging them with getting to the bottom of the matter. The responsibilities would be manifold: analyzing the technology and duplicating it if possible, forecasting the level of public panic in the wake of Disclosure, determining the level of vulnerability to industrial or financial interests, managing media and academia, ensuring secrecy from hostile nations, and certainly learning everything possible about these other beings.

The group's existence would have to be kept secret, even from Congress. For once the rest of the world learned of America's possession of such awesome technology, they would jealously demand to be a part of its harvest.

The available evidence points exactly to this turn of events. During the mid-1980s, a seven-page document surfaced mysteriously—almost certainly leaked from within the U.S. intelligence community—which purported to be a briefing memo prepared in 1952 for President-elect Dwight Eisenhower. It described the recovery of crashed UFOs and alien bodies, and referred to "Majestic-12" or "MJ-12" as the group responsible for managing the secret.

Ufologists have argued over the authenticity of this document, as well as many similar documents subsequently leaked. Yet, following the event at Roswell, Truman would have been negligent had he not authorized some kind of group to respond.[5]

The documents list the names of the alleged members of MJ-12. They included: the director of the CIA, a man who helped organize the Manhattan Project, the head of the Air Materiel Command at Wright Field, the Air Force Chief of Staff, the Chairman of the National Research Council, the head of MIT's engineering department and leading aircraft designer, the Executive Secretary of the new National Security Council, the Director of the Harvard College Observatory, the head of the CIA's Psychological Strategy Board, the base commander of the Atomic Energy Commission installation at Sandia Base, and the Secretary of the Joint Research and Development Board. All of them together would be the group one would want to examine the reality of flying saucers, to examine what happened at Roswell, except for one person: Harvard astronomer Dr. Donald Menzel. While it may seem reasonable to include an astronomer on a team to study presumed extraterrestrials, Menzel's inclusion baffled UFO researchers. During the 1950s and 1960s, he was the world's leading debunker of UFOs. For years, he maintained that UFOs were simply misidentifications of prosaic phenomena: stars, clouds, airplanes, balloons, et cetera.[6] This was surely true for some sightings of odd lights in the sky—people are fallible, after all. But many of Menzel's so-called explanations of UFO phenomena were threadbare, even embarrassing. Yet, as a leading astronomer of his time, his presence in the debate prevented many other academicians from entering the field.

Menzel's inclusion in the documents was odd. Were the forgers making a joke? His name raised doubts. The MJ-12 papers were volatile enough, and such doubts further undermined them. Then came the story's twist.

UFO researcher Stanton Friedman—that dogged, inveterate burrower in government archives, that meticulously detail man—discovered that Donald Menzel had led a double life. Not even Menzel's wife had known about it. It turned out that Menzel had been a prominent, classified consultant for the U.S. intelligence community.

Not just any part of the intelligence community, but the CIA and the code-making, code-breaking National Security Agency (NSA). This was when no one knew the NSA existed, despite its probably being the most powerful of the U.S. intelligence agencies. The spooks cared little about Menzel's knowledge of the stars; they were more interested in another of his talents, for Menzel just happened to be a world-class cryptographer, an expert in codes and ciphers. In a 1960 letter to President-elect John F. Kennedy, he mentioned his Navy Top Secret Ultra Security Clearance, and his association with this activity for almost 30 years. He told Kennedy that he probably had "the longest continuous record of association of any person in the country."[7]

When considering that it just might come in handy to have a smart fellow who knows how to crack difficult communications, Menzel's inclusion makes a great deal of sense. His stature as a Harvard astronomer was a bonus, enabling him to slap would-be academic conspiracy theorists firmly into their place.

If the MJ-12 documents really were faked, it would seem that whoever created them knew of Menzel's intelligence activities and background. That would have been very rarified information. Or perhaps, as Friedman believed, the documents were real after all.

The term *Majestic* has been used occasionally in this book to describe the group charged with managing the many problems posed by these Others. This may be its actual name, or it may not. Either way, it is logical and reasonable that President Truman—not wanting to pass the buck—created it from the most trusted members of the U.S. military, political, and scientific establishment.

Once that decision was made and the group formed, a machinery was created and set in motion. Machinery that was so complex, so labyrinthian, and so powerful, that it became alive.

Choke Points

Threats and intimidation, such as those made with Frankie Rowe and others, are not the only ways to keep a secret. Management of the press is also critical.

By the early 1950s, the CIA had developed relationships with most major media executives in the United States. This does not mean something so crass as CIA agents telling executives what to print or broadcast. Rather, it means that some executives voluntarily killed stories that would damage perceived American interests. Sometimes, when necessary, the CIA would be consulted. Sometimes stronger medicine was prescribed, like planting disinformation or even stories that were flatly untrue.

Even a partial list of the participating organizations is breathtaking: the *New York Times*, the *Washington Post*, the *Christian Science Monitor*, the *New York Herald-Tribune*, the *Saturday Evening Post*, the *Miami Herald*, Hearst Newspapers, Scripps-Howard Newspapers, and Time-Life. Major news wire services, such as Reuters, the Associated Press, and United Press International, also coöperated. So, too, did television and radio broadcast concerns such as CBS News, the Mutual Broadcasting System, and others. In addition to these, the CIA owned many newspapers and publishing houses overseas.

Some of this information came out during the 1970s, when the CIA admitted to having paid relationships with more than 400 mainstream American journalists.[8] Consider the possibilities available to any person or group covertly employing 400 journalists. Although the CIA claimed it ended such relationships, it tacitly acknowledged the need to cultivate them in cases of national security. More recently, one inside military source told the authors that CIA influence among freelance journalists today is "pervasive." Former CIA Chief William Colby, a cold man who made his mark during the murderous Project Phoenix, who rose to the top of the Agency during the 1970s, and whose life ended in a boating "accident" on the Potomac in 1995, once told a confidant that every major media was covered by the long reach of the CIA.

But the CIA sought to manage more than the media. It also gained influence over the world of the intellectuals by funding all political flavors: those on the right, in order to promote American global interests; and those on the left, to wean socialist-leaning Americans away from Communism and toward an acceptance of "the American way."[9] This also happened in the world of academia, which several studies have amply exposed.[10]

The CIA's management of information is deft. Naturally, one cannot control all journalists, professors, and independent researchers. However, one can create chokepoints of information guarded by leading figures. If some maverick publishes something dangerous, the appropriate CIA proxy at the *Los Angeles Times* or Harvard University makes sure to attack it, and if necessary ridicule it. It is always the nail that sticks out that gets hammered.

More typically, unwelcome stories were blocked from going national. Throughout the 20th century, the wire services, collaborating with the CIA, simply neglected to carry them. Today, in the 21st century, this happens to be one area in which there is potential to turn the tables. Now, local stories can be spread far and wide via the Web. In the future, this may prove to be a problem for the secret-keepers.

So far, however, a preponderance of power remains on the other side of the fence. In fact, the revolving doors connecting academia, journalism, and the national security community are openly acknowledged. An abundance of intellectuals actively court the national security world. Why not, when the connections, prestige, and paychecks are so compelling?

As it happens, most UFO debunkers have been connected with the national security community. In this regard, Donald Menzel has already discussed, but during the 1960s, a successor to Menzel was in the wings: Philip J. Klass.[11] Klass was no scientist like Menzel, but he was the Senior Avionics editor for the prestigious defense publication, *Aviation Week and Space Technology*. For more than three decades, Klass used any and all means to throw cold water over the idea of UFOs. Some explanations were astronomical, even to describe large objects that were tracked on radar. Some he quickly labeled as hoaxes, such as a 1964 landing case witnessed by a terrified police officer, in which ground traces were photographed and studied. Other explanations were more creative, such as "ball lightning" to describe an enormous structured craft hovering at treetop level. When these failed to impress, Klass plied the trade of the propagandist, often via ridicule, invective, and furious letter-writing campaigns to smear reputations.

Throughout his career, Klass was under widespread suspicion—not proven as of this writing—of being an intelligence community asset. That he lived in the Washington, D.C. area, had consistent and exceptional access to the mainstream U.S. media, and worked within the defense community made such suspicion understandable.

People such as Menzel, Klass, and their successors have been important as vocal, media-savvy debunkers who seem independent, but are actually tied to the defense and intelligence community. Their work sets the tone for the mainstream media, which generally follows along happily.

Denial and Ridicule in Service to the State

Today, most professors and journalists—who have nothing to do with the national security state—have internalized the sanctioned opinions. They have learned to discuss UFOs the way a weary parent chastises a child for reading too many comic books. These things are not real. If you speak about them too much or too openly, people may think there is something wrong with you.

That is one reason why the cover-up has stood for so long. Had we followed our own glasnost policy from the beginning, the UFO argument would be over. People would have discussed this problem in the editorial pages, on the nightly news, and over hot dogs at their children's ball games. They would have concluded that something was there. Except that the architects of the cover-up stumbled upon the twin concepts that enabled them to hide the truth from the people they were sworn to protect. Two pillars, each one lending strength to the other in service of the common goal.

Denying the witnesses. People who saw "flying saucers" were often marginalized and ridiculed. One of the two famous McMinnville Photos from May 1950, strongly believed to be authentic. Photo by Paul Trent.

Denial and Ridicule

Official denial works. When a general or leading scientist explains there is no fire, that the smoke is an illusion, our natural instinct is to believe—despite what the crazy neighbor thinks, sometimes despite the evidence from our own eyes. We want to believe our authority figures.

Ridicule gives denial its power. When official statements are made, language is of the utmost importance. It is easier to smirk at a "flying saucer" than an "unidentified flying object" or "unknown aerial phenomenon." It is easier to dismiss alien intelligence when it is characterized as "little green men" instead of "extraterrestrial biological entities." Alien agendas can be dismissed when boiled down to science-fiction scenarios in which the occupants land on the White House lawn and declare "take me to your leader." Even the apparent widespread abduction of innocents has become the subject of ridicule on comedy shows. Even today, questions about the subject are often presented simplistically, often with a derisive sneer: "Do you believe in flying saucers piloted by little green men?" Imagine saying yes to that question.

No one wants their reputation smeared. Such false and misleading framings of the question quickly convinced the world's academic and journalistic institutions to run far and fast from the UFO subject. Indeed, in this dance of disinformation, it is sometimes hard to tell whether these institutions lead or follow. Craving public acceptance of their knowledge and authority, very few scientists, professors, or journalists can afford to show interest in the topic. As a result, the secret keeps itself, with only occasional government intervention.

We live in a world in which more than half of us believe that UFOs are real vehicles not of this Earth. Yet, official denial and ridicule continue to rule the day. This may be the greatest cognitive dissonance that any society has ever maintained about something so important.

On November 7, 2006, for 15 minutes during the afternoon rush hour at Chicago's O'Hare airport, a disc-shaped object hovered silently near the United Airlines terminal, then cut a sharp circular pattern in the cloud bank while zooming off.

A pilot announced the sighting over radio for all grounded planes; a United taxi mechanic moving a Boeing 777 heard the radio chatter and looked up; pilots waiting to take off leaned out their windows and saw the object. There was a buzz inside the airport among United Airlines personnel. One management employee received a radio call about the hovering object, and ran outside to see it. He then called the United operations center, made sure the FAA was contacted, and drove out on the concourse to speak directly with witnesses.[12]

United Airlines took statements from the witnesses and instructed them not to discuss the matter further. But one did, and the account soon reached *Chicago Tribune* reporter John Hilkovitch. Soon, the O'Hare UFO story became the most widely read news item in the history of the *Tribune*'s website.

The FAA and United Airlines initially denied any knowledge of the incident. That is, until it became obvious that they knew all about it. Investigating the case was not easy. Journalist Leslie Kean found that most of the witnesses chose to remain anonymous, citing fears of job security. When a recording was finally released of a supervisor's call to the air traffic control tower, Kean listened. She heard the tower operator and a second man laughing at the witness on the other end. The operator asked the witness if she had been celebrating the holidays early. Such an attitude forced the witness to waste valuable time, stating to another operator in a later call, "I'm not high and I'm not drinking."

The devastating effectiveness of denial and ridicule cannot be overstated. After years and generations, their effects have fully pervaded our culture. They have enabled intellectual bullies to roam free, to intimidate people who know what they have seen, and keep the truth covered.

Yet, there has always been a fight to end UFO secrecy. During each decade following the Second World War, there have been attempts to unlock the door. Each time, however, there were counter-measures that minimized any gains or defeated the attempt altogether.

In 1953, a classified CIA study known as the Robertson Panel recommended that the intelligence community tightly control UFO-related information reaching the public. This meant not only monitoring the newly formed civilian-based UFO research groups, but using its relationships with media giants (such as Walt Disney Corporation) to debunk UFOs.

Direct evidence has been found to show that, more than a decade later, the Panel's directives were still being followed through. A 1966 letter by former Panel member Thornton Page addressed to the former Secretary, Frederick C. Durant, stated that Page had helped organize a recent "CBS TV show around the Robertson Panel conclusions." This was a reference to the CBS television show UFOs: *Friend, Foe, or Fantasy?* narrated by Walter Cronkite, which had taken a stridently debunking tone toward UFOs.[13]

The debunking tactic worked up to a point, but never completely. One reason was simply because the UFO operators, whoever they were, did not seem to get the memo that they did not exist. UFO reports within the United States spiked upward during the mid-1960s, even receiving Congressional attention. Something had to be done.

In late 1966, the U.S. Air Force commissioned the University of Colorado to conduct an independent, scientific study of the phenomenon. This became known as the Condon Committee, after the project leader, Dr. Edward U. Condon. From the beginning, the project was plagued by dissension. It wasn't because Condon was an arch-skeptic on the matter, but that his attitude toward investigating UFOs was anything but scientific. His statements were limited to jokes and obvious crackpot cases. Even skeptics who had taken the time to look into the matter knew there was much more than this.

It became evident to some members that the project was rigged. Condon even admitted as much privately to Dr. David Saunders, one of the project scientists. If he were to receive information confirming UFOs as extraterrestrial, Condon said, he would withhold it from the public and take it personally to the President.

What drove project scientists to mutiny, however, was the discovery of a hidden memo written by Condon's number-two man, Robert Low. "The trick would be to describe the project so that, to the public, it would appear a totally objective study," wrote Low, "but to the scientific community would present the image of a group of nonbelievers trying their best to be objective but having an almost zero expectation of finding a saucer."[14]

When the project scientists discovered this memo, they complained *en masse* to Condon. He then summarily fired them. Incidentally, Robert

Low had been a combat intelligence officer during the Second World War. He also appears to have been a CIA operative who performed clandestine missions for the Agency during the late 1940s. The pervasive relationship between the CIA and academia appears to have played an important role in this project.[15]

By the time the Condon Report was completed in late 1968, it had been cobbled together by a replacement team of scientists. Despite Condon's and Low's skeptical lead, the report failed to explain roughly 30 percent of its cases. Condon was barely interested, however. His conclusion, which is all the mainstream press cared about, stated that UFOs were of "no probative value." In other words, further study of them was unlikely to lead to greater scientific knowledge. He recommended that the Air Force close Project Blue Book, its official investigative project regarding UFOs.

Now that the Condon Report had dismissed UFOs, there was ample scientific justification for ignoring the topic altogether, and ample reason for political and military authorities to deny any interest in it.

But the struggle against UFO secrecy did not end. During the 1970s and 1980s, thousands of pages of government documents relating to UFOs were released via the Freedom of Information Act. Many of these documents proved that the phenomenon was being monitored by military agencies, and that they were very concerned. Some of these documents were embarrassing to agencies which had long denied that they had anything to do with UFOs. Once again, it seemed as though that secrecy surrounding UFOs was in danger.

Then came the Roswell story, adding fuel to the fire. The story had been buried for more than three decades. But it was rediscovered during the late 1970s, and brought a new dimension to the idea of a government cover-up. After all, if an alien craft had been recovered by military authorities, this takes the cover-up to new levels. It would mean that the government could not merely be accused of incompetence in investigating the mystery of UFOs (which many had argued). Because now it would be in possession of alien technology and probably even bodies. For a few years, the momentum seemed to favor those seeking to end UFO secrecy. The Great Wall appeared to be cracking.

By the early 1980s, however, two things stopped this momentum. One was a 1982 Presidential Executive Order signed by President Ronald Reagan. No longer were federal agencies obligated to provide fast and affordable searches for citizens—a serious blow to the Freedom of Information Act. The process became slow and expensive. Certain agencies, such as North American Air Defense (NORAD), were exempted from FOIA. The NSA and CIA also became all-but-impervious to UFO-related requests.

The other development was the influence of military-intelligence elements within the UFO research field. In 1983, and again in late 1984, Air Force intelligence officers operating out of Kirtland Air Force Base in Albuquerque, New Mexico, quietly leaked documents to researchers that described the recovery of crashed UFOs and alien bodies. This included the MJ-12 documents. Whatever the actual truth contained within them, researchers have been distracted by the debate over their authenticity. Are they genuine? A hoax? Some incarnation of both?[16]

But then came another attack against secrecy, one that remains important to this day. That is the development of the Internet from around 1990 onward. As late as the 1980s, very few people foresaw the dramatic changes that would soon come. From the beginning, the UFO subject was a prominent part of the Internet. Many researchers found their voice by speaking to thousands—and then millions—of people via cyberspace.

Taking its lead from the Internet, television programming soon offered more sophisticated portrayals of UFOs. Several shows during the 1990s, most notably *Sightings*, *The X-Files*, and *Dark Skies* suggested a darker, grittier side to the story than had been offered in previous television fare. In the process, UFOs and gray aliens entered popular culture. Although watching fictionalized stories is not a cover-up ending activity by itself, it does expand the dialogue about the topic and promotes a desire for the facts. The more that people discuss this, the more they realize that UFOs may actually be real.

Of course, pop culture immersion is a double-edged sword. Public awareness may be raised, but so is the threat of contamination. For instance, the very success of *The X-Files* in one sense worked against public acceptance of the UFO-ET reality. It became typical to dismiss UFO believers for watching too many episodes of Mulder and Scully. To this day, mocking news stories about UFOs lead with the ubiquitous *X-Files* musical theme.

There is a wide rift between popular belief and "official truth" on this matter. Major media corporations, which have drastically consolidated in recent decades, still control most newspapers, radio, and television. In these venues, with occasional exceptions, UFOs continue to be ignored or ridiculed.

But the Web is another matter. For the most part, it continues to serve as a true voice of the people. It contains a massive trove of UFO information. Some of it is unreliable or just plain wrong, but some of it is excellent and sophisticated. The battle over UFO secrecy, and over information in general, is now on the Web, where major media continues its efforts to increase its share of traffic, and governments continue their efforts to restrict websites in the interest of "national security" or "public safety."

Such has been a short history of the struggle against UFO secrecy. Whether or not that secrecy was originally justified is a matter of debate. The answer can only come from what is known about the UFO reality and the intentions of the Others. Still, it is reasonable to concede the initial necessity. However, secrecy eventually became policy, buried deeper and deeper, boxes within boxes within boxes.

During the 1950s and 1960s, Ohio State University astronomer J. Allen Hynek served as the lead scientific consultant to the Air Force's Project Blue Book. Hynek was a team player, publicly debunking many cases for his employer, even at the cost of his personal reputation. In 1966, he speculated that UFO sightings in the state of Michigan might only be marsh gas caused by decaying vegetable matter in the swampy areas. In other words, "swamp gas." In his later years, Hynek took a more favorable public attitude toward the UFO mystery, and during the 1970s and 1980s was widely held to be the "Dean" of ufologists. Still, he maintained close relationships with the U.S. Air Force throughout his life.

Hynek died of brain cancer in April 1986. The year before, wracked by the physical pain of the disease that was destroying him, he had a tumor removed from his brain. In the recovery room as the anesthesia began to wear off, his thoughts were elsewhere, his pain more emotional than physical. In a frail voice, he was overheard by his wife Mimi asking a question that had nagged at him for decades. "Why can't they tell me?" he asked. "Even now?"

By the time Hynek passed away, the "they" that would not level with him were no longer exclusively within the United States, nor were they all taking orders from a military chain-of-command. In the same way that the UFO phenomenon is worldwide, the concealment of this explosive information had moved beyond the U.S. governmental structure.

Let us now examine this element of the cover-up, widening our sweep while going deeper at the same time.

An International Cover-Up

Through the years, and with increasing speed, other nations have made public statements about UFOs and released their own data. The nations of France, the United Kingdom, Belgium, Norway, Italy, Mexico, Brazil, Russia, and many others, have either made important statements about UFOs, or released sighting information that is available for anyone to examine.

Britain, France, Brazil, Sweden, and New Zealand, for instance, have released thousands of pages of UFO reports. Even if some of these were for purely bureaucratic reasons (for example, to relieve government agencies from the burden of answering individual requests from citizens), there is no question that their data will be studied by many researchers for some time.

There is also the fact that key leaders of several nations have made statements about baffling UFO cases. This has happened in Belgium, Mexico, Brazil, Canada, Russia, Spain, Japan, Zimbabwe, South Africa, the United States, and elsewhere. Each time, however, the spokesperson has stopped short of admitting that UFOs represent something truly alien (unless giving a private opinion, which has happened many times).

Some official statements have come close, though. Case in point: the 1999 French COMETA Report. This was a government-sponsored study of UFO data that made the startling admission that UFOs strongly appeared to belong to an alien intelligence. Yet, the report was not considered an official statement of the French government, and became an orphan. It generated no public policies. No major political figure followed up.[17]

So, yes, there have been "disclosures" of varying types. But these are not Disclosure.

When we zoom out from merely a U.S. perspective to a global one, we can see that an international UFO phenomenon needs a coordinated international cover-up. It may seem difficult enough to control and manage this story within a single country, but it feels impossible to do so on a global level. Yet, this is what has happened.

A good analogy of how this international cooperation might work can be seen in the program known as Echelon. Echelon is a global intelligence operation involving, at the least, the National Security Agency (NSA) of the United States, in cooperation with the NSA-equivalents of the United Kingdom, Canada, Australia, and New Zealand. Only Australia has admitted its participation, and America's NSA refuses even to answer inquiries from Congress about its activities.

The program involves a comprehensive electronic sweeping and sharing of information among its members. This includes all forms of electronic communication, most notably emails, text messages, and telephone voice communications. Anyone, anywhere, can be monitored by Echelon.

Echelon's significance in relation to the UFO cover-up is two-fold: it appears to be independent of national laws, and the American NSA holds the rank of first among equals.

In the same way that the Manhattan Project clarifies how Roswell could be swept under the rug, Echelon helps us understand how Majestic can operate successfully and maintain anonymity, even while controlling a global team of secret-keepers. In both cases, there is precedent from similar projects that have managed to pull off their own missions.

Paint It Black

The secrecy of the UFO reality has been matched only by the money that has gone into it. The decades-worth of moves and countermoves with an otherworldly intelligence have cost a great deal of money just to build the infrastructure and coordinate manpower.

Asking Congress to fund such a program is not an option. By its nature, the UFO/ET issue created an "end run" around the traditional American constitutional governance, for even elected representatives could not be trusted to maintain secrecy over such an awesome reality. As the secret-keepers saw it, funding needed to be covert, and even included such illegal non-governmental sources as drugs and guns. Think of such publicly known scandals as the Iran-Contra scandal of the 1980s, then multiply.

Still, public tax dollars also pay for such activities. The funds come from the black budget—that is, classified federal spending, much of which is hidden from Congress. The black budget has evolved throughout the years into a system of Special Access Programs (SAP). From these have grown "unacknowledged" and "waived" SAPs. Publicly, these "do not exist"—except that they do. Better known as deep black programs, a 1997 U.S. Senate report described them as "so sensitive that they are exempt from standard reporting requirements to the Congress." Persons involved in them were ordered to deny that their program existed, even to superior officers. Saying "no comment" was not good enough. Physical security for the program normally included "elaborate and expensive cover, concealment, deception, and operational security plans."[18] Such is a glimpse of the complex, compartmented, Byzantine system of Pentagon spending and secrecy.

We are talking about huge amounts of unaccounted money. During the last two decades, several Congressional inquiries have noted that many billions of dollars have gone missing from the federal system; some have even put the figure into the trillions of dollars. In 1994, a law was passed requiring the federal government to account for its money in a business-like way. As a result, several reports described the loss of gargantuan sums of money. The most perplexing of these claims came from Secretary of

Defense Donald Rumsfeld on July 16, 2001, when he spoke to the House Appropriations Committee regarding the Pentagon's Fiscal Year 2002 budget and stated, "The financial systems of the department are so snarled up that we can't account for some $2.6 trillion in transactions that exist, if that's believable."[19]

The amount of $2.6 trillion seems incomprehensible, especially when the Pentagon had an annual budget of about one-eighth that amount. Lest one believe this was a simple mistake, members of Congress discussed the amount, and the Pentagon's accounting office later amended it to $2.3 trillion. The number was clearly offered as legitimate. Secretary Rumsfeld could make such a statement because it was part of the fiscal mess he inherited from the Clinton administration. It should be noted, incidentally, that the amount of $2.3 trillion reflected accounting discrepancies, not necessarily "missing money." In later months, a good portion of the discrepancy is said to have been resolved. Even after that, however, many hundreds of billions of dollars were apparently gone.[20]

How is it possible to lose track of so much money? How long had this problem been developing? Although answers are not forthcoming, others have occasionally asked.

One person was aviation journalist Bill Sweetman. In one of the few public investigations of Special Access Programs, Sweetman estimated there were roughly 150 SAPs within the Pentagon at the close of 1999, many of them unacknowledged. They often had independent systems of classification, with total control exercised by the program manager. Most interesting, he concluded that most SAPs were dominated not by Defense personnel, but private contractors. He had no idea how these programs were funded.[21]

The sprawling secrecy apparatus was discussed again in 2010 by *Washington Post* journalists Dana Priest and William Arkin. After a two-year investigation, they concluded that America's classified world "has become so large, so unwieldy and so secretive that no one knows how much money it costs, how many people it employs, how many programs exist within it or exactly how many agencies do the same work."[22]

This structure applies to UFO secrecy. Considering the obvious importance of the UFO phenomenon and the need for a secret infrastructure to deal with it, a detached analyst can assume that there are several UFO-related black budget programs, and that some of the lost money has gone into funding them.

Follow the Wreckage

The U.S. has a history of government agencies existing in secret for long periods. The National Security Agency was founded in 1952, its existence hidden from all but a handful of Congressmen and Senators until the mid-1960s. Even today, little is known about the actual activities of the NSA. More secretive still is the National Reconnaissance Office, ostensibly charged with monitoring America's network of spy satellites. Founded in 1960, the NRO remained completely secret from the American public for 30 years.

Secrecy develops its own *raison d'etre*. For it breeds not only power, but private gain, and it appears that much of the UFO secret went private. Consider the scenario of a crashed disc recovery, like the Roswell incident. An exotic object goes down, the U.S. military arrives on the scene, keeps the civilians away, collects all material and bodies, sanitizes the area, and transports everything to relevant facilities, whether these be at Wright-Patterson Air Force Base, Los Alamos National Laboratories, or Nevada's Area 51.

Once the bodies and materials have been transported, then what? Clearly, they would need to be studied. While the branches of the U.S. military employ many brilliant minds, the fact remains: if the military wanted unfamiliar or extraterrestrial technology studied and replicated, then private contractors would be the answer. That is where most of the talent works and cutting-edge knowledge exists. When something needs to be built, one turns to General Electric, Lockheed, Boeing, McDonnell Douglas, SAIC, E-Systems, Hughes, Raytheon, Bell Laboratories, Bechtel, and other companies that could incorporate exotic technologies into new weapons and applications.

Through time, this would require giving up some amount of "ownership" of the technologies to the corporations. This is not such a bad option for the military. In the first place, generals and admirals know that once they retire, their best financial outlook will come from employment with some defense contractor. Privatizing the UFO secret also helps with secrecy. It means that all the secrets concerning UFOs and related technologies become not merely classified but proprietary. As such, they become even more impervious to public scrutiny. Responsible military and government officials could now say in all honesty that there are no known U.S. agencies charged with managing the UFO situation. Plausible deniability is critical.

Several sources from the covert world support the argument that control over the UFO secret has gravitated to the private world. One well-placed individual, with upper level connections to the CIA, told the authors that early in the 1980s, if not before, "the [UFO] program was transmogrified and became private, just as many, many other projects become private." Another source, equally well placed, said that enormous sums had been spent on a deep black program to study extraterrestrial technology, providing the interesting fact that security for the program was seven to eight times more expensive than the science. The source held a strong opinion that private contractors had taken the lead role in the secrecy structure. Two other insiders with high-quality credentials also arrived at this judgment.[23]

In this vein, the story of Vice Admiral Thomas R. Wilson is revealing. During the late 1990s, Wilson was Chief of Intelligence for the Joint Chiefs of Staff, a position known as J-2. In 1997, UFO researcher Dr. Steven Greer and Apollo 14 astronaut Dr. Edgar Mitchell obtained an audience with Wilson. The two expressed their concern about the "rogue" nature of certain Special Access Programs connected to the study of alien technology; that is, their concern regarding these programs were dominated not by government personnel, but by private contractors, possibly as runaway programs beyond formal government control.

According to statements later made by Greer and Mitchell, as well as another corroborated source, Wilson did look into the matter.[24] After two months, Wilson found that the claims were true. When he was finally able to meet with a representative of the SAP (not the program manager but its attorney), the Admiral was told that he lacked a need to know about it. Indeed, the only reason he was even granted a meeting was to determine how he learned about the program.

But saying that the UFO secret has been privatized is not completely right, either. We are talking about a quasi-public, quasi-private matter, like parents with joint custody of a child. Indeed, the U.S. military and intelligence community serves as the ideal shield behind which this private-public entity operates. The team-up makes the entire organization more impervious to public requests for information. And the continuing connection to the black budget feeds it with intelligence and resources that exist because of America's global military footprint.

Over time, however, the U.S. government lost a great deal of control over the secret, and even lost track of what it knew. A cloak of confusion descended over this important and life-altering matter.

When outgoing President Dwight Eisenhower warned the nation in 1961 of the growing influence of "the military-industrial complex," he might well have had the UFO situation in mind. He certainly saw the future.

Presidents and UFOs

There is much evidence that past U.S. Presidents have been interested in UFOs, and there is some that failed to learn all they wanted to know.

Given that Truman did know and probably formed Majestic, and that Eisenhower probably received a briefing upon entering office, it appears that these two presidents had some level of knowledge and control over the issue.

There are rumors about President John F. Kennedy, of how he told Marilyn Monroe, and of how his own intentions toward Disclosure ultimately may have gotten him killed. President Lyndon Johnson is thought to have been disinterested and to have passed the responsibility off to Vice President Hubert Humphrey. President Richard Nixon is widely perceived to have had knowledge, and there is a story that in February 1973, he took his close friend, the comedian Jackie Gleason, on a wild ride in Florida, showing him alien bodies at Homestead Air Force Base.[25]

Long before he was a U.S. President, Gerald Ford was a powerful U.S. Congressman. In 1966, when UFO sightings in his Michigan district had peaked, he called for a Congressional investigation. "In the firm belief that the American public deserves a better explanation than that thus far given by the Air Force, I strongly recommend that there be a committee investigation of the UFO phenomenon," said the future president, adding, "I think we owe it to the people to establish credibility regarding UFOs, and to produce the greatest possible enlightenment on the subject." The result was the Condon Report, that masterful manipulation initiated by the U.S. Air Force, which debunked the phenomenon. As president, Ford had nothing to say about UFOs, though in retirement he replied to an inquiry from a UFO researcher. "During my public career in Congress, as vice president, and president, I made various requests for any information on UFOs. The official authorities always denied the UFO allegations. As a result, I have no information that may be helpful to you."[26]

Jimmy Carter saw a UFO when he was governor of Georgia and promised to open the files when he became president. "If I become president, I'll make every piece of information this country has about UFO sightings available to the public and scientists," said the candidate. "I am convinced that UFOs exist because I have seen one." He tried for a year to get NASA to accept UFO reports, but gave up. This much is part of the public record.

The actress Shirley MacLaine, who was close friends with several U.S. Presidents, stated in a 1995 appearance on the *Larry King Show* that, "[President Jimmy Carter] told me many times...that it was true, that there were crafts, that he believed there were occupants."[27]

There is also a story told to the authors by a high-level intelligence official about a UFO briefing President Carter received in June 1977. It was unknown to the source what specifics were discussed, only that when the president was seen in his office, he was sobbing, with his head in his hands, deeply upset.[28] If it is true, then Carter got the briefing he wanted, but did not like what he heard. Moreover, he was influenced never to mention the subject again.

Ronald Reagan not only saw a UFO while Governor of California, but had his pilot chase after it. He told several people, including members of the press, until he realized the story would undermine his credibility. At that point, he back-pedaled. Years later, as president, he mused more openly. On several occasions during his presidency, Reagan discussed the scenario of how an alien invasion would unite humanity. Addressing the United Nations on September 21, 1987, he stated, "I occasionally think how quickly our differences worldwide would vanish if we were facing an alien threat from outside this world.[29]

Reagan is also alleged to have told filmmaker Steven Spielberg at the *E.T.: The Extra-Terrestrial* White House screening, "You know, there aren't six people in this room who know how true this really is."[30]

George H.W. Bush, a man with longtime connections to the world of intelligence, and who had directed the CIA for a year under President Ford, is believed to have known much about UFOs. While campaigning for President in 1988, he was cornered by a UFO researcher named Charles Huffer, to whom he said, "I know some. I know a fair amount." As president, Bush was tight-lipped about the subject, although there are sources who allege that there were high level discussions on a possible UFO Disclosure in 1990, which was canceled following the abortive coup in the Soviet Union that summer.[31]

Shortly after he became President, Bill Clinton instructed his friend Webster Hubbell, whom he had named Associate Attorney General, to investigate and report back to him on two things. "First," asked Clinton, "who killed JFK? Second, are UFOs real?" According to Hubbell, he found no answers, although it must be said Hubbell's tenure in office was brief, and he did not seem to have searched very diligently.[32]

One source of the authors, a man who has worked extensively within the national security establishment for many years, met with Bill Clinton at a social gathering during the late 1990s. After a few moments of one-on-one time with the president, the man delicately raised the topic of UFOs. Clinton's only comment was, "There's a lot there, and I wish I could do something about it."

George W. Bush built an administration which prided itself on secrecy, but it is quite possible that he was never fully briefed on this subject. At least, this is according to a senior intelligence official speaking on the condition of anonymity to the authors. It is, however, a reasonable speculation that his vice president, Dick Cheney, did have the clearance. Early in the Bush administration, the Vice President appeared as a guest on the Diane Rehm PBS radio program. Grant Cameron, a Canadian UFO researcher specializing in Presidential policy, was lucky to be the first caller. Cameron asked Cheney whether he had ever been briefed about UFOs while in the government. Cheney replied, "Well, if I had been briefed on it, I'm sure it was probably classified and I couldn't talk about it."[33]

President Barack Obama has avoided discussing the topic in public, at least not in a way to give it any credibility. When asked about the subject during the 2008 Presidential campaign—having just seen his rival Congressman Dennis Kucinich savaged for admitting to his own UFO sighting—Obama deflected with humor: "I don't know, and I don't presume to know. What I know is there is life here on Earth, and that we're not attending to life here on Earth. We're not taking care of kids....we're not taking care of senior citizens.... As President those are the people I will be attending to first. [audience laughter] There may be some other folks on the way.... [more laughter]."

Some individuals made well-publicized claims that Obama would be the "Disclosure President." Specific predictions (forever the bane of the alternative research community) were offered repeatedly for such Disclosure announcements, which of course never occurred. The predictions were based on alleged inside sources that clearly existed only in the realm of fantasy. If any further evidence were required to throw cold water on the notion of Obama as the Disclosure President, the White House statement of November 4, 2011 more, than suffices. This was in response to the "Disclosure Petition" organized by Stephen Bassett's organization, Paradigm Research Group, asking the Obama Administration to acknowledge an extraterrestrial presence on Earth. The reply was only granted because more than 17,000 signatures were attached to the petition. Yet, a low-level functionary drafted the reply that there is no credible UFO evidence, nor any to suggest a cover-up.[34] Whether or not Obama was ever briefed is not certain, although unverified sources told the authors that he had been briefed on the basics of the situation, but has no authority over the program.

Despite the importance of the subject, it is not clear that all U.S. presidents are briefed on it. Knowing details of black budget programs has become a liability. Moreover, presidents are transitory players on the national and world stage. They come and go. From the perspective of lifelong program managers, they cannot be trusted to deal with the issue in a secure manner during their term, nor after they leave office.

Who Is Really in Charge?

If the UFO secret is real, someone or some group is in charge and doing an acceptable job at keeping it quiet.

During the 1950s, American sociologist C. Wright Mills described a "power elite" in the United States comprised of corporate, military, and government elements. It was a radical analysis at the time. But Mills was onto something. Today, we can see that corporations—or more accurately, transnational corporations—have gained a dominant role in this relationship.

Right or wrong, globalization is the reality of today's world. By the late 1980s, it created new opportunities for corporate visionaries, primarily by access to cheap labor. The goal became to create an international legal structure to facilitate this process. There have been many facets of this transformation. One was the creation of the North American Free Trade Agreement (NAFTA), others included strengthening the International Monetary Fund (IMF), World Trade Organization (WTO), and World Bank, all of which promote privatization of natural resources and have often been accused of undermining national laws regarding health, food safety, and the environment.

It was a silent revolution. Until the 2011 "Occupy Wall Street" demonstrations in Manhattan, followed by similar "Occupy" demonstrations elsewhere, the question of who is in charge had not been up for much public discussion. Yet, a new global structure of power has been created that heavily influences, even dominates, nation states. Old-fashioned national sovereignty has become a quaint relic, like a old portrait of a forgotten family member, fading to yellow in a worn-out frame.

It is natural that these same private interests would eventually take charge of the UFO secret as well, albeit through the auspices of the U.S. government and military. The money is certainly there with which to do it.[35]

Worlds Within Worlds

By now, the classified world has moved far beyond the reach of the public world, and far beyond in its power and capabilities. This has great implications for UFO secrecy.

Consider the story of a former NSA scientist who spoke with the authors. According to this individual, the NSA was operating computers during the mid-1960s with a processing clockspeed of roughly 650 megahertz (MHZ).[36] To put that in perspective, it took 35 years for personal computers in the consumer market to reach that speed. Indeed, in 1965 there were no personal computers at all. Immediately, the near-fatal Apollo 13 mission in 1971 comes to mind, with its reliance on slide-rulers by mission specialists to guide the damaged NASA space craft back to Earth. When presented with this image, the NSA scientist shrugged and stated that secret computational capabilities were too important to share with NASA.

So, in computing, the National Security Agency was an amazing 35 years ahead of the rest of the world. This leads one to wonder not only what its computational capabilities are today, but what might be the capabilities of an organization charged with managing the UFO secret (in which the NSA is almost certainly involved). With a head start in studying exotic properties from materials obtained, say, at Roswell in 1947, is it not likely that some scientist would have a *Eureka!* moment at some point? Perhaps he might not be able to duplicate all the features of the object under study, but could important improvements be developed toward such things as better integrated circuits, high tensile fibers, laser technology, and fiber optics? Naturally, such claims have been made—and denied—for years. But there is a logic to them.

Here is where it becomes interesting. For sure, there would be a great profit motive at work. One would assume that there would be spin-off products introduced at great commercial value as a useful money-making venture. Ideal ground-floor business opportunities.

But what if some of the innovations derived from such exotic technologies were so advanced, so radical, that their very existence was deemed to be too sensitive to share with the rest of the world? What if, for instance, a true breakthrough was made with propulsion technology, and the black-world scientists produced some form of field propulsion—in other words, anti-gravity? Or biotech breakthroughs such as super-longevity? Such developments would transform the world (which we will return to).

If the clandestine world did invent a "flying saucer" of sorts, as an example, something that operated on principles of gravity-negation, why would the U.S. military refrain from using it during warfare? Surely, such a technology would be of immense value in fighting the wars that have severely strained the U.S. economy, to say nothing of the immense damage caused to Iraq, Afghanistan, Libya, and elsewhere during the past decade as a result of military actions. Would it not be logical, sane, and even humane to employ such technology to end warfare in a region that is being destroyed by it?

Cynics would state that the prospect of never-ending warfare is desirable to certain groups that influence U.S. policy. True, but there is another reason to consider. Within the history of U.S. military technology, we have examples of the military withholding the use of its best weapons because their existence was classified.

One of the better-known examples of this was the U.S. air strike against Libya in 1986. The raid employed F-111 fighter aircraft. Left out of the mission, however, was the F-117A Nighthawk, better known as the stealth fighter. It had been operational since 1983, but was still classified in 1986. In a form of logic both perverse and rational, the F-117A was so radically advanced that keeping it secret was more important than using it for this military mission. As it turned out, the strike on Libya failed to achieve its main objective, which was the elimination of Libyan leader, Muammar al-Gaddafi. The stealth fighter was reserved for a more important military engagement, which turned out to be the U.S. invasion of Panama in late 1989.

Applying this logic to the world of reverse-engineered UFO technology, one might see how something even more exotic than the stealth fighter would be reserved for missions considered more important than mere geopolitical struggles. If, as may very well be the case, some form of flying saucer was "made in the U.S.A.," what possible missions would it have?

The answer is obvious: to deal with the beings responsible for the UFO phenomenon in the first place. Whether these beings are extraterrestrial, long-term transplants, home-grown, interdimensional, time travelers, or something even more fantastic, the technology used to develop man-made UFOs must be used specifically to deal with them. We will expand on this theme in Chapter 4.

And so, the years turned into decades, the world entered the 21st century, the U.S. military structure became dominated by private contractors, and the world became a global village. Meanwhile, the secret-keepers of the UFO mystery became more fully international, and also became private to a large degree.

Given the mixture of a treasure chest of government money, private connections, and an extraterrestrial secret, the likelihood exists that six decades later there is a clandestine group that possesses:

Technology that is vastly superior to that of the "mainstream" world.

The ability to explore areas of our world and surroundings presently unavailable to the rest of us.

Possible interactions or encounters with the Others who are here in our reality.

Scientific and cosmological understandings that give them greater insights into the nature of our world.

A significant built "off the grid" infrastructure, partially underground, that affords them a high degree of secrecy and independence of action.

This might well qualify them as a separate civilization—one that has broken away from our own, in effect, a breakaway civilization. Still interacting with our own, its members probably move back and forth between the official reality of what we are supposed to believe, and the other reality which encompasses new truths and challenges.

When Disclosure finally comes in the future, it will reveal the existence of a group that has pulled the strings on the UFO secret for years. It probably has a name, one that we are unaware of now, that will be exposed and become infamous.

In this book, we refer to the leadership council and those men and women who answer to it as the Breakaway Group. Bolstered by tremendous co-opted assets worldwide, they have gained independence from the established political and military authorities. For it is likely that this Breakaway Group answers not so much to the President of the United States as it does to private, internationally based individuals and groups. These have been the quiet leaks from the classified world which have reached both of the authors for years, and which have reached many other researchers of this topic.

With the Breakaway Group in mind, one might be tempted to dismiss our formal government as mere window dressing. That would be a mistake. The Breakaway Group is able to exist in part because it draws from established, powerful institutions of government, finance, and military authority. Nationalistic governments exist, and they are powerful, even if they are infiltrated and co-opted by the Breakaway Group and individuals who serve it. In fact, most of the people who work in these existing institutions have no knowledge of their own manipulation.

The point is that, despite their co-option, the world's institutions still have a life of their own. In an A.D. world, they will still be engaged in the debate, held accountable for actions taken by their members, and will still be reactive to their constituencies—sometimes with and sometimes without the direction of the Breakaway Group.

Let us hope that those people in the Breakaway Group who are dealing with the presence of the Others are doing so in a way that is responsible to humanity as a whole. For now, we have no way of knowing whether this is so, and no way of holding them accountable to the people.

Disclosure presents the opportunity for a structural change in how the world does its business. The Breakaway Group fears the public blowback and loss of power from such an act of honesty, however, so they will maintain the secret as long as possible. They will do this because once their existence is intuited, then acknowledged, and then scrutinized, their long-standing role as puppet-masters may be coming to an end.

Yet even the power-brokers of the Breakaway Group cannot control everything. Although they will never disclose of their own choice, circumstances are in place that could force a decision, no matter how closed to the idea they might be today.

A secret once thought necessary to save the world has taken a quiet toll on many lives. Now, in order to save the world, that secret must be dragged into the light of day. Ready or not, here it comes.

Vignette #2:

Air Force Veterans' Petition on Behalf of Captain Thomas Mantell

✧✦✧

**AIR FORCE VETERANS' PETITION
ON BEHALF OF CAPTAIN THOMAS MANTELL**

To: The President of the United States

From: Veterans Supporting Recognition of Pilots Lost Contact

Date: July 1, 2023

The following is a petition posthumously to award Air Force pilot Captain Thomas Mantell the Congressional Medal of Honor for valor displayed in the line of duty while protecting his country on January 7, 1948.

Thomas Mantell died on that day more than 70 years ago while attempting to intercept an unknown flying object. This object was reported to be large and round and descended over Kentucky, where it was seen by the commanding officer and others at Godman AFB, by state police, and various citizens. Captain Mantell, a veteran pilot, was scrambled to intercept, along with two other fighter planes.

Mantell climbed his jet aircraft to more than 22,000 feet, leaving the other two pilots behind, and apparently blacked out and crashed to his death.

At the time, the Air Force gave the official explanation that Captain Mantell had inadvertently chased the planet Venus. Although the planet was visible in the sky, it was 5pm and the sun had not set. It is unlikely that Venus could have been that bright at that time so as to fool Mantell and the other witnesses. Three years later, the Navy disclosed that a secret, high altitude photographic reconnaissance Skyhook balloon had been nearby at the time, and that became the official explanation.

But in 1985, the transcript of Captain Mantell's transmission to Godman AFB was declassified. His last words were: "It appears to be a metallic object... tremendous in size... directly ahead and slightly above... I am trying to close for a better look."

Even astronomer and Project Blue Book consultant J. Allen Hynek conceded long after he blamed Mantell's death on the planet Venus, "Sometimes, I stretched too far."

Given the disclosure of the reality of an alien presence on Earth dating back to at least the 1940s, we, the undersigned, believe that Mantell's last words should be taken literally and that his honor be restored by awarding him his posthumous Congressional Medal of Honor.

Sincerely,

Undersigned

Chapter 3

Endgame: When the Impossible Becomes the Inevitable

You may fool all the people some of the time;
you can even fool some of the people all the time;
but you can't fool all of the people all the time.

—Abraham Lincoln

Change can happen with breathtaking speed. Consider the fall of Communism. For more than 70 years, the Soviet Union stood as a seemingly implacable enemy to America and its allies, an enemy that defined the lives not only of its own citizens, but those who lived in the "free world." Then, like flashes of lightning, the Berlin Wall was down, the Soviet Republics were independent, and all of Eastern Europe was holding free elections. No one saw it coming.

Complete change happened again on September 11, 2001. As that fateful day began, the world was as preoccupied and complacent as ever; by nightfall people went to bed frightened and focused.

However, sometimes the change we expect keeps us waiting like a date that never shows up. Disclosure of the UFO reality is like that. It is a truth obvious, clear, and absent from our public discourse.

Indeed, UFO Disclosure comprises a neat paradox: it is impossible and inevitable.

Twelve Angry Insiders

For years, the insiders managing UFO secrecy understood the problem.

Disclosure is impossible. Secrecy is the immovable object. The powers-that-be have no incentive for revealing the truth about UFOs, so dramatic its transformative power would be, so threatening to established interests. Surely, too, the years of official silence and cover-up might make people powerless to effect change.

Disclosure is inevitable. Truth is the irresistible force. Something this large cannot be held back forever. It is easier to stop a tsunami from reaching the shore.

Let us imagine a situation that sparks a crisis, a "trigger" to action. It could be an event in which many credible witnesses record what appears to be a genuine UFO. It might be the unauthorized leak of sensitive data. It might be a surprise detailed statement by a prominent figure about the UFO cover-up—something that allows for fact-checking and verification. The event that triggers Disclosure will probably involve multiple factors that will turn into an avalanche of truth, rushing over everything in its path.

As we have said, the decision to disclose the UFO reality will probably not be made on Capitol Hill or even in the West Wing. The power center of this secret—the Breakaway Group—will meet, maybe virtually, but probably in person. Although it may not be called Majestic-12, this UFO "Control Group" or "Silence Group" will come together and hash it out.

The first thing on the agenda will be a review of the event itself—the event that is pushing Disclosure beyond its normal habitat of radio shows like *Coast-to-Coast AM* and Discovery Channel specials. In this future turn of events, the growing momentum toward Disclosure will be discussed on the front pages and covers of newspapers and magazines, and become the lead story on network newscasts.

The discussion begins. One of the Majestic members will argue that, as bleak as it looks, the group has weathered previous storms like this one. The Phoenix lights in 1997 came close. Someone else will mention the sighting over Stephenville, Texas, in 2008, and the near-panic they felt as a result. Another member will note ruefully that, ever since Roswell, they have skated near the edge.

They take an informal, anonymous straw poll, just to gain a sense of where they are at. Imagine their surprise when, after counting the votes, they find they are deadlocked, six votes to disclose and six votes to stonewall. Every time Disclosure came up in the past, the idea had been defeated soundly.

Wishful Thinking?

Since the beginning of the UFO cover-up, interested observers have expected an imminent disclosure. In some of the earliest flying saucer books, U.S. Marine Corps Major (ret.) Donald Keyhoe predicted that the "Silence Group" could not keep the lid on much longer. As far back as 1950, in his book *The Flying Saucers Are Real,* he wrote "the official explanation may be imminent."

Opening the floodgates. Six decades of secret contact means a massive amount of suppressed evidence. Image by Mastersfx.

The feeling that Disclosure is imminent surfaces every few years, like Ahab's White Whale. It appeared again during the mid-1960s, when there were so many American UFO reports that even Congress wondered what was going on. Then again, during the late 1970s, when the Freedom of Information Act provided a new weapon against secrecy, some activists thought it just might be possible to pry the lid open. Even after the weakening of FOIA in the 1980s, researchers periodically believed that leaks from sympathetic insiders would turn the tables.

Some believe that Disclosure has been happening slowly over the years, via a policy of public acclimation to the UFO reality. To some, it is an article of faith. Indeed, Keyhoe himself believed this. "If we were fully prepared, educated to this tremendous adventure," he wrote, "it might come off without trouble."[1]

But if there is a public acclimation program in place, how would it be undertaken, and how would the public be prepared without causing panic?

No Business Like Show Business

Some UFO researchers believe that the entertainment industry is part of the effort to acclimate the public to accept the concept of alien life. Hollywood, it has been argued, has collaborated with the intelligence community to release disinformation, and at other times leak a few details to prepare people for eventual contact with non-human life.

Certainly several 1950s movies look like CIA-sponsored attempts to deal with Roswell. Researcher Bruce Rux cited 1951's *The Thing from Another World*, considered to be the first realistic flying saucer movie, which reflected certain elements of the crash and recovery at Roswell four years earlier. The film's maker, RKO, was up to its eyeballs in intelligence assets. It was owned by billionaire defense contractor and test pilot Howard Hughes, plus it was a subsidiary of Time-Life, which was owned by CIA-connected Henry Luce. The movie also captured the essence of the Top Secret government study, Project Twinkle, which was then classified.[2]

Some of the other movies of the era look suggestive, also. Several key industry players had connections to military intelligence and later the CIA.

Edmund H. North, the screenwriter of the 1951 UFO film, *The Day the Earth Stood Still*, had worked in the Army Signal Corps during the Second World War. It would seem that the secret-keepers wanted to float some trial balloons before the public, and that Hollywood producers were happy to oblige.

If so, their message seems unclear. Although *The Day the Earth Stood Still* demonstrated alien tough-love, many other movies from this period were invasion-oriented. They included *Earth Versus the Flying Saucers, Invasion of the Body Snatchers,* and *The War of the Worlds*. Were these also examples of CIA influence? And were they the result of official policy, or some unauthorized leak?

If there is continued intelligence community influence amid the outpouring of ET-related movies today, it is even harder to know what the message is.

Consider the career of Steven Spielberg. When he developed *Close Encounters of the Third Kind* in 1977, some wondered if he was part of a government acclimation program. Spielberg has always denied this, saying that he simply believes in extraterrestrial life and knows a good story when he sees one. Although such a denial is to be expected, Spielberg's choices in this genre support his position. His films have hardly been limited to a monochromatic meme about contact, something one might expect if he were receiving inside information. His early films, such as *Close Encounters* and *E.T.: The Extra-Terrestrial,* both portrayed the Others as benevolent scientists. His later treatments, however, showed no such optimism. *Taken*, his epic television series, depicted abductions as the core UFO secret, *The War of the Worlds* presented Martian predators wiping out humanity, and his television series *Falling Skies* featured the resistance against an alien invasion of Earth. Spielberg has also been behind such diverse projects as *Men in Black*, featuring Earth as a cosmic way-station, the historical fantasy *Cowboys and Aliens*, and *Transformers*, with its robotic threat. The easiest explanation for this extraordinary diversity of treatment is that Steven Spielberg, like other people, reads the literature.

The same can be said for the rest of Hollywood. During the 1990s, TV series like *The X-Files* ("The Truth Is Out There") and the historical conspiracy *Dark Skies* ("History Is a Lie") portrayed the government as involved in a UFO cover-up and willing to go to almost any lengths, often extra-legal, to maintain the secret. Both were subject to much speculation, usually either as a means to prepare the population, or else to provide disinformation.

Yet, why would the covert elite authorize dramatic content highlighting their own lies and deceit? If anything, Hollywood's natural method of operation may work in opposition to Disclosure. Its product is of such uneven quality, its messages so diverse, that any citizen hungering for its truth will receive only confusion.

If the Breakaway Group indeed had been using Hollywood as a means either to prepare the public for the eventual truth, or else to obfuscate and bury the truth still deeper, the moment of Disclosure will have caught them off guard, as it will have caught everyone else.

Points and Counter-Points

Let us imagine that the Breakaway Group has decided to break its deadlock by allowing one member from each side argue their respective positions.

First up is the member who supports the *status quo*. His argument will boil down to three fundamental points.

First, the public's right-to-know is not an absolute, especially during wartime. Moreover, he adds, there is evidence that at least some of the Others are hostile, given the abduction and mutilation phenomena. National security concerns dictate that they maintain control as long as possible in order to reverse engineer hardware and develop defensive capabilities.

Second, Disclosure will not stop with a simple acknowledgment of the presence of the Others. The world will be unable to grasp the complexity of this collection of disparate intelligent life-forms. And the Others themselves (or some of them) may have a negative reaction that we will have brought on ourselves. Since they have not made their presence clear, why should we go first?

Third, the results of telling the truth are unpredictable. The economy of the world is based on the *status quo*. Disclosure will cause it to falter and may create another Great Depression. With national unity weakened and governments undermined by years of lies, they will not be able to mount an effective response.

Public panic, he adds, is a real danger. It's not impossible that 1938 can happen all over again, he says gravely, only worse this time.

This refers, of course, to that iconic moment in American history when, on Halloween night, radio listeners who changed stations during the popular *Chase and Sanborn Hour* to avoid the singing of Nelson Eddy got the surprise of their lives. They heard a frightened eyewitness in Grover's Mill, New Jersey, stating that large tube-like spacecraft were on the ground. People were riveted, they called their friends, and the audience grew. As it did, listeners were informed that the human race was under attack by Martians. The aliens were massacring American troops and marching on New York City, as other spacecraft were landing across the United States.

These terrified listeners had tuned in to Orson Welles's *Mercury Theatre of the Air*. They were listening not to a news broadcast, but a radio play—an adaptation of *The War of the Worlds*, the book authored by H.G. Wells four decades earlier.

Orson Welles told the drama as a news story based on breaking events because he wanted it to be realistic. It certainly was. But many people never heard the disclaimer that the broadcast was a play. People heard the names of real places and government officials and assumed the broadcast was "real." In the streets, people were seen packing their prized possessions into their cars and speeding out to the countryside. Some became hysterical and others simply prayed and waited to die.[3]

The speaker might well add that panic was repeated several times. When *The War of the Worlds* was rebroadcast in Chile in 1944, it caused riots. Five years later, it happened in Ecuador. As late as 1988, citizens of Portugal panicked.

It is also possible he will add the comments of Winston Churchill, if a declassified report from the British Ministry of Defence files can be believed. The story came from a scientist who said his grandfather was one of Churchill's bodyguards during the Second World War. It had been passed down to his mother and then to him.

According to the scientist, his grandfather was present during a meeting between Churchill and General Dwight Eisenhower when they discussed an intriguing UFO incident. This involved a Royal Air Force reconnaissance plane returning from a mission that was approaching the eastern English coastline when it was intercepted by a strange metallic object that matched the aircraft's course and speed for some time. Then it accelerated away and disappeared. Churchill appears to have been more concerned about the social repercussions than the military implications of such a device. He said the report should be immediately classified because it would "create mass panic amongst the general population and destroy one's belief in the Church."[4]

No doubt some of the secrecy insiders know whether this story is true or not. If it is, it may be invoked to bolster their position.

It takes two sides to make an argument, however. One member supporting Disclosure now stands.

Facing his debate opponent, he states firmly, "First of all, the hype over the Wells radio broadcast has been overblown for years." Most people who listened in did not panic, and those who did lived in a much less sophisticated time. Besides, that broadcast was about an attack, accompanied by death rays and destruction. If there is any attack going on today, it's a silent one, and public reactions will be much more modulated.[5]

Secondly, he continues, despite what you claim, the public *does* have a right to know, no matter what the truth is, at least in time and on issues that are large enough. We are talking about a planetary issue that has to be dealt with by bringing in the talents and experience of the entire population, not just an elite few.

Moreover, he continues, the initial reason for the cover-up has long passed. The cold war is over. We've had enough time to assess and prepare the public. We know a great deal about who the Others are and what they want. And the signs point to the likelihood that the public will be able to assimilate this information and deal with it.

Finally, the world has too many problems to ignore this any longer. We can finally unleash the technology that has been developed in secret throughout the past seven decades for the betterment of humankind. Why not?

Just before taking his seat, he recalls a statement made by the famous Swiss psychologist Dr. Carl Jung. During the 1950s, Jung had made a thorough study of UFOs. Despite being portrayed by skeptics as dismissing UFOs as psychological in origin, Jung believed there was something important to the phenomenon. A quick search on his tablet retrieved the quote he was thinking of:

✧✦✧

> What astonishes me most is that the American Air Force, despite all the information in its possession and its so-called fear of creating panic, seems to work systematically to do that very thing since it has never yet published an authentic and certain account of the facts ... this is the most unpsychological and stupid policy one could invent. It is self-evident that the public ought to be told the truth, because ultimately it will nevertheless come to light.[6]

"It will nevertheless come to light," he repeats and takes his seat.

✧✦✧

The question on the minds of everyone at the table on this fateful day is whether or not this is the moment when Jung can say "I told you so."

What It Will Take

What will it take to create a condition where all the secret keepers can do is simply to get it over with?

Considering that seven decades of secrecy have given them no incentive for changing the status quo, the answer can only be something so public and so undeniable that the decision has been taken out of their hands. Ex-officio Disclosure must be in progress, based on some event that is causing the exponential growth in the numbers of people who understand that UFOs are real. Under those conditions, the Breakaway Group's only real choice will be to manage the revelation the best they can.

That is the moment when the impossible act of Disclosure becomes inevitable. Not because the men and women managing the secret have decided to release it, but because they will have seen their own credibility plummet until their only option is change. When that becomes the sole alternative, we will finally have Disclosure, and a not a minute sooner.

There are several avenues by which the truth will be placed so boldly in front of us that we will have to pay attention. We have considered them carefully, talked to other researchers, and even consulted our potential readers through private polling. Taking it all into consideration, we believe the road to Disclosure could begin with one of the following triggers which have been ranked from least likely to most likely. They are:

- Photographic evidence.
- Investigative journalism.
- Whistleblowers and leaks.
- Public confessions.
- Physical evidence.
- Foreign declassifications and public statements.
- Political instability.
- A heavily-documented mass sighting.
- Finally, in a class of its own, a decision taken by the Others themselves.

Photographic Evidence

Without a doubt, some UFO photographs have received detailed analysis from scientific teams and passed the test of authenticity. Two of the earliest were taken by an Oregon farmer named Paul Trent in May, 1950. Trent and his wife, both shy people, never tried to capitalize on their extraordinary images. Local friends, however, realized their importance, and the photographs were soon featured in *Life* magazine. Nearly two decades later, they were analyzed by the University of Colorado's UFO study. Even though the Committee's leader, Edward Condon, had been predisposed to debunk all UFOs, the Trent photographs passed muster with the staff specialists. In 1968, the Condon Report concluded that "all

If she does her job well, she will also learn that UFOs appear to pose national security problems. She would learn of the air space violations, the attempted interceptions, the absurd denials by the government. She might just find her world on the verge of being turned upside down.

At this point, her mind might recoil. Reporters are born and bred to be skeptics, sometimes arrogant ones. She thinks, *if UFOs were real, I would have known about them.* After all, she is a smart journalist who went to a good college. If these vehicles are flying in our skies, she reasons, it could never have been covered for so long.

Having taken the bait, she meets the inside source, her Deep Throat. She is given classified documents. These make it clear to her that UFOs are actual physical craft, and that the government has known for a long time. Suddenly, the story becomes very real. If she can convince an editor to start covering the story aggressively, she might have the distinction of being the reporter who pushed the Disclosure story forward. She might win her place in the history books.

So there is hope that the mainstream journalistic world can redeem itself. Yet, a more likely way of starting the fire is the emerging phenomenon of WikiLeaks, the organization that encourages submissions of classified or otherwise hidden documents by allowing the sources who leak them to remain anonymous. In July 2010, WikiLeaks released the Afghan War Diary, more than 90,000 documents about the war in Afghanistan. In October, the organization released about 400,000 documents relating to the Iraq War. The Pentagon called it "the largest leak of classified documents in its history." Then, just a month later, on November 28, WikiLeaks released the U.S. State Department diplomatic cables, which it described as seven times the size of the Iraq War Logs.

Just a decade earlier, these leaks of classified information were not possible, because there was no global technological infrastructure in place to enable it. But times have changed, and they will continue to do so.

It is not hard to imagine that key UFO-related documents could come into the possession of Wikileaks. Indeed, Wikileaks leader Julian Assange stated that some of the "yet-to-be-published" parts of the State Department cables include references to UFOs.[12]

A few days later, Assange's lawyer, Mark Stephens, told the BBC that WikiLeaks had information that it considered to be a "thermo-nuclear device," which it would release if the organization needed to defend itself. Could this be a reference to the reality and seriousness of the UFO phenomenon? As of this writing, the "device" has not been released.

Even if Wikileaks were to release incriminating UFO data, obstacles to Disclosure would still remain. First, the WikiLeaks managers would have to not censor the material. Then, even if the documents were published, we could expect the usual sources to attack them as fabrications. We need only look to the 1980s and the MJ-12 documents to see how such a scenario might play out. Still, it is undeniable that action by Wikileaks, or a similar type of organization, can play a major role in crashing the walls of secrecy.

Public Statement or Deathbed Confession

It might seem reasonable that a statement from an informed and presumably reliable source, especially from within the U.S. national security community, might be enough to spark the debate that ignites Disclosure. But such comments have happened before with little impact.

As previously noted, the former Director of the CIA, Admiral Roscoe Hillenkoetter, stated in an open letter to Congress in 1960 that high-ranking Air Force officers were "soberly concerned" about UFOs, but that the policy of secrecy and ridicule made citizens believe UFOs were "nonsense."

Whether Hillenkoetter was floating a trial balloon for Disclosure at the behest of Majestic, or had broken from them, or was simply speaking as a private citizen—press follow-up was non-existent.

There have been several statements during the first decade of the 21st century by Apollo 14 astronaut, Dr. Edgar Mitchell, about his knowledge of a UFO cover-up. Mitchell was the sixth man to walk on the moon, so his statements might be considered worthy of some journalistic gravitas. Mitchell's most explosive claim has been that two associates of his—individuals of highest national security clearances and of unimpeachable character—described first-hand knowledge of the deeply secret programs to study ET technology and bodies. He also spoke about Roswell as a true case of the crash of an extraterrestrial vehicle.[13]

The Roswell case has largely been cracked by virtue of the men and women who were there in 1947 who have talked to researchers before their deaths. Roswell researcher Donald Schmitt described his task as "racing the undertaker." One spectacular end-of-life confession came from Lieutenant Walter Haut, who was the Public Information Officer of the Roswell Army Air Field in 1947. Haut had written the initial press release about the recovery of a "flying disc." Shortly before his death in 2005, Haut signed a sealed affidavit, which was opened after he died. In a matter-of-fact tone, Haut stated that he saw samples of the Roswell wreckage, which "was unlike any material I had or have ever seen in my life." He added that he saw several bodies under a canvas tarpaulin. "I am convinced," he concluded, "that what I personally observed was some type of craft and its crew from outer space.[14]

These statements by Hillenkoetter, Mitchell, and Haut all failed to make a dent. They did not generate any journalistic or scientific response, nor even spark a public outcry for more facts.

In addition, there have been several impressive statements made by prominent figures around the world, none of which achieved a true media breakthrough or forced open a public discussion on UFOs.

During the 1950s, the Commanding General of the French Air Forces, Lionel M. Chassin, wrote: "We can therefore say categorically that mysterious objects have indeed appeared and continue to appear in the sky that surrounds us. What intelligence is it that guides these objects?...Human intelligence? Perhaps...nonhuman intelligence? Why not?"[15]

The British Admiral, Lord Peter Hill-Norton, who was Chief of the Defence Staff of the United Kingdom, also openly discussed the UFO reality. "There is a serious possibility," he said, "that we are being visited by people from outer space. It behooves us to find out who they are, where they come from, and what they want."[16]

The French Minister of Defense, Robert Galley, stated during a 1974 radio interview that, "if your listeners could see for themselves the mass of reports coming in from airborne gendarmerie, from the mobile gendarmerie, and from the gendarmerie charged with the job of conducting investigations...then they would see that it is all pretty disturbing."[17]

The Spanish General, Carlos Castro Cavero, told a journalist in 1976 that "the nations of the world are currently working together in the investigation of the UFO phenomenon. There is an international exchange of data."[18]

Japanese General Akira Hirano, Chief of Staff of Japan's Air Self-Defense Force, stated in 1977 that "we frequently see unidentified objects in the skies. We are quietly investigating them."[19]

Former Canadian Minister of National Defence Paul Hellyer made several statements in the mid-2000s, including "UFOs are as real as the airplanes that fly over your head," he said, adding, "The United States military are preparing weapons which could be used against the aliens, and they could get us into an intergalactic war without us ever having any warning."[20]

In a television interview from May 2010, President of Kalmykia, Kirsan Ilyumzhinov, the only Buddhist Republic in Europe, claimed that he had been taken aboard an extraterrestrial craft 10 years earlier. The abduction occurred, he said, in a Moscow apartment while on official business. Benevolent alien beings took him on a craft to another star system. Ilyumzhinov, incidentally, was also elected President of the World Chess Federation (FIDE) in 1995, a position he retains as of this writing.[21]

Any time a head of state, anywhere in the world, makes a claim like this, one might think that people would take notice. Ilyumzhinov's statement, however, received a modest amount of coverage and then was quickly disabled. BBC News spoke about his "reputation as an eccentric character." This, apparently, was because he had spent millions of his own dollars to promote chess within his republic. A great deal of speculation followed: Was Ilyumzhinov pulling a publicity stunt? Was he delusional in some way? No mainstream journalist ever asked whether his claims might be true. Ilyumzhinov, after all, was an intelligent and serious man. By making the claim he did, he was exposing himself to certain ridicule. The story quickly died.

Clearly, it will take a very big name making specific statements to tip the public to the breaking point; someone such as Colin Powell, a former U.S. Secretary of State and a man who had been the head of the

U.S. Joint Chiefs of Staff. Imagine a deathbed confession from Powell, or perhaps a signed affidavit from him to be read at his funeral. Such an event would trigger a massive public outcry, and would even shake the media into action. Other names that could qualify as trigger events if they spoke out at the end of their lives include former Presidents Jimmy Carter and George H.W. Bush Sr. (who was also CIA Director), and National Security Advisors Henry Kissinger and Zbigniew Brzezinski.

They could certainly start a discussion. However, even their last-minute statements might not end it. None of them would be immune to counter-attacks. He suffered mental deterioration toward the end of his life, it might be claimed. Or, he had a personal ax to grind.

Ultimately, these individuals are precisely among those who would be most implicated in the cover-up. None of them are likely to lead the charge, or they would have done so already. If one of these prominent individuals speaks out publicly, it will probably be after Disclosure has begun.

Physical Evidence

Just because these strange visitors have not seen fit to meet our blockbuster film fantasy of contact and hover above the Earth's major cities demanding our surrender, they may still, accidentally or on-purpose, leave us something with which we can do business. Indeed, this happened at Roswell and subsequent crash sites.

Clearly, if we could get a civilian lab to study such wreckage, it could prove the existence of the outsiders. For example, researchers Donald Schmitt, Thomas Carey, William Doleman, and others conducted an archeological dig at the Roswell crash site to search for wreckage that the Army may have missed in its cleanup from 1947. In particular, they hoped to find a piece of the so-called "memory metal" that several witnesses described. They did not. Yet, perhaps a piece of hardware continues to hide in the attic of some soldier, something that will not be found until his grandchildren clear it out after his funeral.

It may also be that a new crash occurs. If so, might somebody besides the government gets there first? Or, perhaps a government other than one of the main co-conspirators in the cover-up takes possession of an object, sends materials to multiple labs for analysis, and alerts the media. Given the dominant reach of the U.S. military and intelligence community, this is a long-shot. Moreover, based on what happened at Roswell where authentic wreckage was swapped out for a weather balloon, the possibility of fraud and illegal activity to prevent materials from being adequately analyzed is a strong likelihood.

There is an entire sub-section of UFO research that focuses on physical traces, not necessarily of crashes, but of landings where either heat or radiation has modified the Earth's surface. Indeed, thousands of ground trace cases have been studied throughout the years. Many are compelling evidence of unusual phenomena; a handful are of outstanding evidentiary value that something anomalous occurred. Yet they have not broken through into mainstream discussion.

We have not yet given much attention to alleged alien abductions, but to the extent that some portion of it is true, there are disturbing claims of implants being inserted into the bodies of the abductees. So far, the lab results on some of these are tantalizing but inconclusive. Some appear to be conclusive but not substantiated by multiple labs. That may not always remain the case.

Global Discussion and Declassification

Might some country other than the United States decide to end UFO secrecy?

Several other nations have released their official UFO files; little political forward-motion has come of them. The 1999 release of the French COMETA Report, a sophisticated analysis of many French UFO cases, received precious little mainstream comment. It was the same with the various releases of documents by the United Kingdom, although David Cameron, who became U.K. Prime Minister in 2010, did promise that he would aggressively release more files. Yet, expecting the U.K. to trump the U.S. on UFO Disclosure is fantasy. Some of the U.K. files are intriguing, but most are little more than "raw reports" called in by citizens, which received little to no investigation. They will not be weapons in the battle for Disclosure.

Other nations offer more interesting possibilities. Brazilian officials have occasionally made fascinating statements about the reality of UFOs. In 2010, they cleared the way to study and release UFO reports, including military encounters. In 2009, the Russian Navy announced it would declassify some of its underwater encounters. Both Russia and Brazil have a history of extraordinary military encounters with UFOs; if either of those nations announced that UFOs existed, the landscape would shift.

The greatest challenge to secrecy might come from a country that has practiced deep secrecy for its entire history—China. During the 1990s, just before its transformation into a full-fledged global power, China was still willing to follow the lead of the U.S. on this issue, at least according to C.B. Scott Jones, who for years was a special liaison for Rhode Island Senator Claiborne Pell. Jones shared Pell's interest in matters pertaining to UFOs and extraterrestrials. During the early 1990s, Jones was in China on Pell's behalf, and had occasion to talk to certain Chinese officials with some knowledge of the UFO issue. Impressed by the quiet, sophisticated study they had taken, he asked why they did not publicize some of their findings. Their answer startled him: "We are waiting for the United States to take the lead."[22] Whether this will continue to be the case for China is one of the world's great unfolding dramas.

But the UFO secret is too important for the United States to abdicate on. If some other nation decided to reveal it, it would be seen as a hostile act. Not only by the United States, but also the secret-keepers who work behind the scenes of governments and nations (that is, Majestic or the Breakaway Group). In fact, it *would* be a hostile act, most likely made in order to seize the initiative and move into a position of authority during the coming transformation. Such a decision would have to be carried out in the most extreme secrecy, lest the wrong people learn in advance. One could envision quiet assassinations taking place if things go wrong and the NSA and its allies learn of the plan.

It would also be conceivable that, if all else failed to stop the renegade government from disclosing, the United States might decide to jump ahead on the matter, if only to retain the initiative and its position of primacy among nations. Such a scenario would be worthy of a page-turning spy novel, and it might happen.

Mass Sighting

The event that forces Disclosure could be a mass sighting, one that is recorded independently on radar and videotape by officials, journalists, and the public. Perhaps, too, it prompts a visible military response that cannot be denied.

Through the years, some UFO sightings have combined some of these elements. These include events over Norway (1980s), New York's Hudson Valley (also 1980s), the Florida town of Gulf Breeze (late 1980s and early 1990s), Belgium (1989–1990), Moscow (1990), Mexico City (for years, starting in 1991), Phoenix (1997), and Stephenville, Texas (2008). They posed a challenge to the forces of secrecy. Some of these produced fascinating video evidence, and received at least some press coverage. In several of the American cases, there were behind-the-scenes pressures to prevent mass panic. Frequently, the Federal Aviation Administration (FAA) was on-the-spot, charged with stonewalling public inquiries with absurd explanations that were intended to prevent further press inquiry.

The non-American cases were comparatively easier to deal with. The Soviet Union in 1990 had a media apparatus that could hardly compare with its American counterpart. Mexico's and Belgium's media systems were certainly better developed, but it would be unrealistic to have expected either of those nations to flout the wishes of their powerful ally, the United States, by unilaterally ending UFO secrecy.

Clearly, for a mass sighting to be effective, it needs, at minimum, multiple video recordings. The extraordinary Stephenville sighting did not make further headway because it lacked video or photographic evidence. But even video is not good enough; it must be absolutely clear and undeniable. For instance, the Phoenix Lights of 1997, although recorded on multiple camcorders, never showed a clear object—only a huge formation of lights that admittedly defied easy explanation. Some of the Mexican sightings of the 1990s, although recorded from multiple vantage points, showed white dots in the sky. These white objects were undeniably strange, and moved in ways that were not normal, but once again they were not definitely recognizable as something "not ours." There could always be some reserve of doubt associated with them. Some of the Gulf Breeze photographs and video were compelling, but were typically shot by lone operators (and many of these by the same person, Ed Walters). The Hudson Valley cases, while utterly spectacular, occurred during the early 1980s, when camcorders were rare, and people didn't really travel with cameras. In the case of Belgium, there were several interesting photographs, some good video, and Air Force radar data. They were not, however, simultaneously recorded.

Today's cellphone video cameras are widespread, and they will continue to improve in quality and capability. Every major city in the world is "covered," so to speak, by citizens who have the ability to record strange things in the sky. Many of these objects are already being recorded; a quick web search will turn up hundreds of video recordings of UFOs from around the world. Some are hoaxes, which only serves to complicate the issue. Yet, it is only a matter of time before an unusual object of exceptional capability is clearly seen by hundreds or even thousands, and recorded by enough of them to force the hand of the powers behind the secrecy.

That is what is needed to start a chain reaction.

It is clear that major media groups have been complicit in downplaying the UFO reality, partly due to alliances with the national security apparatus, but also—after generations of denial and ridicule—from sheer terror at taking a risk on this subject. It would help, therefore, that the mass UFO event occurred while members of the major media were present with cameras already operating live. Better still would be to get unrehearsed reactions from on-the-spot television reporters or other major public figures.

A Combination of Events

Whatever the trigger event to Disclosure, it will certainly feel unique when we experience it, and it may well draw from different categories. For example, while we are not optimistic that investigative journalism in today's environment will be successful, it may be that a mass sighting leads to greater interest by reporters and then, finally, an investigation. Intrepid journalists may play a part, but will probably not start the ball rolling.

By the same token, although no one believes that a photo, by itself, will break the cover-up, a photo can be part of an ensemble of evidence. In the event of a mass-sighting, photographic and video evidence will be paired with hundreds, if not thousands, of witness testimony. This can get covered in the media, may generate leaks, and so on.

The future is unwritten on this topic, but there is one fundamental reality of our current era that may play a powerful role in the end of secrecy.

Political Instability

Throughout the past decades, there has been an undeniable relationship of political instability to the release of volatile UFO data. Mostly, this seems due to the likelihood that uncertain times provide greater opportunities for insiders to talk openly to journalists, as well as for initiatives that force greater degrees of government openness. In addition, it seems that there may be a connection between heightened UFO activity with locations and periods of instability.

It happened in the United States during the 1960s. At that time, extreme social agitation appeared alongside a willingness by Congress, for the only time in American history, to question the official line on UFOs. Perhaps one can chalk most of this up to coincidence, but it is true that during the late 1960s, everyone was questioning authority. Members of Congress did so because their own constituents demanded answers. In this case, the result was the Condon Committee Report, which admittedly was not a victory for Disclosure advocates. The point, however, is that the issue was brought into the open. It also happened that this was a time of heavy UFO activity, indeed one of the greatest in U.S. history.

A better example of political turmoil and UFO openness occurred after the scandal of Watergate and the collapse of U.S. power in Vietnam. It was during this political climate, one of great liberalism by the standards of the American system, that the Freedom of Information Act (FOIA) was strengthened in 1974, then strengthened again in 1976. Although these new laws were not designed with the release of UFO data in mind, they did result in an avalanche of formerly classified UFO documents being made public. From the mid-1970s until the early 1980s, FOIA was behind the most important release of official UFO documents there had ever been, roughly 10,000 pages. The result was not the end of denial regarding UFOs, but truly an exposure of the cover-up itself, for it became clear that many government agencies that had denied an interest in UFOs were simply lying. It is also noteworthy that during this period, large numbers of leaks began to discuss secret retrievals of crashed UFOs, or the possession of alien bodies. In several cases, retired military people quietly came forward to UFO researchers, because they believed that the new openness portended an official announcement that would come from the Jimmy Carter administration. Finally, we must also note that late 1973 to 1978 were extremely active years of reported UFO activity within the United States, as well most of the world.

Other nations offer their own examples of political turmoil and transformation linked to the release of UFO data. In Spain, following the death of longtime *Caudillo* Francisco Franco in 1975, UFO information began immediately to reach the public via official channels.[23] It is also noteworthy that Spain was the scene of an impressive wave of UFO activity from 1974 through 1976.

China, too, appears to show a relationship, especially regarding the death of longtime dictator Mao Zedong in the fall of 1976. China had previously been a blank spot on the map as far as UFOs were concerned. That changed dramatically with the leader's death. Immediately afterward, Chinese ufology began to grow and thrive, and Chinese UFO reports became frequent, many of which were spectacular.

Similar to China, UFO activity in the Soviet Union had scarcely reached the West. This changed as the nation began its final convulsions prior to dissolution at the end of 1991. All through 1989, 1990, and 1991, UFOs were reported throughout the country. This was possible because, similar to the United States, Spain, and China, important laws were relaxed, which allowed people to make such reports and encourage public discussion. For a few years, not only did many well-documented and disturbing reports come out (including one of a large UFO just east of Moscow on March 21, 1990), but several statements by leading Soviet defense figures confirmed a serious UFO problem. This could never have happened under the old regime. However, in an era in which all bets were off regarding the future, powerful people, such as Deputy Minister of Defense Ivan Tretyak and Chief of the Soviet Air Defense Forces, General Igor Maltsev, spoke in a surprisingly candid fashion. Maltsev, discussing the March 1990 object, told the press that it was a disc 100 to 200 meters in diameter, and it was able to perform an "S turn" flight horizontally and vertically, as well as hover and then fly "with a speed exceeding that of the modern jet fighter by 2 or 3 times." All the while, it had been silent while doing these things. "At the present time," he added, "terrestrial machines could hardly have any such capabilities."[24]

The outbursts of openness in these nations all occurred during periods of regime change or extreme instability. Of course, this is no guarantee that UFO information will leak, and there are many counter-examples in which regime changes did not result in the release of such information. But such periods of instability appear to lend themselves to this kind of openness in one form or another.

Reaching critical mass. In the final days, citizens will band together to demand the truth. Night Falls in Tahrir Square, February 1, 2011. Image courtesy of The Associated Press/Tara Todras-Whitehall/AP Images.

This leads to the obvious question: How likely will the global situation of the early 21st century lead to another spectacular release of UFO data, one that may push the world past the tipping point and into Disclosure?

By all accounts, the current situation is unstable. The global financial crisis of 2008 is not over; the U.S. economy and much of Europe continue in a free-fall of deindustrialization; Greece and several other European nations are close to bankrupcy; in the United States many states have cut major services and several have flirted with bankruptcy; tensions in the Middle East have peaked; nuclear fears dominate the India-Pakistan, North Korean, and Middle Eastern regions; the wars in Iraq and Afghanistan continue to bleed global resources dry; an environmental crisis struck the Gulf of Mexico; and other eco-crises have engulfed much of the rest of the world. These problems do not describe the full weight of the world's problems, but they show that the global kindle is dry; a spark may well set major crises into motion. Not long ago, the movement to "Occupy Wall Street" gained worldwide recognition, and continues to be a sign of widespread dissatisfaction by people with the current structure of political and financial power. Perhaps the global spark has been ignited, or perhaps this is a precursor to the main event.

If history is our guide, the current unrest may jar UFO secrecy loose.

Finding Out for Ourselves

Behind any of the specific events that may result in UFO Disclosure, however, there is one great, inexorable force, relentlessly pushing us all into the future, into the light of truth. That is the steady growth of human technology and capabilities.

The Endgame could happen tomorrow, it could happen in 20 years. It might even wait longer, although we doubt it. There are a few reasons: the increasing rate of change of our society, the greater volume and acknowledgment of truly mysterious sightings, and the global need to get on with business. We may be at the tipping point, or at least at its beginning. Even if the Others do not wish to be found, those of us who for so long have been on the outside of this secret may find them first.

Consider the change of pace in our civilization. For thousands upon thousands of years, human society went on with very little change. More than a century ago, European farmers commonly used hand scythes not much different than those used by the earliest farmers from 10,000 years ago. As recently as the 19th century, most human production was based on muscle power, whether human or beast, just as it had been since time immemorial. In the realm of the mind, too, our condition was marked, century after century, by the replacement of one set of superstitions with another. That is, until the introduction of scientific thought throughout the last four centuries—a blink in cosmic time.

Following eons upon eons of life that went on in a certain way, human civilization has reinvented itself in the last century. Using science as its basic tool, we have unlocked Pandora's box, releasing our vast potential for good and ill. From the relatively recent reality of horses pulling carts, we have invented: the light bulb, the automobile, the airplane, the radio, motion pictures, mechanical robots, insulin, television, frozen food, liquid fueled rockets, the electron microscope, radar, jet engines, helicopters, computers, the atomic bomb, transistors, bar codes, the hydrogen bomb, solar cells, optic fiber, the hovercraft, the modem, integrated circuits, the microchip, compact discs, hand held calculators, cell phones, personal computers, super conductors, the World Wide Web, fuel cells, the sequencing of the human genome, the iPod, optical camouflage systems, YouTube, and smart phones.

And time will not stop; emerging technologies today are of incredible diversity and transformative power. In the area of transportation, they include: nuclear fusion power, biofuels, nanowire batteries, ultracapacitors, wireless energy transfer, and electric cars. In material science they include high-temperature superconductivity and superfluidity, carbon nanotubes, cloaking devices, and self-healing materials.

But it is in the area of information technology that the most dramatic (and for our purposes, relevant) changes are likely to take place. For here, we are on the verge of entering a completely new world in which computing power achieves capabilities we could not dream of just a few years ago. Within the next few years, we are likely to see widespread use of solid state drives, making computers and portable electronics devices lighter, stronger, faster, quieter, and requiring less power. There will be breakthroughs in the areas of holography and virtual reality, enabling people to immerse themselves within realistic artificial environments. We should also expect improvements in the ability of the human brain to interface with the World Wide Web via direct interface with computers or even implants.

Most profound will be the improvements in artificial intelligence and quantum computing. According to computer and AI experts such as Ray Kurzweil, by around 2020 we can expect to see computers embedded everywhere throughout our world, even more so than today. Virtual reality environments will be more common, as will "computer assistants." By then, it is expected that the computational power of a leading edge consumer brand computer will be equal to the computational power of one human brain. That does not mean that your computer will necessarily be "smarter" than you are. But it does mean it will possess an awesome computational and "thinking" ability that current computers lack (excepting computers within the classified world, where this ability may have already been achieved).

By 2030, it is possible that a typical computer will have the processing power of 1,000 human brains. The human brain itself may well be mostly "decoded"—that is, digitized somehow. And if it is digitized, it can be uploaded. There will probably be direct neural pathways between human and machine, implants of all sorts to enhance human abilities, and computers that claim to be "conscious."

Within such a period of dramatic technological change, can we really expect that our ability to create forward motion on the matter of UFO Disclosure will not somehow be enhanced? Consider how portable electronic devices—smart phones—have changed the way we communicate within the short span of five years. We are all communicating with each other in ways that were unforeseen just a few years ago.

Indeed, the world of the next twenty years promises a transformation of global civilization. It may also see the beginnings of a transformation of the human species itself via developments in biotechnology. All of this will happen whether or not the Others are acknowledged.

The Breakaway Group may not have considered this, but they should. Even though they have had a head start thanks to exclusive access to alien technology, the rest of us will soon have the capabilities necessary to find the Others, definitively, without anyone's help.

The Others

Finally, however unlikely it seems, there is one trigger that trumps all others, and brings Disclosure instantly and openly.

No one really knows how these "Others" think in the most general terms, much less how they think about the prospect of revealing themselves to us. It may be that they do not think about it much. They have not landed in a public space and announced their presence, like the extraterrestrials from *The Day the Earth Stood Still.* Nor have they been entirely successful at remaining hidden. Indeed, they have been seen by millions of people.

If the Others have anything to do with maintaining the status quo, then they are not apt to announce their presence in any new way. However, it may be that the idea of slow acclimation is not a human one, but theirs. Perhaps their craft do not really crash accidentally. Could it be that, although they could disguise themselves from our radar and our eyes, they choose not to? Maybe one day they will decide to end the debate here on Earth once and for all.

Facing the Light

Throughout the years, this discussion had come up among the human secrecy elite, the Breakaway Group. Always, the rule of secrecy prevailed. On this occasion, the deadlock could well go on for some time, except for one thing: *The world already understands what is going on.*

There are many routes by which Disclosure may arrive. Some undoubtedly will merge with others, and what starts as a trickle will become a river, then a flood. Once the process starts, there will be a free-for-all by many people and institutions to reach the truth first.

When that moment comes, the people of the world will offer less resistance than prior generations would have. By now, the public has seen it all. Our collective capacity for shock is lower than at any time in history. We have lived through the death of Soviet communism, impeachments, natural disasters, rogue nuclear states, 9/11, destructive wars fought on false pretenses, disputed elections, collapsing economies, and an African American in the White House.

The old choice between the truth and the lie will vanish. The accumulation of knowledge by ordinary people, the cracks in the stonewalling response, the expanding consciousness of our planetary condition; all of these together will move the world closer and closer to the tipping point. For the insiders, it will now come down to either getting in front of the issue and leading the discussion, or remaining hidden and letting it slip from their grasp. Such a result will be unacceptable for the secret-keepers.

So, at the end of the debate, members may discuss the state of planning for Disclosure. As far back as the purported November 1952 Eisenhower Briefing Memo, it was mentioned that "contingency plan MJ-1949-04P/78 (Top Secret - Eyes Only) should be held in continued readiness should the need to make a public pronouncement present itself."

Whatever the authenticity of that document, there can be no doubt that a contingency plan of some sort has been periodically dusted off and updated throughout the years. Studies would have been commissioned, polls taken. At the meeting, this data will be available, and expert testimony will be read.

When the next vote is taken, the ayes will have it in a super-majority. As looks are traded around the room, the chairman realizes the enormity of what has taken place. He asks, "Well, who's going to tell the President?"

Vignette #3:

One Family's Story

✧✦✧

Today on the eve of the one year anniversary of Disclosure, commonly referred to now as AD1, we begin a series of "Where Were You?" articles, prepared by our staff, detailing the moments immediately before the news broke and immediately after. Some of these people are famous, and were involved directly in the events of that day. Many more were just average people, like the Franklin family of this first in a series.

One Family's Story

Looking back, Bob and Jennifer Franklin remember AD1 for how normal it felt when it started. With three children that spanned junior high school to junior college ages, the breakfast table was typically chaotic for a Friday. Rides were being arranged, plans for movies and sleepovers were in progress, dress codes were being discussed, and reports were waiting to be printed until a new ink cartridge could be found. Bob had a presentation to go over with the CFO that was three days overdue and he was scared and frustrated when he left without kissing Jennifer goodbye. She barely noticed because today was the last day she was working with her partner who was retiring from the police force and she was in charge of the cake. The kids were left to sort out their own schedules for themselves. But they would see each other again in a couple of days for the family's regular Sunday dinner. That much was for sure.

At lunch, Jennifer's partner got the news that his retirement party had been canceled, or at least postponed. Apparently, the Department of Homeland Security had just raised the threat level to orange. She paid for lunch, got her partner a slice of pie with a candle, and gave him a long hug. Both had been approved for overtime until a department re-evaluation following the President's speech. The cake would have to wait.

The CFO made Bob wait in his outer office for 45 minutes, where he watched CNBC's coverage of the stock market fluctuations over all the rumors. Bombing Iran was emerging as the consensus for the announcement, but Bob thought it was stupid beyond belief to telegraph your punch like that. No wonder the markets were freaking out and had just closed down 237 points.

In the hour before the President was to speak, it became clear that other world leaders had reserved similar times to also speak to their own people. When the president soon stood at that familiar lectern and uttered the phrase "intelligent non-human species," both Bob and his boss uttered the same expletive. Bob instantly dialed Jennifer and got through. "Are you seeing this?" She answered that the word was the governor was going to call for martial law and that Bob should leave the office immediately and head back home. She would call the kids right away and call him with their locations, providing she could get through what was sure to be a monumental overload of the cell tower infrastructure.

That night Jennifer did something she had never had to do before in her law enforcement career, which was to discharge her service revolver. She fired it into the air to stop a crowd of looters at Stark and Whitman, and three were arrested. It took twice as long as normal to book them at the station, not so much because of the extra perps that were getting fingerprinted, but because all the intake personnel could not stop watching the TV—and neither could the perps. When Jennifer got off her shift at three in the morning and came home, she found Bob still watching with both younger kids under his arms asleep like they used to do when they were in grade school. As she filled the coffee maker with water, she looked up at the stars and thought she saw something, but she wasn't sure.

Other types have also been reported. Reptilian-type beings, who by all witness accounts are formidable creatures, both in terms of their intelligence and technical capabilities along with insectoid or mantid-type beings. Each one of these has been reported with variations: some taller, some shorter, some with a mixture of features and colorations. Sorting all this out is daunting, as one cannot be sure of how much actual memory is being recovered as opposed to screen memory or confabulation. Yet, the patterns are there.

Human-looking entities have also been reported. These, however, are not your run-of-the-mill human. They are very different, and seem to be "beyond human." Often termed "Nordics" or "Blonds," they typically appear as majestic, even angelic. They often demonstrate deep intelligence and a kind of paternal empathy for the humans who encounter them. It is difficult to say that they "abduct" people. It is true that many of the people who have allegedly had encounters with these beings did not ask for contact (although some claim that they actively sought contact with these beings). It is, instead, that the encounters are usually described as a positive experience.

There is also a body of research that describes "almost-human" beings, something that appears to be a hybrid species: part-human, part-something-else. A program to create a genetically modified human being? It might appear so.

What do we make of these varied beings? Do they represent different groups? If so, what might their own relationships be? Do they cooperate or compete with one another?

During the 1960s, Ivan Sanderson, a biologist by profession and one of the most original writers about UFOs, methodically asked not what UFOs were, but what they *could* be. He developed a six-page outline of the possibilities.[1] Therefore, suggested Sanderson, they could inanimate or animate. If inanimate, they might be natural, or artificial, each possibility with several subsets. If animate, they could also be natural or artificial. Natural forms might include life-forms indigenous to space, or to atmospheres, or to solid bodies. Artificial forms might be domesticated natural life-forms, genetically created life-forms, or biochemically created life-forms. And so on.

Keeping a similarly open mind, and with an eye toward comprehending all the evidence offered by this most challenging of subjects, we can summarize the existing explanations for whom the Others actually may be.

Extraterrestrial

Based on humanity's built-in sense of time linearity and spatial relationships, it is easy to understand why this explanation has been the most obvious and durable. Our own perceptions of time involve moving forward, and our perceptions of space involve moving from one place to another.

Deepening the riddle. Who are they and what do they want? Photo courtesy of NASA/STSci.

Extraterrestrials have always been at the heart of the debate about UFOs. Because the beginning of the modern UFO mystery, speculation both informed and otherwise has considered that these unknown objects might be "interplanetary." This includes analyses from within the United

States Air Force, which at various points during the Cold War had substantial factions stating that this was the most likely possibility. Certainly, the extraterrestrial hypothesis (ETH) has been the dominant theory among UFO researchers since the first books on the subject appeared in the 1950s. We have also seen the ETH demonstrated in countless space alien movies, depicting intentions both hostile and benign.

There is a powerful logic to the ETH. Astronomers now estimate that the Milky Way galaxy alone contains from 200 billion to 400 billion stars. These numbers are staggering, even considering that only 7.6 percent of all stars in our galaxy are sun-like "Type 2" stars. If we accept the lower estimate of 200 billion stars, this means there could be 15 billion sun-like stars in the Milky Way. Indeed, within the scant astronomical distance of a mere 50 light years, we know of at least a dozen such stars.[2] If we consider that inter-galactic travel might be feasible in some manner wholly unknown to us at present, the field opens up to the hundreds of billions of galaxies estimated to exist.

But let us confine ourselves merely to our own, cozy galaxy. We do not know how many planets orbit around the estimated 200 billion stars, nor how many of those planets might be similar to Earth. Yet, recent discoveries give us cause for a liberal estimate. By late 2011, astronomers have made confirmed detections of 693 planets beyond our solar system. Most of these are gas giants like Jupiter, presumably unsuitable for life (although this leaves out the question of possible moons around a gas giant that might support life). However, the high proportion of gas giants is a function mainly of our detection methods, which generally have not been sophisticated enough to find many smaller, rocky planets, like Earth. It is now thought that most of the extrasolar planets are rocky—like Earth. In particular, recent studies indicate that most sun-like planets are likely to have rocky planets orbiting them.[3]

Understanding that, from this point, we are estimating using logical guesses more than hard data, let us press on a little. If we consider that only one-third of sun-like stars have rocky planets orbiting them, and that only one-third of those have a planet that is roughly the size of Earth, and that one-tenth of those developed life of some sort, and that one-hundredth of those were home to a species that attained intelligent life akin to birds, reptiles, and mammals, and one-hundredth of those gave rise to a species that mastered science and technology, we would be left with more than 16,000 technologically proficient civilizations that have existed in the Milky Way alone.

Some exobiologists might think these estimates are very high; others might consider them conservative. But let us stay with the estimate of 16,000 technologically proficient civilizations. What might be the odds that some of them currently exist? Here, too, we can do little more than guess, but surely it seems reasonable to suppose that there may be quite a few. Have many of these mastered the art of space travel, as humanity is only now just beginning to do from its home on Earth? Even if some of them rejected the idea of reaching out to other life forms, perhaps for philosophical reasons, there may be others who have embraced it.

Clearly, there are hindrances to them contacting us. There is the problem of distance. We are constantly reminded by astronomers of the astronomical distances separating the stars. These are far beyond what human beings can travel. There is also the question of how long technologically advanced civilizations can last. Considering how quickly we have brought ourselves to the brink of global disaster by means of nuclear weapons, natural resource depletion, and environmental pollution, we wonder if other technologically advanced societies last very long before collapsing. Yet, as we will discuss shortly, there may be a good reason to suppose that advanced civilizations can be durable. They may even be more durable than their planets. It is possible that at least some of the UFOs are extraterrestrial visitors who no longer have a home world, or have exhausted its resources, and are travelers in space, stopping to re-source their ships for the rest of their journey.

It is certainly possible that *all* of the diverse beings associated with UFOs have extraterrestrial origins. This scenario is still the odds-on favorite as an explanation for UFOs. A Las Vegas oddsmaker would have to make this likelihood the one to beat.

Still, other long-odds answers do exist.

Intelligent Machines

It may be possible that the Others are not alive in the sense that we are. Given our rapidly approaching abilities in machines and artificial intelligence, and the fact that other civilizations could be hundreds, thousands, or even millions of years more advanced than us, it is possible that we are encountering contact with the products of advanced machine intelligence.

Most scientists involved in artificial intelligence research are convinced that we are on the verge of a new era in civilization: the age of intelligent machines. Many of them also believe in the inevitability of an event they call the Singularity.[4] This is believed to happen when computer intelligence becomes able to upgrade itself, to reprogram itself continuously, and become self-aware.

Such a process could involve a rapid, exponential increase in computer intelligence, far surpassing human intelligence. Consider Moore's Law. In 1965, Gordon E. Moore predicted that the number of transistors per integrated circuit would double every 18 months. Incredibly, this has held true. In 1971, the leading integrated circuit had more than 2,000 transistors; by the year 2000 that number was 42 million. In 2010, Intel unveiled the world's first 2-billion transistor microprocessor.

Is there a critical mass in terms of hardware, software, connectivity, and storage that will enable machines to foresee their own technological needs and redesign their software? Instead of requiring 18 months to double their power, what would be needed when artificially intelligent computers are assisting with the research? Could the time be cut to 12 months? And when it becomes more powerful still, to six months? Then three months, then one month—then what? At that point, as one AI writer put it, "our crystal ball explodes" and everything we know goes out the window.

When will this happen? Many AI experts believe it could be anywhere from 2020 to 2080. Some prognostications are unsettling. More than one scientist has predicted, for all intents and purposes, a god-like level of intelligence residing within machines. Some, like Bill Joy, co-founder of Sun Microsystems, have issued warnings. Others believe that Singularity may be the only way our species can be saved from itself.

Human beings are not suited to live in space, nor anywhere other than Earth. We evolved here, with Earth's unique gravity, magnetic fields, temperature, microbes, atmosphere, and food. To live elsewhere, we would need to be modified, perhaps so much that the result would be something entirely different than what we are now. A new species, created with some of our DNA, would probably be the most logical means of sending biological organisms to distant worlds. Unless, of course, it is a better choice to let the machines go it alone.

Was such a scenario played out somewhere else in our galaxy? Perhaps the answer is yes. If so, it could explain many elements of the UFO phenomenon. Why, for instance, has no one announced themselves formally to us? Perhaps because establishing relations with human beings on any level of parity makes no sense to a machine or artificial organism.

On the other hand, an advanced machine intelligence might be interested in our biological resources. In order to interface with natural worlds, a machine intelligence might create biological entities for expressly that purpose. Presumably, the best way to do this would be by custom-creating entities from the DNA native to that particular planet. Our scientists are only beginning to unravel the secrets of DNA. But to an intelligent machine wanting a supply of biological organisms, such raw material could be very important.

This brings us to the Grays. These creatures seem to be perfect candidates for artificially created beings. They appear to be gender-neutral, and many witnesses claim they lack sex organs. This makes sense. Why would you want a drone-worker to have the ultimate distraction of sex organs, when you can make such creatures yourself? Author and abductee Whitley Strieber has described his impressions of the Grays as mechanical, working in a tight unison that would be unusual for biological creatures, but reasonable for mechanical ones.

Abductees often describe a single Gray taller than the rest, who is "in charge." They often report a procedure, sometimes called Mindscan, when the entity probes the person's mind telepathically and "sees" their innermost thoughts. This might be interpreted as tremendous psychic power possessed by the entity, but perhaps such a thing could be done by implants within the brains of the alien being and abductee. For instance, it is now possible for chimpanzees to move a computer cursor across a screen, solely by the power of thought—and a conveniently placed chip in the brain.

Such news gives one pause when considering claims of alien implants within human abductees. Could implants be more than mere tracking and storage devices? Could they also function as conduits to an advanced machine intelligence?

Consideration of this theory weakens one of the main skeptical arguments against UFOs: that advanced technological civilizations may not last very long. Skeptics see our own civilization spinning rapidly out of control and extrapolate this feature to intelligent life elsewhere. Now, advanced technology wielded by biological entities may indeed be inherently unstable, but it is not so clear that such a condition applies equally to advanced machine intelligence. If not, the extraterrestrial hypothesis—combined with advanced AI—becomes more tenable as a way to explain UFOs.

As for understanding the motives of any artificial intelligences that are here, this might be as difficult to fathom as life beyond the Singularity. After all, if UFOs are the product of advanced machine intelligence, they passed that point long ago.

Earth-Based Entities

Maybe we know less about the Earth than we think we do. Under this theory, we are not the only intelligent life-form living on this planet. It might seem counter-intuitive that another intelligent species could have evolved here on Earth without our knowledge. But one interesting possibility would be a branch of humanity itself. Is there enough time in the prehistory of humans on Earth for a technologically capable civilization to have evolved and then, somehow, gone into hiding from the remainder of the human race?

We might call this "the Atlantis theory." Among scholars of alternative ancient history, there is a major school of thought contending that there was in fact such a civilization, and that it suffered a cataclysm around 12,000 years ago. This cataclysm left its mark on later human groups in the form of myths about the Great Flood.

Perhaps an early civilization, one which attained great heights of science and learning, did exist during such an antediluvian period. Could it be that representatives of that civilization continued on, but kept their knowledge to themselves? Would they have interacted with the rest of humanity—mere savages by comparison—and passed themselves off as gods? Could they then, over the following thousands of years, have continued to develop as a quasi-secret society, partly interacting with the masses of humanity, but also continuing their own esoteric tradition, one in which they eventually developed flying saucers?

As difficult as it might be to accept for many people, there is an undeniable neatness to the idea. It would explain the human-looking "extraterrestrials," which would now not be extraterrestrial at all. Perhaps, too, these highly advanced humans conducted genetic manipulation to create the other types of "alien" entities.

Again, we are left with the question of why we fail to see evidence of such a human civilization. But perhaps that is because they have merged themselves with us, effectively living among us. Another possibility is that the human-looking entities that people encounter are indeed human, but were taken millennia ago by extraterrestrials. After thousands of years, they have been enhanced and made to seem like gods to the rest of us.

Whatever the answer, we might wonder if they control human civilization while still maintaining themselves as a separate society. It also seems possible some of them have established permanent residence here. After all, we do have a beautiful planet.

Extra- or Ultra-Dimensional

The people who lead the way in "out-of-the-box" thinking are the physicists. They openly discuss reality, perception, and nearly every other once-crazy idea in ways that demonstrate how the universe is much stranger than we ever considered.

It should not surprise us, then, to learn that some of them do not confine their cosmology to just one universe. Increasingly, they theorize about a "multiverse," which includes other universes existing beyond the boundaries of our own reality. There are several variants of this idea. The idea of "bubble universes" is that some regions of space do not continue to expand or stretch along with the rest of the universe. They form bubbles, which may contain different properties and physical constants, effectively resulting in multiple universes. Physicist Michio Kaku has skillfully argued that our universe may be just one in an endless multiverse, a single bubble floating in a sea of infinite bubble universes. Another version of this idea is through an interpretation of quantum mechanics by which something that is possible, but not realized in our universe, may exist in another universe. A common analogy is that reality is a many-branched tree in which every possible quantum outcome is realized.[5]

Common sense would have us believe that the Others have been separated from us by space; that they have traveled long distances to reach us. But could it be that they coexist with us in the same space, only in a parallel reality? If so, traveling from "there" to "here" may not be about long journeys. Perhaps it involves some other form of transportation that simply crosses over the barrier in one way or another.

It is conceivable, based on statements made by sober physicists, that there may be multiple Earths in existence, perhaps an infinite number. Is it possible that one of them has achieved the capability to travel from their version of our planet to ours? The mind reels, but scientists increasingly allow themselves to muse about such matters and are (usually) not laughed at by their colleagues.

This is hardly to say that the idea of multiple universes is established science. It is extremely difficult, if not impossible, to test the theory. This means it is possibly "unfalsifiable," and therefore outside proper scientific methodology. Some critics also argue that it seems contrary to Occam's Razor as an explanatory principle of our reality. More to the point, it is not clear which of the several concepts of a "multiverse" would explain how beings could travel from one reality to another.

There are many cases in the UFO literature describing objects that appear to "wink in" and "wink out" of our reality. Perhaps this means that they have mastered some sort of cloaking technology, or perhaps it means that they truly enter and exit our reality.

If an interdimensional explanation is true to some extent, it could explain certain phenomena ranging from UFOs to ghosts and other paranormal activity. It may turn out they are "bleed-throughs" from other legitimate realities.

Angels and Devils

The written evidence from the earliest human societies suggests that people believed they had interactions with highly intelligent and powerful beings. We have described them by many names, including gods, fairies, angels, and devils. One possibility is that these are names we gave to arriving extraterrestrials, or perhaps to members of a lost, Atlantean civilization.

The idea that ancient humans believed extraterrestrials were gods was made popular in the 1970s by author Erich von Däniken. "If our own space travelers happen to meet primitive peoples on a planet some day, they too will presumably seem like 'sons of heaven' or 'gods' to them," wrote Von Däniken, in *Chariots of the Gods*. "Perhaps our intelligences will be as far ahead of the inhabitants of these unknown and as yet unimagined regions as those fabulous apparitions from the universe were ahead of our primitive ancestors." Von Däniken's writing inspired others, notably linguist Zecharia Sitchin, who wrote a series of books on ancient Mesopotamia. Together, their speculations have been criticized and ridiculed by professional scientists, historians, and archaeologists, yet found expression in films such as *Stargate* and *The Fourth Kind*.

In a discussion that includes time travelers, multiverse visitors, intelligent dinosaurs, and self-replicating AI machines, let us now turn the argument around. If extraterrestrials can be interpreted as biblical angels and demons, can the opposite be true?

If there are truly angels and demons that exist as part of God's cosmic tapestry, perhaps early humans saw them for what they truly were. Perhaps it is modern humanity, with its technology and sci-fi movies, that errs in interpreting the Others as extraterrestrials. From our perspective we like to see our ancestors as confused, but could the confusion be ours?

The late John Keel believed that UFOs were related to the demons, angels, and fairy tales of the past. The events described in that literature, he wrote, "are similar, if not entirely identical, to the UFO phenomenon itself.... Strange objects and entities materialize and dematerialize in these stories, just as the UFOs and their splendid occupants appear and disappear, walk through walls, and perform other supernatural feats."[6]

On various websites and ministries, many evangelical Christians have seconded this belief. Although it may strike some as odd, there are many evangelicals living in America who know chapter and verse of the UFO cover-up, can lecture at length on the difference between Project Grudge and Project Sign, and discuss famous sightings in great detail. They believe; they simply happen to disagree as to the origin and the intention of these Others.

Time Travelers

For science-fiction writers, time travel stories are catnip. Of course, they usually work best when you don't think too much about the scenario—just as Sarah Connor mused while on the run in Mexico at the end of the first *Terminator* film.

In 1993, the first original film for the Sci-Fi (now SyFy) Channel was *Official Denial.*[7] Although it was about the UFO cover-up, it contained a twist ending in which the question turned out to be not where the aliens were from, but *when* they were from. The visitors were not alien after all: they were ourselves. Having bred diversity from their DNA in order to survive an environmental collapse, they had returned backward in time to save us, and thus to save themselves. The abduction of certain people was part of a protocol to follow specific bloodlines that were important in DNA development and ancestry.

Although such a left turn makes for a dramatic surprise, it also answers several questions about the Others, and in a surprisingly consistent manner. It explains why sightings increased markedly after the Second World War. That could simply be the "jump time" when the modern age began truly to unfold. It also might explain why they have been seen throughout human history. Could it be that, in a different time stream, there were no "ancient aliens" visiting our ancestors, but that future time traveling humans made the decision to appear in our past? From our present-day perspective, we would perceive these visits as ancient when, conceivably, they might be occurring at the same time as ours.

The notion of "aliens" as extratemporals, or time-traveling humans from the future, is intriguing, if a bit convoluted. Still, the idea of the Others as evolved, time-traveling, versions of ourselves has its own puzzles and inconsistencies. If people of the future are our visitors, then presumably there is another time stream in which we do not have a UFO phenomenon—at least in the original time stream where the decision was made to go back into the human past. Or does the whole thing go in some bizarre loop? For now, at least, time-travel is only theoretical (and according to many physicists, just barely). Moreover, the full weight of UFO sightings and reports do not easily fit the time-travel thesis.

All of the Above

The universe is not only bigger than can easily be grasped, but the rules by which it operates may be odder than we realize. Given this emerging scientific reality, it may be that there are multiple extraterrestrial groups who visit us, a real life *Men in Black* way-station.

By way of analogy, if the United States is a tourist destination, why should the only tourists come from Japan? What about the United Kingdom, China, Brazil, and a hundred other countries? If there is something on Earth that is interesting to one species of intelligent life, and if the universe is "teeming" with such life, then Earth may be a destination stop for many other life forms. Even within a single group there may be multiple agendas.

We can mix it up further. If they are not all extraterrestrial, there may be multiple types of entities that are here, some of which include our other theories. We may have extraterrestrials mixing with ultraterrestrials, and neither group may think much of the "home-grown" Earth-based Atlanteans. At the same time, there may also be artificially intelligent and genetically enhanced creatures tossed in for good measure.

If the universe is as huge and diverse as we now believe it is, and life is rare enough to be interesting, but common enough to facilitate interaction, then anything is possible.

Question #2: What Do They Want?

Obviously, this is a difficult question to answer. If only we knew who they were, we might better grasp their intentions.

It is clear that whoever these Others are, they have interacted with us on their terms. This is not a relationship of equals. For many years, they have determined when they choose to encounter us, where they have encountered us, and the nature of the encounter itself.

It is distinctly possible, given the fact that we are so deep into a continuing contact without a singular disclosure event, that they want little to do with us, or at least have no desire for open contact. The Brookings Report anticipated this in 1960, stating "If the intelligence of these creatures were sufficiently superior to ours, they might choose to have little, if any, contact with us." As *Star Trek's* Gene Roddenberry would put it, they might have a Prime Directive.

There is a school of thought that sees the intentions of these beings as predominantly peaceful and benign. This is the position of Dr. Steven M. Greer, director of the Disclosure Project, which has lobbied members of Congress and other government officials for full disclosure on the ET presence on Earth. "Obviously, any civilization capable of routine interstellar travel could terminate our civilization in a nanosecond, if that was their intent," Greer wrote in the "Disclosure Project Briefing Document," released in April 2001. "That we are still breathing the free air of Earth is abundant testimony to the non-hostile nature of these ET civilizations."[8]

Implicit here is the idea of social evolution leading to the elimination of suffering and want. Accordingly, civilizations older than ours would have achieved advances in everything from health to politics to resource distribution. For such civilizations, war would be unnecessary, perhaps unthinkable. With the attainment of all physical needs, the next journey would be spiritual.

Among people interested in the UFO/ET topic today, the idea is often taken further still. Some, for instance, claim that they communicate with such beings via telepathic messages or channeling. Usually, they claim that the message and intentions they receive is positive, that these beings are humanity's teachers and even spiritual masters, nudging us to raise our level of consciousness, and possibly gain admission into a larger galactic community.

Although some of these foregoing assumptions, like those gained via channeling, are essentially unverifiable, those regarding the peaceful nature of advanced civilizations can at least be argued for or against with a certain degree of logic on either side. After all, it is not impossible to argue that if there an advanced civilization came from elsewhere to Earth, they must have found a way to avoid the species suicide currently facing humanity. Somehow, they would have discovered a way based on peace, not war. Author Michael Michaud described this perspective as "contact optimist."[9]

It is not difficult to point out logical flaws in such a perspective, and indeed Michaud found it unpersuasive. First, just because the Others have not annihilated us so far, there is no inherent reason why they might not do so in the future. Secondly, possessing advanced science and technology does not indicate superior ethics or spiritual evolution. The Nazi war machine of the 1940s made use of very advanced technology and weapons for its time. Similarly, the warfare and weaponry of more recent years does not indicate any ethical or spiritual advancement on the part of humanity.

Imagine our own time-travel experiment, in which a small group of 21st-century humans were transported to medieval Europe, carrying a few of our trinkets of contemporary life. We arrange a meeting with some of the leading lights of the time, perhaps philosophers and other scholars. They would notice our clothing, which would be of a craftsmanship and functionality they had never dreamed of. They would notice that we were substantially taller than they were, and in much better health. Through us, they would learn some of the marvels of the world and universe. Then they would see our iPhones, laptops, e-readers, and bluetooth devices—and probably see them as magical, certainly as vastly beyond their wildest ideas of what was possible. They might very well conclude that we had solved all of our social and political problems, that we had discovered a way to improve human life beyond measure, and that we must be a peaceful race; how could it be that we had not destroyed ourselves—or them—despite our awesome power?

British astrophysicist Stephen Hawking advised caution when contacting aliens. He warned that if they were to visit us, "the outcome would be much as when Columbus landed in America, which didn't turn out well for the Native Americans." These remarks in 2010 stirred up a brief storm, particularly when he speculated that aliens might want to raid Earth for its resources and then move on. "I imagine they might exist in massive ships," he wrote, "having used up all the resources from their home planet. Such advanced aliens would perhaps become nomads, looking to conquer and colonize whatever planets they can reach."[10]

Oddly, Hawking seemed to be speculating about "massive ships" in some kind of hypothetical sense, but quite a few UFO sighting reports, including some by military authorities, describe truly enormous craft. One example came from the Chilean Air Force on December 16, 1978. The pilots of two F-5 fighter aircraft, on a training mission near the Chilean town of Mejillones, saw an enormous object in the sky. Each of the airborne radar systems tracked it, as did ground control, meaning there were three radar confirmations of it. The object gave a radar return equal to 10 or more aircraft carriers. It had been motionless, but as the pilots approached, it took off at an "unimaginable" speed to the west. All at once, the object vanished from all three radar screens. The Chilean Air Force acknowledged the encounter, but offered no explanation. What could it say?[11]

To UFO researcher Vince White, the phenomenon is disturbing. These giant ships, he wrote, "are carrying a giant something…[perhaps] whole armies over our heads…[or] hauling resources out of this world we know nothing about.… Could there be unwilling and unlucky passengers aboard?"[12]

Perhaps they have come to help, as Greer maintains, or to take, as Hawkins suggests. Maybe they just like to observe. In the evidence gathered throughout the past six decades, there appear to be examples of each motivation.

Let us take the example of the Grays, which may well be a type of cybernetic life form. It could be that they are well suited for space travel, but less able to function at their destination. Upon arrival, perhaps they are programmed to abduct some of the native inhabitants and bioengineer bodies that would allow them to colonize. Such a plan would take quite a few generations, maybe even centuries. In our typical human impatience, we might be inclined to argue that, because they have not zapped us into oblivion, they must be peaceful. In addition to the rejoinders offered earlier, we might ask why such visitors would wage open war and thereby destroy the planet they found so desirable in the first place? Second, in their time frame, it could well be that a centuries-long takeover strategy is perfectly feasible and normal to them. Patience may be their dominant trait.

We do not know. To assume their intent is peaceful, based solely on the available facts, is not responsible. It is possible that the Breakaway Group knows the answer. It is even possible that this group has collaborated with the Others. But if any of that has happened, neither side is sharing with the rest of us.

Scientific Research

Scientists who contemplate UFO reality usually consider the Others to be researchers, perhaps in part because they want to see extraterrestrial visitors as being like themselves, only from space.

It could be that we are being observed in a way that mimics our own investigation into native peoples around the world. The research project (humanity) might involve many factors: biology, technology, sociology, and so forth. German rocket pioneer Professor Herman Oberth, a man heavily involved in early space age research, speculated that these "intelligent observers" had observed Earth's lifeforms for centuries, "and more recently…atomic centers, armaments and centers of armament production."[13]

Perhaps some of the abduction phenomenon is explainable as scientific observation. We tranquilize wild creatures, tag them with transmitters, then release them to track and observe them. From time to time, we pick them up.

Dr. Roger K. Leir has removed physical implants from alleged abductees, which he believes provide evidence of an alien tracking system. Many of the surgeries, which have been recorded on video, show bizarre, tiny objects being removed from people. According to Leir, these usually contain very sophisticated technology housed within a bio-membrane of some sort. The analysis of the implants, while intriguing, still awaits independent confirmation.[14]

A vastly advanced race might not see our technology as a sign of civilization. They may instead see us as inferior life forms, curiosities worthy of study.

Membership Committee

Maybe they see us in a more interesting light. It could be that we are currently *The Greatest Show in the Galaxy,* about to transition to the next level of whatever it means to be a civilization.

Perhaps a dormant project was kick-started when the human race crossed the nuclear threshold and created nuclear weapons. Thus, the Others could be observing us as we are about to develop even more sophisticated technologies, enabling us to jump into their world, so to speak. If that were so, it seems reasonable that they would observe us to determine our suitability to join a greater galactic community. That may be the reason behind the scientific research study.

The example has been used that we might remotely observe a native culture from the sky in an aerial search, simply establishing that they exist. We might later move in for a closer look, avoiding being seen. Later, we might allow ourselves to be seen by members of the tribe who go back and describe strange visitors. Eventually, we might approach them, sit down, and talk.

In such a manner, the UFO phenomenon might be seen as an acculturation and acclimatization process, whereby the Others allow us to see them more and more through time. Eventually, as years pass, perhaps they will initiate open and formal contact of their own accord, regardless of our own agenda and readiness.

A continuing thread of UFO contact through the years has been the idea that the Others are here to save us. Sometimes the impending danger is galactic, like an approaching comet, and more recently the 2012 doomsday scenario. A dominant idea is that humanity is a threat to itself, that the planet cannot sustain human over-population, weapons, pollution, and mismanagement. This line of reasoning dates to the Contactee reports of the 1950s, and has found some voice in abduction research to this day.

They Want Our DNA

Many abduction accounts include a sexual and reproductive dimension. When we add in fairly consistent witness testimony concerning human/alien hybrids, we get a disturbing scenario. In 1997, Temple University professor David Jacobs published his book, *The Threat*. After extensive research into the alien abduction phenomenon, Jacobs argued that the Grays were creating a hybrid species designed to replace humanity and relegate humanity to an inferior status. As a result, they have kept their program remarkably secret, especially considering that they are integrating themselves into our society and world.[15]

The creation of an apparent alien-human hybrid species could mean one of two things. First, that they seeking a way to merge with the existing human population. This does not necessarily portend evil for humanity. It might imply the continued existence of our species, albeit with an element surreptitiously added into the mix. The second possibility is a replacement scenario, such as envisioned by Jacobs. Human genetic material would be necessary in order for the extraterrestrial species to adapt to Earth's ecosystem. This scenario is especially disturbing, because some of the interactions recorded by Jacobs between the hybrid beings and normal humans have shown them to be cruel, sadistic, and emotionally dysfunctional. He believes their plan to be well-organized, systematic, and a true threat to the human race.

They Want Our Souls

Whitley Strieber has said that his abductors told him, "We recycle souls." Other researchers have occasionally come across startling references from abductees regarding the interest that these beings have in the human soul.

This is a challenging topic to discuss, even in a book dealing with such impolite topics as extraterrestrials, abductions, secret governments, and the like. In the first place, not all people even believe in the existence of a soul.

Can a soul be taken? Can it be "rewritten"? Can it be of value to others possessing the ability to "take it"? Such claims have been made by people professing to know the truth. They may prove to be inherently unverifiable. One anonymous source, someone who claimed to have a lot of knowledge and wrote detailed posts on the Usenet bulletin board system, claimed that during abductions, "sometimes a person's soul is temporarily removed" and placed in a lead box, which effectively contains it. The reason is to prevent what happens next from being recorded upon that soul, from becoming a part of that person's history. "But, perhaps more importantly," the author concluded, "it doesn't become a part of his history for others to read, either."[16]

Can such a thing be true, or is this complete fantasy? Can it go deeper than this? Does it?

Another theory of abductions and the soul is connected to the belief in reincarnation. Eastern religions have maintained that the soul can incarnate within creatures of all types. Could it be, as some people claim, that souls having previously been in an extraterrestrial race are now incarnating into human bodies? Are there Star People among us—people who are human in every biological and genetic sense, but who have the soul (literally) of an extraterrestrial?

They Want Our World

If the Others are here, on our world, in our reality, interacting with us in some manner, then *why*? Could it be as simple as coveting our planet? Within the context of our vast cosmos, Earth is surely a paradise, blessed with natural resources and an abundance of life. If beings from elsewhere come from a world less abundant than our own, they may be developing a strategy to make Earth their new home.

The idea of extraterrestrials coming to Earth to enslave humankind has been a science fiction staple since H.G. Wells invoked it more than a century ago in *The War of the Worlds*. "Yet across the gulf of space, minds that are to our minds as ours are to the beasts that perish, intellects vast and cool and unsympathetic, regarded this Earth with envious eyes," Wells wrote in the opening to his book, "and slowly and surely drew their plans against us." Ever since, in books and film and television projects, aliens have taken to trashing our world.

Yet, it has hardly been the sole purview of sci-fi writers to invoke alien threats. American war hero General Douglas MacArthur twice alluded to the possibility of a future war between humanity and aliens from space. On one occasion in 1955, he reportedly told a journalist that "because of the developments in science all the countries on Earth will have to unite to survive and to make a common front against attack by people from other planets." In 1962, while speaking to the graduating class of West Point, he referred to "ultimate conflict between a united human race and the sinister forces of some other planetary galaxy."[17]

Ronald Reagan's several statements concerning hypothetical alien invasions come to mind. As someone who had been a UFO witness himself, and who (according to sources of the authors) was also briefed on the topic, it seems unlikely that he was merely being whimsical.

They Want Nothing

What if they are so far beyond us that we offer them nothing at all? Such a possibility has been raised many times throughout the years. Consider the insights of Whitley Strieber, one of the few people who has openly discussed his abduction and contact experiences, and is probably the most articulate of them. In our "classical" reality, he points out, when you flip a coin, you get either heads or tails. You cannot get both. But at the scale of the very small, reality works differently: matter can be both wave and particle at the same time. Normally, this is because there is a strong interaction that prevents atoms from going into "superposition" and becoming "indeterminate," essentially everywhere at the same time.

But, Strieber asks, what if we could control the degree to which our bodies were in such a state? What if, in addition to possessing quantum entangled neurons within our own brains, we could have quantum entanglement with all other human brains, and therefore have access to the knowledge and intellect of billions of brains? In that case, writes Strieber, "we would be radically, fantastically different from what we are. We would have the ability to spontaneously change our appearance, or even become invisible. We would be able to not only extend our awareness across the whole of reality, but also to draw on our collective understanding to interpret what we see. We would, in short, be like our visitors."[18]

Of course, he points out, we are most certainly not like them. Their consciousness may exceed our own as much as ours exceeds that of the family dog. With perhaps total knowledge of the universe, such beings, according to Strieber, are at "the end of innovation," something that "would be the most profound catastrophe that could befall an intelligent species." In such a situation, "the quest for the new would take on an almost mythic urgency." Thus, it would not be entirely true to say they want nothing from us. In effect, they might be voyeurs who desperately seek to experience, if only vicariously, the feeling of discovery accorded to humanity.

In the same essay, Strieber argued that Disclosure could well "devastate the human mind." For, if the Others appear in numbers, they will enter our minds. "And, I can assure, you," he writes, "that kind of contact is as hard a thing as a human being can experience. It is an agony beyond terror. I know. I have been there." He concedes that a few people will be able to handle it, but many will not. They simply will not be ready, nor are they ever likely to be.

Question #3: Are We Safe?

In the news business, the question "Are we safe?" is the key question that people want answered in any story, whether in an international story like 9/11 or a local shooting. From our current perspective (observers who have been denied certain key facts), trying to determine the threat posed by the Others is guess-work.

Still, our "safety" involves some assessment of three criteria. First, how advanced their technology happens to be. Second, how physically close they are to us. Third, what they want.

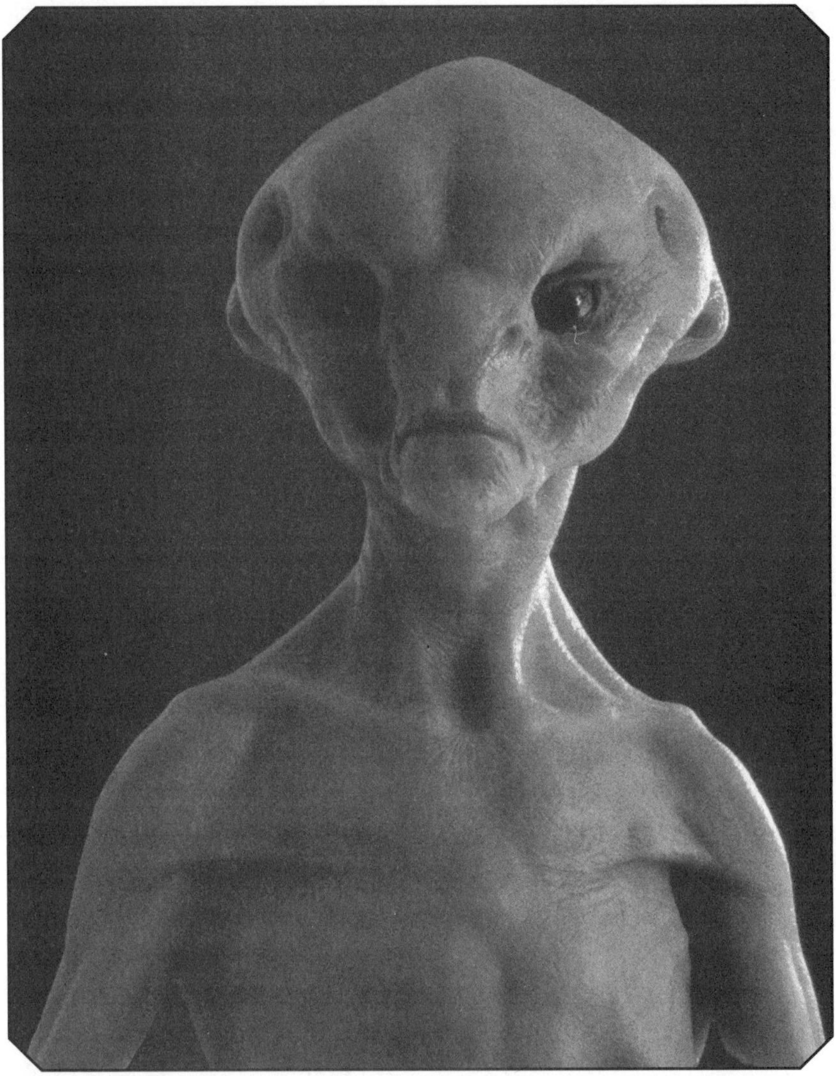

Hiding their agenda? If they have come in peace, why have they not contacted us in an open way? Image by Amalgamated Dynamics, Inc.

"If we believe their technology is not much better than ours, that they are basically 'good guys,'" wrote UC Davis psychology professor Albert Harrison in 1997. "We will feel less threatened than if they have an overwhelming technical superiority, are already in our neighborhood, and seem unfavorably disposed toward humans."[19]

There are military men and women who have studied these questions, but we can give quick provisional answers to them right here.

First, their technology is clearly superior to our own. Despite scientists who assert that interstellar or interdimensional travel is impossible, these beings have managed to reach us, whatever and wherever their origins. Second, they are here, and not phoning us from 50 light years away. Third, although there are neutral and even positive examples of interaction, there are some examples indicating a lack of concern or empathy for humans, and even a few that appear decidedly hostile.

Their Technology

The capabilities of the Others are clearer to us than their intentions. A review of more than a half-century's worth of UFO encounters gives us an idea of what they have, and what they can do. The results are unsettling.

- Craft that can hover silently, indefinitely, and accelerate instantly in any direction.
- Craft that can negotiate upper atmosphere as well as undersea conditions.
- Exceptional stealth characteristics when desired, including physical invisibility of craft and occasionally demonstrated radar stealth.
- Advanced energy weapons that can disarm sophisticated electronics, communications, and avionics systems in fighter aircraft (1976 Iranian jet fighter incident), or disarm nuclear weapons (1967 Malmstrom AFB incident).
- Apparent negation of gravitational effects, possibly by creation of gravitational fields, making them independent of the need for energy as we define it.
- Management of space-time, possibly indicating some level of mastery of time itself, even possibly including knowledge of "time streams."
- Creation of physical paralysis in human beings by means of apparent light beams or related phenomenon.
- Induction of a range of human physiological or emotional responses, including terror, unnatural calm, lethargy, or sleep ("switching off" people during abductions).

These might be considered some of the more standard military capabilities. We will ignore the possible existence of more substantial weapons, whether these be nuclear, scalar, laser, or some other obvious offensive weapon. These may well exist, and could certainly be intuited from the technical abilities of the craft themselves, but the open UFO literature does not give us much information regarding such weaponization.

Infiltration of Society

There may be another capability that exists, something potentially more nefarious. Is it possible that some of *them* have found a way to infiltrate human society? If so, have they infiltrated the human power structure? Such speculation seems better suited for the plotline of a novel, movie, or video game than for real life. However, from the point of view of any alien species here on Earth, it would be valuable to have some of the native population working for them. Perhaps this is best achieved through bribery, or through a combination of implants and mind control. Or, possibly, by means of breeding their own human population, and even providing them with various enhancements—genetically, biologically, technologically—to make them more functional, more formidable.

Included in the legacy of the late abduction researcher Budd Hopkins is his emerging conclusion that not all aliens look "alien." In his 2003 book, *Sight Unseen*, coauthored with Carol Rainey, Hopkins published several accounts that suggested human-looking people who were decidedly odd in various ways, and who were connected with abduction experiences, often in a helper-type of capacity. It was unclear who these beings were; Hopkins and Rainey suggested they were a type of "transgenic" being, or alien-human hybrid. If so, they were human-enough looking to "pass" without too much problem, essentially being seen as eccentric and little more.[20]

Two other anecdotal pieces may fit in the puzzle.

During the late 1980s, retired government scientist Dr. Eric Walker conducted a series of correspondence and telephone interviews with various UFO researchers. Walker had been a friend of President Dwight Eisenhower. Similar to Ike's brother Milton, he had also been president of Penn State University. Most significant, Walker was a former chairman of the Institute for Defense Analysis, one of the most important think tanks in the nation. Simply put, Walker knew everybody who was anybody.

Now, Walker decided to talk. After he confirmed the existence of MJ-12 to a researcher, he told him that he was "chasing after and fighting with windmills.... You are delving into an area that you can do absolutely nothing about.... Forget about it!" Yet, the persistent researcher was later able to get Walker to say more. There was a "machine" recovered, said Walker, "obviously a landing vehicle only, fully within the realm of current knowledge. Four normal looking males were with it, very much alive. Yet, Walker's implication was that they were not human.

For the next few years, Walker had sporadic communications with other researchers with whom he continued to discuss this topic. One of his more intriguing statements was, "How good is your mathematics?" The researcher answered, "As good as it could be for a doctor in physics. But why?" Walker replied, "Because only a very few are capable in handling this issue. Unless your mind ability is like Einstein's or likewise, I do not think how you can achieve anything." Then Walker asked more questions: "How good is your seventh sense? How much do you know about ESP? Unless you know about it, and know how to use it, you would not be taken in. Only a few know about it."

To all appearances, Walker decided to let his guard down with an occasional researcher or two. If so, could it be that beings looking perfectly human, but with exceptional abilities, have merged on a limited basis into society?

Another account concerns the government "remote viewer," Ingo Swann. During the mid- to late-1970s, Swann was engaged in nothing less than psychic espionage on behalf of the U.S. intelligence community. As part of the cadre of remote viewers, his job was to learn things that were difficult to learn otherwise, including such things as the location of Soviet submarines, the inside layout of certain Embassies, and so on.[21] In the course of such work, it was not unusual for the remote viewers to catch the attention of clandestine programs to participate in various projects. On one occasion, Swann was contacted by a "Mr. Axelrod," and met with him at a secure underground facility, where he was brought blindfolded by two military-looking men whom he described as "the twins," because of their identical appearance and coordinated movement.

Axelrod never told Swann what agency he belonged to, but was very interested in testing Swann's ability to remote view the moon (whereupon Swann claimed to see beings who became aware of him). Axelrod also took Swann to a remote forested area, where they waited until a triangular UFO appeared, as if on cue, and Swann was later asked for his impressions of the object. The program, in other words, had all the earmarks of a counter-intelligence operation by a group of ETs who happened to look human.[22]

The human race may have a serious challenge not only from advanced weaponry, but a fifth-column. Presumably, the military and intelligence forces of the world—the U.S. in particular—have already caught the assignment of dealing with this. The question is, are they up to it?

Our Military Preparedness

If our feelings are mixed After Disclosure, nowhere will this be more true than when we consider the military. After all, it will be seen as the initial architect of the secrecy, triggering feelings of anger and hostility. Yet, there will be a strong feeling that it is necessary for possible defense, at least until people understand who these other beings are.

There will be much second-guessing, and many forthright questions. Has the military succeeded or failed in protecting humanity from a dire threat? Has it acted in an aggressive manner with peaceful visitors? Can we expect it to be truthful now, after generations of denial and deception?

Some will fault the military for its secrecy, and for failing to keep citizens safe. To this, it will undoubtedly respond that it *has* kept people safe, or at least as safe as possible, and that secrecy was the only rational path toward accomplishing this goal, given the potential threat.

Of course, the U.S. military will continue to be secretive. It will have no interest in revealing that it failed to protect its own airspace, nor that a superior force was able to engage and defeat its best technology and pilots. The physical evidence of bodies and wreckage will not be forwarded without a legal battle. Photos and reports will need to be subpoenaed. Its assessment of the capabilities of the Others will need to be pried out, if that is even possible.

Still, it is inevitable that the long history of military encounters with UFOs will come out. Our history of contact in the skies includes hundreds of confirmed, excellent cases where military pilots and observers saw actual physical craft. In a number of these instances, jets were scrambled to intercept and fire on them. An unknown but possibly substantial number of pilots have been lost through the years.[23]

Many former high-level military officers have spoken publicly about the reality of UFOs and their evaluation of our own capabilities. Consistently, they have indicated that our militaries are outclassed.

In an A.D. world, however, will the military protect us? To what extent will it need to? If, as it appears on a basic level, humanity has had a confrontational relationship with the Others, a logical question will be whether we have created revolutionary technologies with which to defend ourselves.

Do We Even Have a Chance?

The history of abductions, mutilations, and attempted jet interceptions make it reasonable to suppose that at least some of these Others are not here for science or diplomacy. If so, we may assume that Earth's militaries have worked diligently to play catch-up.

If the limits of current military capabilities were what is known publicly, it would still be a powerful arsenal of weapons.

Consider the most advanced fighter aircraft in the world today, the Lockheed Martin F-22 Raptor. It employs stealth technology for such missions as air superiority, ground attack, and electronic warfare, along with signals intelligence. In addition to stealth, the aircraft is renowned for its speed, agility, precision, and situational awareness.

Or the "stealth cruise missile," also developed by Lockheed Martin. It is said to cost less and work better than the famous Tomahawk cruise missile. It carries a 1,000-pound warhead, which can be fitted with nuclear, chemical, conventional, or biological weapons. As a stealth aircraft, it is able to reach its target undetected (by known human technologies) and fire its low observable payload from a distance. Enemies that are hit are taken by total surprise.[24]

Lasers would be of obvious interest in any military engagement with the Others. Currently, the U.S. military uses lasers for targeting and other nonlethal purposes. No doubt these are helpful for battlefield troops, but they are not the kind of offensive weapons needed to shoot down a flying saucer. Yet, open literature indicates that we are fast approaching significant capabilities. In 2009, Northrop Grumman announced it had built and tested an electric laser capable of producing a 100-kilowatt ray of light, the long-sought-after "magic number," which is powerful enough to destroy an airplane or a tank.[25] The U.S. Navy is expected to incorporate lasers in the near future. One of these, a solid-state laser system designed by Northrop Grumman, was described by a program manager with the Office of Naval Research as "like a high-powered sniper rifle, except with much more range."[26]

Whether these weapons would be capable of knocking out UFOs, however, is debatable. Effective military action against the Others would surely require a range of sophisticated technologies. It is a good bet that within the deeply clandestine world of the Breakaway Group, there is still more.

The idea that a breakaway civilization may have developed parallel to our existing society, fueled by black-ops money for generations, is the ultimate double-edged sword. On one level, it is outrageous for governmental authorities to have operated on such a massive scale with no citizen oversight. On the other hand, if we have recovered alien technology throughout the years, we may have developed our own program that is aimed at the likelihood of conflict some day with the Others.

If the motives of at least some races of the Others are harmful, then the world after Disclosure will be faced with an ends-justified-the-means argument. Although that issue will be sorted out in all its complexities by future officials and courts, it is possible now, through a combination of leaks, logic, and observation, to gain a reasonable idea of what "the program" might be all about.

It appears that a portion of the time, money, and effort has been expended toward trying to make a flying saucer of our own. Testimony regarding the recovery of crashed UFOs, reverse-engineering programs, insider claims (such as one to aviation journalist James Goodall that "we have things out there that are literally out of this world"), and the many eyewitness accounts of UFOs over Groom Lake and Antelope Valley all support this hypothesis.

There is evidence that man-made flying saucers have existed since at least the 1960s. One confirmed photograph from 1966, taken not far from Dugway Proving Ground in Utah, hints strongly of terrestrial manufacture, as it is nearly identical in shape to a craft video recorded inside Nevada's Nellis Test Range in 1994, and which was leaked to the television show *Hard Copy*. The movements of the Nellis UFO have been analyzed in detail, indicating extraordinary performance characteristics (such as making a right angle turn at 140 mph). That it was recorded deep inside one of the most secret U.S. testing ranges gives us reason to suspect that the Nellis UFO was of terrestrial manufacture. That is, one of *ours*.

In between the 1966 Utah UFO and the 1994 Nellis UFO are a multitude of leaks concerning a clandestine program to manufacture flying saucers. The most intriguing of these concerns three craft that were said to be in a large hangar at Lockheed's facilities in Helendale, California, in November 1988, just after the presidential election. The main witness, aviation designer Brad Sorensen, told only a few people of what he saw, but what he claimed was astounding. Accompanied by a senior member of the Defense Department, Sorensen says he saw, "three flying saucers floating off the floor—no cables suspended them from the ceiling holding them up, no landing gear underneath—just floating, hovering above the floor." These are the words of aviation illustrator Mark McCandlish, the first person to whom Sorensen told his story.

Nearby, a general was speaking at a lectern to a group of people. He referred to the vehicles as "Alien Reproduction Vehicles," as well as Flux Liners, because they used high voltage electricity. He mentioned several fascinating features of the ARV. One was that it could perform at "light speed or better." Another was that it ran on energy obtained through the vacuum—presumably this is the so-called zero-point energy field. It was also apparently stated that the ARV had already performed a general reconnaissance of all planets of the solar system in a search for life, and that no life was found. Sorensen noted that the ARV looked “ancient,” and as though it had been used extensively. A video exhibit nearby showed the smallest of the three vehicles hovering over a dry lake bed. It made three quick, hopping motions, then accelerated straight up and out of sight within seconds. It was unclear whether the vehicle was silent, or whether the tape simply lacked sound.[27]

A key point about the ARV that Sorensen described to McCandlish: It was essentially identical in appearance with the 1966 Utah UFO and the 1994 Nellis UFO.

The ARV story, which is unconfirmed, indicates that there is a secret space program. Indeed, there is evidence of anomalous activity in Earth’s orbit. One researcher, Jeffrey Challender, collected hundreds of unusual events that were recorded on space missions from the United States, Russia, Europe, and China. Some of these clearly have prosaic explanations. Others, are not so clear.[28] Also of interest in this context is the collection of satellite data provided by researcher Ron Regehr. During the 1990s, while working with the military contractor Aerojet, Regehr fortuitously obtained a printout of data from the U.S. Defense Support Program (DSP), which made it clear that “fastwalkers” (e.g. space-based UFOs) are tracked with regularity.[29]

If these anomalies are genuine, they provide ample reason to develop a secret space program. It would be necessary to interact with that phenomenon in some way, whether through investigation, communication, or hostilities. For this reason, there is a possibility that the Strategic Defense Initiative (SDI) program initiated during the Reagan years housed a covert component related to UFOs, even if that was not its main mission.

But there is more to “the program” then secret flying saucers and space missions. It also appears to be about studying alien bodies and conducting related biotech research. Less information exists on this, but at least one source described it to a UFO investigator as early as the 1970s. The need for such a program would be obvious if alien bodies were ever recovered.

In terms of military application, clandestine biotech research may have aided in some important areas. Simply having an example of an advanced non-human life form could spark advances in the understanding of our own biology and physiology, let alone that of an extraterrestrial species. Biotechnology has become very important to the military. It has been and will continue to be important in the treatment of war injuries, prevention and diagnosis of diseases, and protection against biochemical toxic agents. It can enhance human battle effectiveness (even to the point of creating "super soldiers"), and enable the creation of small-scale or ultramicro-scale destructive biological weapons.[30]

There may be another activity that deeply clandestine military groups have been conducting in order to meet the real or perceived alien threat: Performing their own abductions, a phenomenon that goes by the abbreviation of MILABs, for military abductions.

MILABs have been discussed publicly since around 1990, although they may have been going on longer than that. One of the earliest writers on the subject, Dr. Karla Turner, interviewed a number of abductees who had been taken by human and non-human groups. Other MILAB victims also came forward to describe their stories. It would appear that some of them were taken by human groups as a counter-intelligence operation, in an attempt to learn the alien agenda. Through a combination of chemicals, hypnosis, and perhaps other technologies, attempts were made to extract the memories of the victims that were then wiped, or at least tampered with, so that it took them years to begin learning the truth of what happened to them.

Just as the idea of alien abduction remains controversial and is subject to skepticism, so too is the idea of military abductions, possibly even more so. To some, the idea is preposterous, as the deeply criminal nature of the act seems beyond the pale, to say nothing of being too risky to undertake. After all, the repercussions of being caught would be catastrophic for any organization performing them.

The problem, however, is that there is a certain amount of abduction research that points in this direction. Moreover, if some of the previously mentioned indications are true, it is not hard to see why the risk of

MILABs would be undertaken. It may be that the Breakaway/Majestic Group is behind the MILAB phenomenon, using its subjects to learn about the Others. But there may be more to all this than simple counter-intelligence. Some MILAB abductees have indicated a strong interest by human black-ops groups in psi phenomena. Indeed, Eric Walker had hinted years before that psi was important in understanding the Others.

This takes us to what may be a crucial element of the abduction phenomenon, both alien and human. Why are the abductees taken in the first place? Jacobs, Hopkins, and others argued it is for breeding hybrids. But that begs the question of whether abductees are taken at random, or specifically chosen for a reason. Information that has come to the authors indicates that some of the answer relates to psi abilities that have been identified in the subject, and that this is of interest to the Others.

It also appears to be of interest to the Breakaway/Majestic Group, which, according to several cases the authors have investigated, puts these people to work as psychic spies of sorts, making sure to manage their memories as much as possible. We know that remote viewing was an active interest in certain parts of the U.S. intelligence community from the 1970s until at least the 1990s, and we also know the program had several spectacular successes. Why close down something that is proven to work, and especially something that may prove useful in the struggle to understand the agenda of the Others?

If the Others have spacecraft that exceed our capacity, it seems likely that humanity would want to build some of its own. And if the clandestine leaders of the human race thought they were fighting a deceptive battle with enemies that employed psychic abilities, they would want to improve their talents in that regard. If Mr. Axelrod, perhaps representing a human-looking group of Others, was trying to test the ability of human remote viewers to detect his group, it could well be that the Breakaway Group employs such people, some who may have full knowledge of what they are doing, but perhaps some who do not.

What has been going on behind the scenes for these many years may be humanity's attempt to fight fire with fire. If that is so, the idea that we could be burned is not outrageous. If relations with the Others becomes aggressive in the world A.D., humanity will be up against formidable strength. Might they have "doomsday" weapons that could shatter our planet?

Again, one sees the irony of our situation. If the Others are hostile, the world will probably not complain that the secret-keepers diverted so much black budget money into creating flying saucers and other weapons. When the cards are laid on the table, people may be thankful that our hand has a few aces.

Who Do They Think We Are?

Whether they have traveled from other worlds or other dimensions, Others have arrived in our neighborhood.

If they are new arrivals, we might gather that they would have passed through an atmosphere filled with satellites processing huge quantities of information, including radio, television, and other digital media blanketing the globe. We have no idea whether this massive amount of information—which overwhelms us—would have the same effect on them, or whether they would have systems, computers, and intelligence that could find patterns and sense in it that might surpass our own understanding. Much of the electronic data they sift would be expendable mediocrity, like a re-run of *Mork and Mindy*. Some of it would have been more edifying, such as our greatest examples of art, music, literature, and philosophy. Some would be the historic record of man's folly—a self-created catalogue of our own sins from the Spanish Inquisition to the massacres of Rwanda and beyond. That is just the material available at a distance.

Of course, they may have scouted and monitored us for a long time. We can speculate that they would quickly come to understand some basic concepts.

First, they would realize that we are not a hive-minded species that practices group-think. Instead, they would see a great variety and complexity in the expression of human thought, culture, and ways of life. They might view this as something positive or—if they are hive-minded themselves—as a fatal flaw. They may have thought that the outpouring of grief over Steve Jobs, a man who urged us to "Think Different," was curious or threatening.

Second, they would realize that we are an aggressive species. Not all of us, but enough of us. They would see that humanity has devoted great resources to a military footprint extending from nation to nation across the planet. Not only are our space weapons, bombs, fighter jets, and wars-in-progress easily seen, but they appear to have tested them as to capability with some regularity throughout the years.

They would also observe the vast disparities in our allocation of resources and wealth, in which billions of people live in abject poverty while a very few live in opulent luxury. Perhaps they disapprove, or perhaps this is the way of their world, too. All we really can say is that they will notice everything from the the groundswell at Tahrir Square to the 2011 anarchy in the UK to the struggle to Occupy Wall Street.

They might also have concluded that we have overpopulated the Earth to the point of impending resource exhaustion, species extinction, and ecological disaster. Abductee reports commonly refer to the Others providing mental imagery of Earthly environmental collapse. Belief that they are here to save us from ourselves may only be wishful thinking on our part, or it could be a clue as to their agenda. They might be here to help us save our sinking boat. Or they could be here to take it away from us, given our careless stewardship.

Perhaps the best that we can hope for is to be viewed as we are: a mixed bag full of highs and lows, capable of deeds both awful and sublime, simultaneously greedy and generous, hateful and loving, warlike and peaceful. If they are here in peace, we may hope that they will see us as an evolving work-in-progress, an intelligent species worth watching and nurturing. If they are here for more selfish purposes, they might see our short-comings as flags of caution for them, knowing that humans can never be counted out, and will fight when cornered.

Vignette #4:

Transcript.
253 Russell Senate Office Building, Washington, D.C.

✧✦✧

LOCATION: 253 RUSSELL SENATE OFFICE BUILDING
WASHINGTON, D.C.

TIME: 9:00 A.M. EST DATE: WEDNESDAY, AUGUST 21, 2021

SENATOR BENTLEY: As Chairman of the National Commission on Extraterrestrial Secrecy, I'd like to convene our sixth public hearing. We continue over from yesterday our witness, a Mister Frank James Bartko. The Sergeant-at-Arms will swear in the witness.

(The witness is sworn and seated.)

SENATOR BENTLEY: Mister Bartko, I believe even the public's sometimes limitless patience for more lies and deceit has been exhausted by current events, so I will simply skip the niceties and get right into it. Will that be acceptable with you?

MR. BARTKO: Yes, sir. It will.

SENATOR BENTLEY: Fine. Now as we concluded yesterday, you testified under oath that you had never heard of the organization known as Majestic-12, Majic-12, MJ-12, or simply Majic, or Majestic. Would you care to revise your testimony today, given that you had the evening to refresh your memory?

MR. BARTKO: No, sir. I'll stand by that statement.

SENATOR BENTLEY: Then why is your name, sir, on this memorandum, dated September 4, 1974? (*speaks to staff*) Please show Mister Bartko, the Committee's Exhibit, 3-B.

(The witness examines the exhibit.)

MR. BARTKO: I can only assume that it is a fraudulent document created by political enemies during this turbulent period where it seems more important to find scapegoats than it does to find the truth.

SENATOR BENTLEY: Three sworn witnesses have testified before this committee, sir, that the memo is authentic and that you were not only a member of Majestic-12 or Majic-12 but that you were, in actual fact, its leader for a period of nine years. Are those witnesses then lying, sir?

MR. BARTKO: It appears they are.

SENATOR BENTLEY: At any time in the last 40 years, sir, have you yourself ever been at a crash retrieval site of an extraterrestrial spacecraft?

MR. BARTKO: Not to the best of my knowledge.

SENATOR BENTLEY: Have you ever seen an extra-terrestrial biological entity, sometimes known as an Eben, currently known as an Other, either dead or alive?

MR. BARTKO: Not one I would recognize.

(Laughter from audience)

SENATOR BENTLEY: By all means, share the humor with us, Mister Bartko.

MR. BARTKO: I find it amusing that with a potential threat of invasion now hovering over us, literally and figuratively, that the United States Congress would focus its energy on the past and not the future. I find it downright laughable that my own service record with the U.S. Armed Forces should be subjected to such innuendo and smear and that my years of service be so diminished before the public I swore an oath to protect. And I believe that it is ludicrous that my 45 years in private business, where I created more than 750 jobs, should be characterized by you and your committee as a front for some nefarious and illicit purpose.
So, yes, Senator, the whole thing does amuse me.

SENATOR BENTLEY: Given that the President of the United States himself has disclosed the reality of an extra-terrestrial presence on this planet, doesn't it strike you as reasonable that an organization created to monitor that presence in the past should come forward and tell the American people what it knows?

MR. BARTKO: You're asking me a hypothetical.

SENATOR BENTLEY: Do you believe an organization called Majestic-12 or Majic-12 existed, or that an organization by a different name but with the mandate of managing extra-terrestrial contact was created?

MR. BARTKO: Senator, I'm a businessman. I have enough trouble getting my employees to stop stealing office supplies and calling in sick when they're not. Aliens, that's above my paygrade.

SENATOR BENTLEY: The committee will recess for 15 minutes to give you time to confer with your lawyer on the penalties of perjury to a congressional committee, Mister Bartko. (gavels) We're in recess.

(The committee recesses.)

Chapter 5

Blowback:

Collateral Damage and Unintended Consequences

Fear defeats more people
than any other one thing in the world.

—Ralph Waldo Emerson

Humans are a very adaptable species. When our living conditions change, whether it involves going to prison or winning the lottery, we alter our attitudes and expectations. Although Disclosure of the reality of the Others will result in a great shock, people will adapt in the long run; there will be little choice.

During the days, months, and even years following The Great Event, however, such optimism may be in short supply. In 1954, Carl Jung warned of the danger of waiting too long to inform the public. In the event that extraterrestrials were confirmed and were visiting Earth, he wrote, humanity as a whole would be in the "precarious position of primitive communities today in conflict with the superior culture...the rudder would be removed from our grasp." The result could be catastrophic. The surest way to avoid this would be for the authorities "to enlighten the public as soon and as completely as possible."[1]

Jung wrote those words more than 50 years ago. If he were alive today, he would probably look at Disclosure as fraught with even greater danger, for our day of enlightenment has been delayed far beyond reason.

After decades of cover-up, in which institutions have been subverted and people ridiculed, simply lifting the veil will not solve every problem. On the contrary, it will create new ones.

More than 40 years ago, the Condon Report noted in its Introduction, "If, as many people suspect, our planet is being visited clandestinely by spacecraft, manned or controlled by intelligent creatures from another world, it is the most momentous development in human history." Nothing has changed since those words were written, except that the cover-up, by its durability, has placed many institutions front-and-center of any backlash to Disclosure.

The world's governments and military powers will be immediately exposed for their deceit. To be sure, they will portray themselves as having hidden the truth for the public's own good. Some people will accept these reasons; others will not. Even under the most favorable circumstances, however, there will be blowback.

We mean "blowback" to signify unintended consequences and collateral damages from a covert operation. This particular one, which has lasted seven decades, is among the greatest secrets ever kept. Who will get singed in the reaction? Who will escape with the least damage?

The specifics of what will happen will be heavily influenced by the Others. Will they have a high-touch or benign-neglect policy toward us? Will they show us how to achieve cheap or free portable energy, or will they make us feel that we are under imminent threat? Or will we simply be forced to live in the twilight, where their agenda remains unclear or hidden? Each possibility will have its own transformative policies. Each will aim the blowback at different institutions.

Being a loser in the eyes of the public is not always catastrophic. During the first year A.D., although the public may distrust the military, it will still want it for protection. The media, too, will be widely condemned as truth bunglers and national security sycophants. Yet, it will still be the main avenue by which people get information about the new circumstances, although not without great challenges. The educational system may have had its head in the sand, but students will still need to go to school.

Indeed, we believe that the greatest blowback will happen on the streets—and it will not matter where they are. From Beijing to New York City and every location around the world where people are dependent on the reliable delivery systems of modern society, the hot wind of truth will set some fires. Expect to see something resembling a global riot to spread like a forest fire, like Occupy Wall Street gone global and on steroids, either feeding on itself until it burns out, exhausted from lack of fuel, or else developing into an even greater conflagration.

The Great Panic of Year One

Not everyone believes that the Great Announcement will lead to panic and mayhem. As we noted earlier, one of the earliest UFO researchers, Donald E. Keyhoe, regularly voiced his belief that people can handle the truth. "We have survived the stunning impact of the Atomic Age," he wrote. "We should be able to take the Interplanetary Age, when it comes, without hysteria."[2]

That was 1950; six decades ago. More recently, Admiral Lord Peter Hill-Norton, who served as the United Kingdom's Chief of Defence and the head of NATO's military committee, argued that even if UFOs turned out to be of extraterrestrial origin, life would go on. People in the 21st century will not panic, he believed. "They are much more interested in doing the pools or the lottery. They would shrug their shoulders and take it as a matter of course."[3]

And yet the keepers of the secret might not agree. One of America's legendary astronauts, Colonel Gordon Cooper, believed fear of panic to be central. In 1985, he testified before a United Nations panel that UFO secrecy was "imposed on all specialists in astronautics." Every day, he said, radar instruments were recording objects "of form and composition unknown to us." But the authorities conceal this information because of how they believe people will react. "So the password still is: We have to avoid panic by all means."[4]

The question of public panic always hangs over this issue, and this must be an important concern of the Breakaway Group. Certainly many people would take the news in stride, as much as one could expect under the circumstances. Although these things are inherently impossible to measure, the argument can be made that people of the 21st century are better able to handle the great shock inherent in a Disclosure statement then their grandparents would have been. A lifetime of popular culture dealing with extraterrestrials may have prepared them psychologically to some extent.

But there has always been a certain percentage of UFO witnesses who experience deep, powerful fear during their sighting. For many, it is the most intense, overwhelming fear of their life. The history of UFO encounters is replete with examples of witnesses who became hysterical, filled with sheer terror. What was happening to them was the shattering of a once-solid worldview, and a sudden feeling of powerlessness in the face of an unknown and alien intelligence. Not everyone collapses at such a time, but some do.

After Disclosure, even the panic of a minority of people will pose a serious challenge to society. If as few as 10 percent of the people have a deeply negative reaction to the news, there will be dramatic repercussions. If that number is 20 or 30 percent, so much the worse. The manner of Disclosure will be all-important, but for some, any Disclosure at all will push them close to the edge. Others will go right over.

It would be nice if the world could plan for this extraordinary event as it did for Y2K, when computer scientists methodically tweaked our technology in preparation for the Year 2000. In order to do that regarding Disclosure, however, it must be handled openly. Books similar to this one can be written, but realistically most people will not see what is coming until it is on top of them. Besides, no amount of planning can conceivably cover all the contingencies. We must expect the unexpected. Exopolitics activist Stephen Bassett once stated, accurately we believe, that Disclosure will "mark the birth of a new world."[5] And how can anyone truly prepare for that?

Reaction will be full of contradictions. Some will see it as humanity's best hope for survival. Others will see it as a harbinger of catastrophe. Only time and shared experience will allow these two groups to begin to see things through the same set of eyes.

None of this is an argument to postpone the event. Despite what anyone wants, what anyone feels is right, Disclosure will happen. It is only a matter of time. In later years, long after the fact, our memories will recall the frightening, thrilling, challenging, arduous, and momentous time.

The Fire Spreads

For a time, however, people may feel like Japanese civilians walking through the rubble in Hiroshima in 1945—dazed, frightened, and unable to fully comprehend what just happened. The first 12 months will be so challenging because the strife and deprivation that accompany them will largely feel self-inflicted by humans, not the Others.

In the immediate aftermath, the world will go to red alert. People will hoard. It is a natural human reaction, seen repeatedly throughout history when people receive destabilizing news. Workplace productivity will drop for a time, as each workplace will have some employees who will not cope well. Distribution systems will sag. Perhaps the driver who drives the truck to your local supermarket every Thursday has a nervous breakdown, or is hurt in a looting incident. Other drivers will be found, but perhaps not immediately nor reliably.

Store shelves will soon look thin and picked over. Bulk buys will be up everywhere and consumers will stock up in massive quantities, beyond what they have done before. The Wal-Marts and Costcos will hire extra security, issue lottery numbers, and limit purchases. Even so, a week after the announcement is made, most of them will be temporarily closed, waiting for re-supply. The black market on the streets for common items like toilet paper, aspirin, and canned soup will thrive.

The shortages will trigger fear, which will trigger more hoarding and more shortages in a vicious cycle that may last the greater part of that first year.

Panic will express itself in two forms of personal behavior. Some people will pull in, shut themselves inside, watch the news, and wait to see how things play out. Others will need to get out, feeding off the company of friends and coworkers in order not to be alone as they sort out the changes.

Sorting the winners from the losers. The Great Panic of Year One starts the chaotic process. Japan earthquake aftermath, 2010. Photo courtesy of Kelly Kaneshiro, via Wikimedia Commons, public domain.

If, during the initial announcement, people shrugged their shoulders, they will not be doing so now. Every day will bring a new set of headlines reporting the forward momentum of contact. Even the old headlines, which will still be with us, will be reported differently. The earthquakes, volcanoes, bombings, assassinations, and other calamities will be seen through a different filter.

Suspicion will rule, not merely directed at the government or the Others, but at each other. Today, only a small, fringe group of people believe aliens walk among us. That will change after Disclosure. During the first year A.D., you may be viewed with suspicion by other people, and if you are an average type of person, you might look at your own neighbors and friends that way.

People with second homes may flee to them. As the days turn into weeks, however, they will realize that supplies in their mountain and sea communities are even lower than where they came from. And the news will carry reports of unattended homes being robbed. They will return home to protect what they have and wait it out. If they are not armed, they will pay a premium to get that way.

Sales of guns will be up at least 500 percent from the previous year. The number of arrests for driving with a concealed weapon will skyrocket. Police officers will stop making routine traffic stops because they will not risk getting shot. The number of domestic gun accidents will reach an all-time high.

Because of the initial looting and riots, martial law will be common in much of the world, and some of the largest cities will be first. As smaller municipalities see how it has worked, they too will experiment with it in order to calm nerves, although martial law will undoubtedly make matters worse in many places.

For those who live through it, A.D. will be remembered as a great surprise, followed by an ominous feeling about how deeply the world changed. People will look back at how they endured it all, just so they could return to a good life that they hoped will still be there, much like how an earlier generation viewed the Great Depression.

Cracked Foundations

Like everything else in life, Disclosure will come with winners and losers.

Certain institutions will suffer a loss of confidence, because they either participated in the secret (government, military) or, by virtue of their niche in society, should have alerted the public (media, academia).

Others will have to adjust their business models because they operated in good faith that UFOs were bunk. Now, realizing they were duped, they will have to cope and change. Those sectors include the economy, industry, and the legal system.

These are all familiar institutions that will be changed by Disclosure. There is one, however, that will be unfamiliar to almost everyone. That will be the Breakaway Group. Its members, hidden for so long, will now be exposed. In the immediate world, A.D., these people will be a target for public anger and hostility, the kind previously reserved for arrogant Enron, AIG, and British Petroleum executives.

Government

There will be great fury directed at the governments of the world, in particular the U.S. government. Their salvation will be to acknowledge their complicity and show the public that they are doing all they can to atone for past sins. The path to renewed legitimacy will be to align with the incensed public against the secret-keepers themselves. One of the great issues of the age will be whether this occurs.

Among the many hard questions will be, "Where were our elected representatives for all these years?" We know that most members of Congress were kept in the dark, but that hardly means they should have ignored the signs, the stories from their constituents, the warnings from experts, and the prodding from a few of their own who were laughed at rather than embraced. Instantly, Capitol Hill will come alive with a fervor to investigate.

The United States Senate has never held open hearings on the subject of UFOs. The House of Representatives has held two, both of which were limited.

The first one was initiated in 1966 by House Minority Leader (and future U.S. President), Gerald R. Ford of Michigan. UFOs were turning up all over his state, and he called for hearings. When the House Armed Services Committee convened them, only three individuals testified. All were connected to the Air Force's Project Blue Book: Harold Brown, secretary of the Air Force; Dr. J. Allen Hynek, scientific consultant to the Air

Force; and Major Hector Quintanilla, Jr., chief of Project Blue Book. As a result, Air Force Secretary Harold Brown announced the formation of an independent review of Project Blue Book and current UFO cases. The University of Colorado was soon contracted to conduct a "scientific study of UFOs." This was the infamous Condon Committee.

The second congressional hearing on UFOs took place in July 1968 by the House Committee on Science and Astronautics. This was during the final stages of the Condon Committee. This time, six scientists testified and six others submitted prepared papers. One who testified, atmospheric physicist Dr. James E. McDonald, recommended the rapid escalation of "scrious scientific attention to this extraordinarily intriguing puzzle." Another expert, UCLA Engineering professor Dr. Robert Baker Jr., called for a government-sponsored UFO action and investigation team. In fact, of the six scientists who testified, five thought UFOs presented a genuine scientific anomaly that demanded further study (only Dr. Carl Sagan disagreed).

But within months, the Condon Committee concluded that there was no convincing scientific evidence for UFOs, and recommended closing Project Blue Book. When Blue Book was disbanded in 1969, the United States government officially got out of the UFO business.

That is the sum total of U.S. Congressional action regarding UFOs. Most members of Congress, more worried about elections and lobbyists, have steered clear of the topic. During the 1990s, however, there was one prominent exception: Representative Steven Schiff (R-New Mexico).

During the early 1990s, when the Roswell case was resurrected in the public eye, some of Schiff's constituents asked him to look into it. In early 1994, after continual Pentagon stonewalling of his inquiries, Schiff persuaded Congress's investigative body, the Government Accounting Office (GAO), to examine Air Force records on Roswell. Shrewdly, the Air Force initiated its own report and beat the GAO to the punch, in which it stated that the crash of a Mogul balloon had caused all the commotion. In a later report, the Air Force announced that claims about seeing alien bodies were probably caused by its dropping of "test dummies" from high altitude parachutes—despite these having taken place in the following decade, and despite the dummies being 6 feet tall and weighing 180 pounds. The GAO, meanwhile, had concluded that key records that would have shed light on the Roswell crash were inexplicably missing.[6]

Schiff's crusade for UFO truth ended in 1998. While serving his fifth term in Congress, he developed a sudden and rapid onset of squamous cell carcinoma, a type of skin cancer. He was dead at the age of 51. Roswell researcher Don Schmitt investigated rumors of foul play, but admits the case is weak. However, one source (well known to the authors) stated adamantly of his knowledge that Schiff was murdered, but declined to name names.[7] Perhaps, as files are turned over in those first days A.D., some of them may shed some light on Schiff's death.

Schiff's inquiry into UFOs was the exception. In the world after Disclosure, the men and women elected to serve the public's interests will be exposed as having missed the most important public policy matter ever.

Investigating for crimes. Asking again, "What did you know and when did you know it?" The Watergate hearings of 1973. Photo courtesy of the Sam Ervin Library (Daniel R. Smith, Curator).

But now, politicians will rally. Scurrying to the nearest microphones, they will condemn being kept in the dark. They will promise congressional hearings. They will allocate money for their own investigations. They will jockey for position to get on the right committees.

And they will put on quite a show. At least one showboating committee chair will reach back to Watergate and resurrect Senator Sam Ervin's famous question: "What did you know and when did you know it?" It will become the refrain once more as humbled secret-keepers apologize and explain under withering questioning.

At that point, the world will realize that some very important people broke some very big laws. The question will be how to handle their criminality.

Truth Commissions

Consider the dilemma facing a president or prime minister. Public anger may be explosive, and without some way to vent it, the results could be violent and revolutionary. National governments everywhere will seek to maintain control of the process, attempting to vent public anger in a controlled way. One way to do this may be to establish a Truth Commission.

In the United States, there has never been a Truth Commission for a major policy issue on a national scale. The odds are about even that Disclosure will create the conditions for the first-ever Truth Commission to become operational.

A model for something of this magnitude is The Truth and Reconciliation Commission (TRC) assembled in South Africa after the abolition of apartheid. Established by President Nelson Mandela and chaired by Archbishop Desmond Tutu, it was tasked with discovering and revealing past wrongdoing by the government. Many truth commissions have failed in their work, but the TRC is the rare exception, and it served as a crucial component for the transition to a democratic political system. Its mandate was to bear witness to, record, and in some cases grant amnesty to the perpetrators of crimes relating to human rights violations, reparation, and rehabilitation.

Although national laws will prevail when it comes to legal remedy, nations are unlikely to conduct Truth Commissions without reference to each other, and in particular to the United States, widely perceived as the heart of UFO secrecy. Within the U.S., Congress may choose to establish such a commission to deal with the stain of secrecy.

If such a commission is formed, certain similarities to the South African experience are likely to take place. Witnesses identified as victims of the secrecy violations will be invited to give statements about their experiences, and some of the better cases will be selected for public hearings. Perpetrators of the secrecy will be given the opportunity to testify and request amnesty from both civil and criminal prosecution. If the history of South Africa is an indication, the most prominent participants in the cover-up will probably take a pass.

After traveling throughout the United States (and possibly, in this instance, being empowered to take testimony in foreign countries), a report will be assembled that will document what happened.

At the end of the process, the central issue will still be unresolved. Truth commissions are sometimes criticized for allowing crimes to go unpunished. Squarely on the table will be the relationship between this truth commission and criminal prosecution.

We believe there is an answer with precedent.

Amnesty and Pardon

If the President of the United States, at the time of Disclosure, was heavily involved in the cover-up either before or during his tenure, and if that connection can be demonstrated, then there will be a resignation in the offing.

However, assuming that the President of the United States himself was not an architect of the cover-up, pressure will be brought to use presidential authority to extricate the country from a very intricate mess.

The mess will be one in which a special prosecutor will have been appointed in the first month or so A.D. As this office conducts its business, it will become obvious that many high-ranking current and ex-officials will be targeted for prison sentences. The charges will vary. Certainly perjury will be common, but an entire shopping list of criminal charges will be under review.

Matters could become dramatic. In the case of a President about to resign, he may use his authority to issue thousands of pardons, triggering a separate constitutional crisis.

More likely, a President who has maintained plausible deniability will find inspiration in the acts of two of his predecessors.

On January 21, 1977, one day after his Presidential inauguration, Jimmy Carter granted a presidential pardon to all of those who had avoided the draft during the Vietnam war. That single act meant the government forever relinquished the right to prosecute hundreds of thousands of draft-dodgers. Such a blanket pardon may well be issued A.D. in an attempt to focus the nation on the future of contact, and not on the past crimes.

✧✦✧

> Acting pursuant to the grant of authority in Article II, Section 2, of the Constitution of the United States, as the President of the United States, I do hereby grant a full, complete and unconditional pardon to: All persons who may have committed any offense between July 2, 1947, and May 17, 2021, while operating under orders that were given by lawful authorities in order to maintain secrecy concerning certain knowledge of extraterrestrial or non-human intelligence operating within the borders of the United States and its military bases worldwide. This includes lying under oath, obscuring facts from the elected representatives of the elected government, funding covert operations through extra-legal means, and all manner of felony acts to be determined as having been in the cause of maintaining this secrecy.
>
> This pardon does not apply to the following who are specifically excluded there:
>
> - All persons judged to have committed murder or other felonious assault resulting in grave bodily injury to another party.

- All persons judged to have committed treason against the United States by using their knowledge of the extraterrestrial presence and the secrecy surrounding it to subvert American interests.

✧✦✧

No matter what else, treason and murder will be crimes that no president can pardon. If lives were lost in such ventures, those individuals will go to prison, possibly for a long time.

It may be that a blanket pardon fails to suffice for the extraordinary times that A.D. will usher in. In that case, specific pardons will be granted for certain individuals. President Gerald Ford's pardon of disgraced President Richard Nixon comes to mind. Imagine if high-level generals or ex-presidents have been connected to the cover-up. They will be pardoned, by name, and for specific acts. If it were to happen today, for example, it might be former President George Bush, Sr., who was also a former CIA director. Perhaps he would be given a pardon in exchange for his full, truthful testimony.

However, the same wildcard disclaimer has to be made here. The way this plays out will be determined by the nature of our relationship with the Others, and whether or not a deal has been struck with them at any point during the last seven decades.

Economy

Economies usually like stability. In the short run, at least, there will be great disruption, as the money markets are shocked and rocked by the news. Permanent damage to the structure of our economy is another matter.

There are many examples in which the financial markets bounce back from bad news. A return to business, even if not business-as-usual, is likely to be the A.D. scenario as well, not because the changes will not be deep, but because there really is no alternative but to go forward, no matter what that means. History teaches us that humans adapt, and the markets that they create in which to transact their businesses also adapt.

The announcement will probably be accompanied by a bank freeze and a temporary shut-down of the stock market. There is precedent for both.

Three weeks before President-elect Franklin Roosevelt took office in 1933, a banking panic spread throughout America, feeding on itself, causing alarmed customers to empty their accounts. The day before Roosevelt took office, more than 5,000 banks went out of business. Roosevelt called for a "bank holiday" and closed every bank in the country. After Congress passed back-up legislation, the banks stayed closed until Department of the Treasury officials could inspect each institution's ledgers.

Following the attacks of September 11, 2001, the New York Stock Exchange, the American Stock Exchange and Nasdaq remained closed for the rest of the week, not opening for business again until September 17. When the markets did reopen, the New York Stock Exchange dropped 684 points in the first day of trading.

Both scenarios are about giving people and institutions time to process changes. Whatever happens after Day One, there will be a need for time to consider things.

Taking Stock of the Situation

One financial advisor the authors spoke to anticipated that the immediate aftermath of Disclosure would be "pure chaos and hysteria." The only reasonable response, he thought, would be to shut things down. If Disclosure occurs on a Friday afternoon, as we anticipate, it is likely that the markets will be closed for the entire next week.

But what happens when they resume? Most traders believe that the only way to calm markets down is to let them open up. Even then, there is bound to be a great deal of panic selling, and this may well trigger the so-called "circuit breakers," which close chaotic markets. Put into place by the major securities and futures exchanges, these are coordinated cross-market trading halts that are activated when a severe market price decline reaches levels that may exhaust market liquidity. Under these contingencies, trading may be halted temporarily or, under extreme circumstances, markets shut down before the end of normal close of the trading session.

These circuit-breakers will probably be triggered repeatedly. During the time period of "close-and-consider," analysts and traders will be getting an earful from their clients. The people we have spoken with expect that anywhere from 20 to 40 percent of stockholders will want to alter their portfolios significantly, if not close them entirely, when they learn that UFOs are real and the government has been hiding this information for generations.

Most financial analysts have spent time considering extraordinary contingencies such as terrorism, nuclear accidents, natural disasters, and criminal acts. Few to none, however, seem to have considered the possibility that UFOs might be real, and that they might have to deal with that. In the world A.D., they will be unprepared, and most of their advice will be made up on fly.

One Certified Financial Manager from a leading financial management and advisory company had some thoughts about how he would behave personally, and how he would interact with clients—although he was told by his management that he could not use his name in an interview with us, presumably because the topic is too alarming. "My biggest job if this happens," he said, "is going to be holding my client's hands over the weekend when I'll probably be freaking out myself."

Day-trader Peter Katz is one of the many financial experts who had never considered the possibility that he would have to take ET Disclosure into account in his stock strategy. When asked about how he would have to adjust, he replied he would not take a strong position until he could see how the market was reacting. "My gut," he added, "is that the market would be heading south instead of north."

Stock analysts from Merrill Lynch to Smith Barney will scramble mightily in the aftermath of Disclosure to bring in consultants and experts to help calm their customers and assure them that they are preparing to adapt to the future. They will create bold new client PowerPoints describing their take on what might be called the After-Market.

But the safe positions of the past may not necessarily apply in this new financial environment. For example, it would seem logical that the price of gold will rise in the panic, and this may happen. Yet, depending on the nature of the announcement, analysts may speculate that the unleashing of new technology will increase gold's value even further or, conversely, diminish it by achieving the ancient alchemist's dream of turning common metals into gold. In general, we can expect that the discussion of radical technologies will wreak havoc on some traditional portfolios.

Because we are not privy to all the information, there is always a caveat. If the Disclosure announcement and news keeps within our more-or-less established view of reality, Wall Street life will continue and adapt. If, on the other hand, there is an unforeseen complexity to it (that is, the Others have the ability to manipulate time), then the entire concept of trading as currently established could be rendered unworkable instantly.

The Biggest Bail-Out Ever

Following the 2008 global financial crisis, Presidents Bush and Obama, along with the U.S. Congress, staged the largest bailout of banks and other financial institutions in history. Responding to the subprime mortgage crisis, The Emergency Economic Stabilization Act of 2008 was enacted to rescue the financial system of the United States. It authorized the U.S. Secretary of the Treasury to spend up to 700 billion dollars to purchase distressed assets and make capital injections into banks. More rescue spending followed. Other countries able to do so staged their own versions of a rescue package.

Disclosure that UFOs are real will trigger instability in the economic system to such a degree that the corresponding response may be even greater than that stimulus package. Global leadership will declare that the situation is one-of-a-kind, and that unprecedented action must be taken. Officials worldwide will reach a consensus that, for the short-term A.D., this is hardly the time for fiscal restraint. They will try to spend their way past the difficulties of Disclosure. The public, to a great degree, will want them to.

Of course, one obvious problem is that if Disclosure is forced before the end of the financial crisis that started in 2008 (still continuing strong as of this writing), further printing of currencies could be ruinous. Aside from this, the grand A.D. economic plan will have strong critics. Recall that Paul Volcker, chairman of Barack Obama's White House Economic Recovery Advisory Board, argued that bailouts signal to the firms that they can take reckless risks. If the risks are realized, Volcker said, taxpayers pay the losses in the future. "The danger is the spread of moral hazard could make the next crisis much bigger."

Bailout defenders will reply that unless the post-Disclosure world is quickly brought to order, we may not make it to the next crisis. Even in the best scenarios, a low-grade panic will be in the air. Governments and politicians are forever focused on the short-term. They will want to do something now, and they will act to keep the money flowing. If the economy remains healthy, it will be easier for citizens to weather the uncertainty of the new circumstances.

Ironically, the entity that will be taxing and spending—the government—will also be perceived as the architect of cover-up. It will take an interesting double back-flip of spin to argue that they have been hiding the truth for decades, but that they need the people to trust them now in order to save the economy. Yet, without a credible alternative, they will probably get away with it.

No matter how successfully the world adapts to the uncertainties following Disclosure, corporations and people will take a wait-and-see attitude. Only a very few companies will expand their spending. Most will sit on their money and observe how things shake down. Ordinary people will do the same. On an intellectual level, people may understand that their global economy demands that consumers spend, but the reaction will be to let someone else do it first. With a world set ablaze by historic headlines, a good amount of hysteria, and rattled institutions, keeping what they have will become priority number one for most people.

There is one fast way to inject money into the economy and be perceived as acting in the national interest. Rather than putting Americans to work on road crews or other public works, the winner will be the military. The military establishments of the Earth—already enormous—may grow larger. They will be tasked with keeping the peace in the homeland

and standing vigilant, ready to protect humanity from the shadow of the Others. More likely than not, those same armies will be primarily employed for keeping the peace among humans.

Energy's New Equation

No blowback could be more disruptive than something that radically alters the engine of the global economy—a one-of-a-kind game-changer. When humanity publicly outs the Others through some form of Disclosure, it will put this dream/nightmare of fundamental change directly on the table.

In terms of dollar value, the petroleum industry is the largest in the world, when one considers its production, distribution, refining, and retailing. It is critical in the maintenance of our civilization, as it underlies an enormous portion of the rest of the world's industrial and transportation sectors. Moreover, it is more than a source of immense wealth for the world's super-rich: of the world's 20 largest oil companies, 15 are state-owned.[8] Therefore, a substantial number of national governments rely explicitly on petroleum for their liquidity.

Within the United States, the oil industry (along with natural gas) is the backbone of the economy. The industry supports more than 9 million American jobs and makes major economic contributions as an employer and purchaser of goods and services. In 2007, the most recent year for which data is available, the industry accounted for more than $1 trillion in value, or 7.5 percent of the U.S. gross domestic product.[9]

Humanity needs a post-oil economy; humanity fears a post-oil economy. We need it in order to save the Earth's environment; we fear it because it will threaten the way we do business with each other.

For humanity, the prospect of moving beyond an oil-based economy is a Holy Grail. The world is addicted to oil, and most of us acknowledge our need to wean ourselves from it. The places where it lies in its greatest abundance are some of the world's most dangerous. Oil accidents can be disastrous: In 2010, a massive spill occurred in the Gulf of Mexico. In 2011, another occurred off the coast of New Zealand.

Once the President acknowledges that "we are not alone," it will be obvious to a number of analysts that at least some UFOs have been real, and it then becomes crystal clear that petroleum is on its way toward becoming obsolete as a source of transportation energy. For many years, leaks have occurred and claims have been made describing radical propulsion systems in alien flying saucers, as well as in the home-grown variety. Certainly, anything that can move in perfect silence, hover indefinitely, and accelerate instantaneously is using something better than high-octane gasoline as its source of fuel, whether this be some form of the fabled zero-point energy field, a clean burning nuclear fusion, or something more exotic.

Oil prices remain high because of the continual state of warfare that has ravaged the Middle East. If the Others have been observing us since at least World War II, then surely they have noticed this relationship. Perhaps they are confused as to why we should allow such conflict to come from a natural resource, but they can hardly miss the connection between war and oil.

Oil experts have disagreed over the fear of peak oil. The bottom-line is, "Will the world run out of oil?" We can presume that because oil is so important to us and we are apparently so important to the Others that this debate has not escaped them. In fact, from their near-Earth observations and more sophisticated monitoring capability they may know the answer to this complex question.

The idea of peak oil is not that the world will "run out" of oil, rather, that it will run out of the easy and cheap oil, the result of which would convulse the global economy.

But even if oil were to continue to be abundant amid a rising global demand for the next 50 years, as some analysts predict, there are still serious questions we need to ask regarding the viability of a petroleum-based world. In the first place, assuming we have enough oil for the next 50 years, what happens then? Second, can the world environment survive another 50 years of full-speed-ahead extraction, refining, and burning of oil? Therefore, what if UFO technology provides us with an energy source that can replace petroleum in many respects? What if this new energy source is clean? What if it is easy to produce, and therefore very cheap?

It does not matter if the Others "give" humanity their energy secret. Once we know there is a viable alternative to oil, the answer will be found. There will be incredible pressures on the world's political leaders on the issue of energy. They may stonewall, but the answer will be found anyway. When it is, the oil industry will face its greatest crisis ever, and this will translate to much of the global economy.

Like it or not, trillions of dollars are invested worldwide in the petroleum industry. Although something better is surely an attractive option for humanity as a whole, it certainly is not for those who own major portions of the world's oil. Suddenly, the long-term value of oil would promise to plummet; suddenly, the portfolio valuations of the world's largest corporations (and wealthiest families) would plummet. Unless these groups are certain that they can control and monetize whatever replaces oil, they will resist any changeover.

In terms of the financial markets, any dramatic change in petroleum futures will affect everything. No matter what product you can imagine, most of its value is in the energy required to make and transport it. If the services of petroleum will no longer be required for much of this, the prices of many products will drop dramatically. Again, this is a good thing for most of us. It may be that the power elite at the top of the human pyramid is happy with this outcome, or not.

This is why Big Oil has been one of the powers behind the UFO cover-up. Breaking its hold over the fabric of our society will alter the structure of economic and political power around the world. Yet, the upside in the long-term promises easily to outweigh the short-term disruptions and uncertainties.

Repealing the Law of Gravity

Replacing petroleum will be one of the major upheavals of the world A.D., but not the only one. Serious researchers of UFOs agree that these craft appear to negate the Earth's gravity. The world's militaries and governments no doubt made that connection long ago. Therefore, the next big upheaval will deal with electrogravitics.

Such ideas have circulated since the 1950s, and they have also received attention in the classified world. During the mid-1950s, several aviation journals discussed what appeared to be imminent breakthroughs in electrogravitics. One of these, a British research company called Aviation Studies (International) Ltd., stated that "electrostatic energy sufficient to produce a Mach 3 fighter is possible with megavolt energies and a k of over 10,000." Another report, by Gravity Rand, Ltd., agreed. According to that report: "To assert electrogravitics is nonsense is as unreal as to say it is practically extant." Then, in 1956, such talk stopped abruptly. Did everyone at once discover that all this anti-gravity speculation turned out to be nothing more than hot air? Or did it go more deeply under cover?[10]

These are the questions that have led some to conclude that Alien Reproduction Vehicle (ARV) is real. Of course, if such technology has existed for some time, it means that every oil-related war was waged under false pretense.

The secret-keepers who will face the harsh questions about their behavior and decisions in that scenario will have their arguments ready. They will argue that even if the technology exists, it would have been dangerous to share it publicly, because the intentions of the Others were unclear.

They will acknowledge that, in the long term, replacing oil with a better source of energy is desirable and perhaps the time has come. The same is true for replacing our current modes of ground-based transportation with something that can quickly, cheaply, and easily get us off the ground. But here is the rub: How would such developments affect not only the profits to those interests in control of the petroleum industry, not only the financial markets, but also the ability of human social and political elites to control society? For what happens when it becomes possible for all of humanity to have access to an abundant, clean, and cheap energy source, combined with knowledge of an electrogravitic propulsion system?

In the first place, it would mean that you could heat your home forever, probably for next-to-nothing. It might also mean that you could make such a system of energy portable, which would enable possibilities never dreamed of with petroleum. For instance, it might allow everyone to be able to power heavy equipment inexpensively. If you wanted to build a deep underground extension to your home, you might very easily be able to do it. A quick trip to Germany, Mozambique, Thailand, or anywhere else could be done easily, and perhaps without government knowledge or control.

How would such new-found wealth and independence sit with those who have been used to controlling the masses of humanity? And, to be fair, let us also ask, what if the capabilities of new energy and electrogravitics can be easily adapted to create very destructive weapons?

The transition away from petroleum and to something better is more than a question of improving our daily "cost of doing business" on Earth. It involves a complete overhaul of our society. The new destinations to which such changes will lead us will be public policy issues of the highest order.

The questions of energy and how they will be resolved may turn out to only be the tip of the iceberg when it comes to sorting out the changed reality. Fortunately, we have a system set up that will begin to address these issues from the beginning.

Legal System

As with most other major issues in American history, from civil rights to health care, the courts will have much to say about how we deal with the acknowledged presence of the Others. Although it may seem a mundane way to deal with something extraordinary, it will be a powerful tool toward helping settle differences among individuals, companies, governments and even, conceivably, the Others, as represented through human surrogates.

The law can be broken down into criminal law, which are injustices against society prosecuted by the State, and civil law, which are injustices against a person prosecuted by the injured party.

Can You Arrest the Others?

Criminal law is not about money. It is about exacting punishment and deterring others who may be tempted to break the law.

When it comes to criminal law's applicability to the A.D. world, we have to discuss whether the Others will recognize authority. We even have to ask whether they will be physically present in a post-Disclosure society, for in fact they may not. Because we are not really clear on who they even are, all we can say is that based on the last 60-plus years, it seems rather unlikely that there could be criminal penalties applied to these beings. As years go on, if relations become normal in some regard, then perhaps. Even this, however, represents a stretch of the imagination.

Can You Sue the Others?

The same would appear to apply regarding lawsuits. But here, things become more interesting. Civil law is all about torts, which range from personal injury and fraud to negligent and intentional misrepresentation. It also includes false imprisonment, defamation, assault, battery, and so on. Given the nature of things that might be disclosed in a coming clean period, there seems to be ample cause to sue regarding human-to-human interaction brought about by contact with the Others. For example, Mac Brazel was supposedly detained in Roswell back in 1947, held incommunicado while he got his head right about what he found on his ranch that famous day in July. Brazel is long gone, but his grandchildren are still around. Or what about *Communion* author Whitley Strieber, who has been ridiculed on *South Park*, no less, for being subjected to an alien "rectal probe"? He may have a case against the people who allowed him to look crazy when he actually was as sane and maybe saner than most.

Civil suits require an injured party. Lawsuits will be filed to seek either money or some kind of injunctive relief. A multitude of new injuries—based on precedent—may present themselves. It may get very messy before order is restored.

The first issue that lawyers will want to resolve is the nature of the Others and whether we have any formal understandings or treaties with them. They will want to know if they are here outside our laws and have presented themselves as a threat to our military, or whether they are as regulated as, say, cruise ships entering a foreign port of call. If the answer is ambiguous, along the lines of "sporadic continuing informal contact," it will be necessary to define a legal relationship with these beings. Lawyers are apt to incorporate this changed reality into our existing legal structure, and the system will continue doing just that on an ad-hoc basis.

On a basic level, attorneys, judges, and officers of the court will want to know if the Others acknowledge the concept of our "jurisdiction." On an even more practical level, they will want to know if the Others accept or refuse "service of process." Although there has been some testimony (and potentially disinformation) about treaties being signed with EBEs (Extraterrestrial Biological Entities) going back to the Eisenhower years, the idea that there is any kind of formal understanding, written or otherwise, between us and the Others is probably a long-shot. This means that lawyers will have to be content dealing with secondary effects and collecting damages from human institutions.

By way of example, consider the abduction phenomenon. Being kidnapped and deprived of your freedom is, by definition, a personal injury. Who to sue? In the first months A.D., it is likely that some enterprising lawyer, prodded by an aggrieved client, will try to sue the Others for damages. This will be a tough sell in the court system, but it is apt to generate publicity for the client and the attorney, something both will probably be seeking if they are the first to initiate such a case.

Once in a courtroom, the judge will ask the sticking question: do the Others acknowledge our jurisdiction? The answer will be no, not really, or at least we do not think they do. We can proclaim our jurisdiction based on precedent and statute, of course, but then the question becomes: how on Earth (literally) do we serve them? The legal answer to that will be some form of publication. If the right judge has been found to hear the case, he or she will accept the plaintiff's argument that any group able to come "here" from "there" (wherever "there" may be) will also have the technology to monitor our communications. The final hurdle a judge would still have to ask is how, if the plaintiff prevails in court, will they ever collect the damages? The lawyer for the case will need to be at his or her best here, but will doubtless argue that while there are no formal relations with the Others now, there are bound to be in the future, and when those relations become clear, they will collect damages as part of that opening agreement.

Bureaucracy Grinds On

On a global scale, many international agreements and understandings will be put to a prolonged and strenuous test.

One area will be the hot-button issue of immigration law. The term *illegal alien* will have a different meaning here, but it will be impossible to avoid the implications. Every government around the world will be forced to discuss whether or not the Others are actually here, on Earth, in their country, walking among the population. If they are, then the nations of Earth have a new immigration issue.

Because we are talking about UFOs, which are flying objects, much of the legal action will focus on the area of aviation and space law.

The International Civil Aviation Organization (ICAO), a specialized agency of the United Nations, codifies the principles and techniques of international air navigation. It adopts standards and recommends practices concerning air navigation, its infrastructure, flight inspection, prevention of unlawful interference, and facilitation of border-crossing procedures for international civil aviation. In addition, the ICAO defines the protocols for air accident investigation. Virtually every aspect of their mandate will be re-examined in light of ET-reality and the fact that UFOs share our airspace.

The International Air Transport Association (IATA) is an international industry trade group that represents some 230 airlines comprising 93 percent of scheduled international air traffic. It will have issues about Disclosure—looking to the past, and planning routes and safety for the future.

The Foreign Sovereign Immunity Act is the statute that establishes the limitations as to whether a foreign sovereign nation or its agencies may be sued in U.S. courts. It provides the exclusive basis and means to bring a lawsuit against a foreign sovereign in the United States.

Where this is likely to become important is in the reverse. Other nations and their representatives may not be able to be sued in the United States, but because most countries are signatory, then it follows that the United States and its own institutions will be protected from being sued in other nations.

What might the United States be sued for?

If the United States government, for instance, has recovered crash wreckage and alien technology throughout the years, it is likely to have submitted it to private industry, discretely and secretly, for analysis and even reverse-engineering. A company that was given this contract may be judged to have had an unfair advantage over its competitors. It is likely, if not certain, that any such contracts awarded by the U.S. government would have gone to American companies.

The Federal Tort Claims Act (FTCA) provides a limited waiver of the federal government's sovereign immunity when its employees are negligent within the scope of their employment. Under the FTCA, the government can only be sued "under circumstances where the United States, if a private person, would be liable to the claimant in accordance with the law of the place where the act or omission occurred." Translated, this means that the government cannot be sued for things it did as a government; in this case, covering up UFOs.

Let us say that the Majestic-12 organization, or whatever else it may call itself, has resorted to extreme measures to keep this secret from time-to-time throughout the years, such as death threats, torture, or even assassination. Under the FTCA, the government is not liable when any of its agents commits the crimes of assault, battery, false imprisonment, false arrest, malicious prosecution, abuse of process, libel, slander, misrepresentation, deceit, or interference with contract rights. However, it also provides an exception. The government is liable if a law enforcement officer commits these crimes. Would MJ-12 agents be considered "law enforcement officers," or simply "agents" of the government? The courts will have to make that call.

There will be a political fight to create a new exemption to the FSIA, so that interest groups—in and outside the United States—can sue the government, based on the "Act of God" status of Disclosure.

Let us say that Northrop-Grumman (an example only) received either crash wreckage or something else of its kind. No Disclosure would have come from the government about its origin; it would have only been referred to as "foreign technology." Engineers at the company would know not to ask questions—the material could have come from the Soviet Union, and it would not be their concern. Yet, the company would have profited from any discoveries, held any patents, and would have reaped incredible advantage in the marketplace.

The government may hold itself as being immune to lawsuits, but private contractors may not be. If details were not forthcoming in a limited disclosure, some people may start by filing Freedom of Information Act requests designed to see what technical details were given, how formalized the sweetheart deal had been, and to what benefit. If technology is patented, then it is publicly available but you cannot use it. On the other hand, if technology has been treated as a trade secret, then other companies can literally tear it apart and try to reverse engineer it for their own patents. Therefore, what if the technology was never patented in order to keep its origin secret and to keep questions from being asked, but its use conveyed an unfair competitive advantage on the company to which it was given? Moreover, the government helped maintain the secrecy from which the company benefited.

The companies who are damaged include virtually all that did not receive favored status. The question grows more complex legally, however, because the history gleaned from the past behavior of our Office of Foreign Technology shows that the government almost never shares the big picture with any one company, preferring instead to share a piece here and another piece there.

The Ultimate Aviation Law Case

The reality of UFOs, given that they are flying objects, may cause members of the legal profession who specialize in aviation law to see this as a golden opportunity to be involved in the thick of the action. Most aviation law deals with accidents, but that may change, too.

There are many lawsuits one envisions following Disclosure. For example, what about a pilot who, in our pre-Disclosure world, saw a UFO come so close to his aircraft that he saw windows on it, so close that he took evasive maneuvers to avoid collision? When the pilot informed traffic control of his situation, he was informed that multiple ground-based radars confirmed his sighting. When he landed, shaken by what he saw, he filed a formal report. His reward for his honesty? His company grounded him from flight status for more than three years. This is exactly what happened to the pilot of a Japan Air Lines jet when he flew over Alaska in 1986.

Was the pilot damaged by the actions of his company? To the extent that he loved flying and derived status from it, yes. His ability to seek other employment may have been diminished as well. He may have lost salary because he was not flying. All of this is actionable even if the airline had no knowledge about UFO reality. But what if an authority figure at the airline did have professional reasons to believe that UFOs were authentic and real? And what about the radar reports and other witnesses that the airline decided to ignore?

In 2010, it was reported that commercial pilots were encountering UFOs in such numbers, creating such an air traffic hazard, that pilots operating out of London's Heathrow Airport started developing unofficial aircrew reports for their colleagues, to ensure that they knew of potential UFO trouble spots. All of this was privately done, without sanction from their employers.[11] When it comes to aviation safety, pilots are educated on wind shear, birds caught in engines, and a litany of other infrequent events, but not UFOs. This may not yet register heavily in a world built around denial, but in the A.D. world it is likely to look like negligence of the highest order.

There are many potential cases affecting aviation law that may emerge A.D. For instance, as documents are released and old stories are re-interpreted, what if it becomes clear that an Airbus crash with hundreds of people on board occurred at the same time a UFO sighting was recorded by military radar operators—but was never revealed? Perhaps the black box recorded something that, in a world where UFOs were fiction, got past investigators. In a world where UFOs are fact, however, the data might now be interpreted as a potential cause of the crash. Would the NTSB—an independent agency—want its own reputation bolstered by proving that the government withheld relevant information to its investigation? What about the airline itself, which paid huge settlement money to the families of the dead? Supposedly settlements are final. In the world of A.D., however, such theories may be tested as airlines try to recover funds and shift responsibility toward the government.

Perhaps all of the airlines will gang up on their respective governments, or perhaps they will specifically target the U.S. government. They could easily claim that the government knew the airways were more hazardous than it acknowledged, and that the FAA (and its non-U.S. counterparts) had not done its job.

Eventually, we may see a sub-specialty within aviation and space law. Particularly if there have not been treaties signed, this specialty may become known as "Extra-Legal," the study of an extraterrestrial presence that operates not above or within the law as we know it, but simply outside of it altogether. Although the rest of the world may refer to these strange visitors as "The Others," it is likely the legal profession will call them by a more specific name: "Extras."

An Entirely New Court System

The court system will be able to stretch, within limits, to accommodate many of the issues that will arise among humans based on an acknowledgment of the Others. Under such circumstances, the Others are simply a factor in the criminal or civil issues that have created conflict between us.

It may seem like bad science-fiction to think that the Others will ever be a part of an official court system. It seems unlikely that they ever will be. Yet, there will be those who immediately push for such a result. They will focus on the need to get these beings to sign a treaty recognizing our courts and jurisdiction. After all, we currently attempt to deal with foreign nationals of countries with whom we have no treaties. It is not always easy, it usually takes time, and often yields less-than-perfect results.

Perhaps the Others would agree to contractual relationships but balk at a nationalistic country-by-country approach. We may have to create an entirely new court system to deal with criminal and civil relations between us and them on a global basis. If there are multiple groups of Others and one of them is responsible for abducting our citizens or mutilating them, we may need a treaty with the "other" Others to police the situation. And if we are trading technology for, say, minerals, then we will need an agreement about how to enforce a contract. Again—assuming they are willing to deal formally with humanity.

The bottom line is that all issues will require discussion about what governing document will apply when trying to resolve disputes between a human and an Other. The term used between residents and companies of different states is "diversity jurisdiction." These are cases that cannot necessarily be heard in one state or another, but have to be heard in the federal courts.

It seems pedestrian to discuss such things. But, depending on the relationship and how it evolves, something of the sort may already exist. If not, it may be created in the first years A.D.

Media

As we have noted elsewhere, A.D. will be the best of times and the worst of times for the major media establishments. It will instantly make reporters relevant again and will make news a commodity for which the public is willing to pay. At the same time, it will reveal the complicity and laziness that the journalistic institutions of the world have brought to this story, now proved to be authentic, The Greatest Story Never Told. To appreciate how badly the media has blown this story, here are three examples from thousands that illustrate its embarrassing lack of professionalism when it comes to this topic.

Example #1: Apollo Astronaut Edgar Mitchell

Edgar Mitchell was the lunar module pilot of Apollo 14, and the sixth man to walk on the moon. In February 1971, he spent a full nine hours walking on the lunar surface in the Fra Mauro Highlands region.

Mitchell also happened to grow up in Roswell, New Mexico. After his NASA missions, he returned there. During the 1970s, before the story leaked to UFO investigators, many people who had kept the story to themselves for years sought him out—seeing him as a national figure who could help tell their story. They told him that what happened in 1947 was the crash and recovery of an extraterrestrial craft, complete with alien bodies.

In the 1990s, Mitchell began to test the waters with his beliefs that we were not alone in the universe. On July 23, 2008, however, he told presenter Nick Margerrison of the *Kerrang!* radio show, that he happened to be "privileged enough to be in on the fact that we have been visited on this planet and the UFO phenomenon is real. It has been covered up by governments for some time now.[12]

The statement was picked up around the world and, at the very least, did manage to surmount the first obstacle to UFO coverage by the media.

This qualified it to go to the second level, where it was ridiculed and marginalized. CNN coverage included the usual raised eyebrow from the anchor while introducing the material, the videotaped package included the musical theme from *The X-Files* and cartoon images of little green men. At the end, the anchorwoman smiled and went to commercial.

In another piece of coverage on the same network, Mitchell's comments were played back, and a statement from NASA read, "NASA does not track UFOs. NASA is not involved in any sort of cover-up about alien life on this planet or anywhere in the universe." The anchorwoman in this coverage also smiled in disbelief, shook her head, and passed off to Wolf Blitzer who managed to say, "Okay, we'll watch this story with you."

This kind of dismissive superiority was repeated by reporters regarding Mitchell's testimony. What was it that made news producers slot this as a silly story? What cue did they receive that convinced them the best reaction was to smile and shake their heads in disbelief?

A man trusted to fly the first moon mission after the Apollo 13 disaster, handpicked from thousands of qualified pilots and engineers, came forward to explain that he believes UFOs are real, that Roswell was the crash of an alien spacecraft, and that the government is complicit in keeping this information covered up. The media's reaction should have been to dispatch investigative teams to learn the truth. Instead, they gave it the kind of on-camera treatment that usually greets the birth of a baby panda at the local zoo.

Example #2: National Press Club News Conference

There is a long history of U.S. military encounters with UFOs, a fact that has been documented many times over. So when, on September 27, 2010, a news conference was held at the National Press Club in Washington, D.C., featuring a half-dozen former U.S.A.F. officers speaking directly to this issue, one might think that the nation's major media would be interested. Even more striking was that these retired officers described cases in which UFOs had been seen near U.S. nuclear weapons facilities. These were events witnessed by multiple soldiers in which nuclear missiles actually malfunctioned in the aftermath.

A few news outlets, including *Fox News* and *The Air Force Times*, covered the event competently. A small number of the major outlets provided neutral coverage in their online content. Yet, despite a great deal of advance publicity and private money expended to promote the event, the news conference was virtually shunned by the media heavyweights.

CNN, the once-proud maverick news organization, allowed a pair of condescending and ill-informed on-air personalities (an anchorwoman and a weatherman) to ridicule these military men for coming forward. The openly skeptical anchorwoman actually laughed, invoked Fox Mulder, and even managed to work in "little green men." One could only see the performance in order to believe it really happened. Most of the other coverage, such as it was, was equally shameful. *Wired*, for instance, titled its hit piece "Tinfoil Tuesdays," while the *Washington Post* sent a lifestyle columnist, John Kelly, who opened his coverage by explaining he arrived late and only came because they offered cookies.[13]

One wonders what it would take to wipe the smirk off the faces of these individuals masking as journalists. Most likely, nothing short of Disclosure itself.

Example #3: Xiaoshan Airport, Hangzhou, China

Another example concerns the sighting of a UFO over China's Xiaoshan Airport in Hangzhou, China, which is the capital of East China's Zhejiang province, on the night of July 9, 2010. According to the report of the municipal government there, an unidentified flying object disrupted air traffic over the airport, causing it to be shut down for an hour while authorities scrambled to figure out what it was.

As reported from several official and unofficial sources in China, the UFO showed up on the airport's radar a little past 8:30 pm. Soon after, airport personnel saw a "shining light" in the air that was later confirmed by passengers who were flying at the time. They described it as a "twinkling spot" that "disappeared very soon" with a "comet-like tail." A striking photo was taken that shows structure and four lighted windows.

Forcing the media. Finally the Greatest Story Never Covered will actually get the attention it deserves. Xaioshan Airport in China closed in July of 2010 because of a UFO. The photo was taken by an anonymous Chinese resident, and has been widely used in the media.

Service was suspended at the airport, which serves as a hub for Air Asia. An extensive aerial search began, leading to a total of 56 minutes of down time, the delay of 18 flights, and the stranding of about 2,000 passengers.

CNNGo reporter Jessica Beaton ascribed it to a publicity stunt. "There's no better way to make headlines," she wrote, "than to have a UFO sighting." Her tone, always important, conveyed amusement. "We're not saying we think little green men landed," she said glibly, "why choose China when Thai beaches are so close by?" To her credit, she did not immediately accept the official explanation. "But really, a reflection from an airplane shut down an airport? They should come up with a better excuse than that."[14]

But why the jokes? After all, one of those Chinese officials also said that the sighting had a "military connection." Further details could not be divulged at the time, he added. Was this American technology? If so, why are Americans flying it in China? If it was Chinese technology, what do they have that looks like the object in the photo, which apparently hovers and then accelerates instantly?

The American media, nearly *en masse*, ignored the event. The "roundtable" on ABC's *This Week* had time to discuss basketball star LeBron James. NBC's *Meet-the-Press* dissected Sarah Palin's YouTube video where she cast herself as a "Mama Grizzly." No enterprising American journalist traveled to China to investigate what happened at Xiaoshan. That, apparently, would be nonsense.

These Are the People Who Will Tell Us About Disclosure?

After Roswell, "deny and ridicule" became policy relating to all matters ufological. We have now reached a place where the mainstream news coverage has been wholly committed to protecting the status quo of the cover-up. One might dismiss this as simply lame behavior and lazy coverage, which it clearly is, but there is also the likelihood of deceit at the higher levels.

Recall that only a few companies now control most of the media, particularly in the United States. These corporate structures have had a long history of collaboration with the U.S. intelligence community. The management of news by the CIA and other intelligence groups around the world is an open secret, and a lot of good analysis has been done on the topic. More than 30 years ago, Carl Bernstein wrote an excellent exposé on the CIA's influence over mainstream U.S. media for an article in *Rolling Stone*, and much follow-up work has been done through the years.[15]

This does not mean that the CIA and its kind control every aspect of news coverage and spin; control is seldom complete. But the indications are that on the big issues, the right relationships have been made with major media. These relationships have continued and deepened through the years.

Disclosure will not change that situation. The national security community will not walk away from the table after having invested so much to control it. Coverage of the post-Disclosure world will continue to comport with the interests of the intelligence community. In the immediate aftermath, all the wrong people will continue to be quoted. As today, so tomorrow: people will need to be vigilant for the truth, and major media will need to be held accountable.

When the smiling anchors and dismissive experts are confronted with Disclosure, will they be honest enough to admit their own ignorance and lack of curiosity? It seems unlikely; about as unlikely as the public feeling good about getting information from these people after the truth is out.

Blowback will singe away whatever credibility remains of the Fourth Estate. They may not notice their hair is on fire, but most people will. The *New York Times*, and institutions like it, with all their resources, will suffer greatly because they willfully failed to give serious attention or investigation into the topic in the past.

It is against this backdrop of ham-handed coverage, at best naive and at worst disinformation, that the world of A.D. will emerge. The question is, how strong will the public reaction against the media be? Will there be a new version of Occupy Wall Street, but one directed at the tightly controlled corporate-intelligence-media complex? Rather, perhaps we should not ask "will it happen?" but "how strong will that reaction be?"

Some truth-tellers, such as Whitley Strieber, whose *Communion* deserves credit for bringing this issue to a wide audience, will gain a new status. What makes him unique today, though, is bravely speaking out against a wall of ridicule. Once authorities confirm his story and thousands of other abductees come forward, he may fade back, like the grandfather who puts on his old military uniform every Memorial Day and marches in a parade. Or—and this is to be hoped—he will be respected as someone who has given more thought to what it all means than most people alive today. Much of the difference will most likely depend on how strong the public reaction is to media portrayal of Disclosure.

The news will spread like a firestorm, blowing everything else away for weeks and months. Everything from quarterly economic reports to local sporting events will be reported through the prism of this contact. Every assignment editor everywhere will be looking at reporting and asking, “Where’s the contact angle in this?” As the media transitions from its steady diet of the trivial into a 24/7 news cycle of contact, it will ignore its own culpability in allowing the cover-up to exist under a rock it chose not to see, let alone turn over.

With no apparent embarrassment, establishment journalists will point the finger of shame and skepticism at the government, the military, and the scientific establishment. Whistleblowers will come forward on a daily basis for quite some time, all now feeling unfettered by previously signed national security agreements, ready to feed the firestorm. Each new revelation will light the flame under a still newer one. Bloggers will have a field day, offering opinion and insight. Every photo released in the first wave of Disclosure will be endlessly circulated on the Internet.

For three decades, local TV reporter Mark Sanchez covered just about everything that came up on his general assignment beat. He sees a firestorm and serious public backlash against the press in the aftermath of Disclosure. Complicity in the cover-up will have eroded public confidence in all public institutions. “Experience tells me disbelief, cynicism and insufficient alarm will greet future proclamations made After Disclosure,” he said. “The truth is liberating, but serious social upheaval will erupt as the truth sinks in…. What follows could be the real legacy of denial the past six decades: public overreaction, intolerance and widespread instability across every level of society.”

Whether or not Sanchez’s pessimism about our ability to handle the truth is warranted, one can hardly argue that widespread instability is bad for the news business. Dislocation and social upheaval are the stuff of Pulitzers and Emmys.

Imagine the golden trophies awaiting reporters who get to cover these kinds of stories:

Sparks Fly Over Majestic's Role at Commission Hearing
The Presidential Amnesty Order
Stock Market and Bank Closure
Man Kills 17 People Thinking They Were Aliens
Cover-Up Architect in Critical Condition After Mob Beating
Abductees File Class Action Lawsuit Against Others
Network News Reporter Fired for Bribe-Taking
Pope Welcomes "All God's Children"
Presidential Candidates Clash Over Contact Policy
Central Park Rally Biggest Ever

As the days and months unfold, however, a legitimate question in the aftermath of Disclosure will be whether or not the media will have the ability or integrity to investigate why it failed so utterly and completely to see this story. Were media owners actually bought-off by those elites managing the cover-up? Will a single news executive actually be fired or held accountable?

We believe that the media institutions that survive Disclosure and thrive A.D. will be the ones that practice a form of "ultimate transparency." By this, we mean that they devote substantial resources to shining the light on their own internal processes of story selection, investigation, and editing. This includes having live cameras in the newsroom streaming the debates and conferences onto the Internet 24/7, so that the people who missed this awesome story no longer have a place to run or hide in the aftermath of their failure.

They Will Survive

Institutions, such as law, media, and government, do not just go away. That is why they are called institutions. They can change, reform, reorganize. They can adapt, incorporate, and morph. Disclosure will blow through them like a hot wind in a summer dry spell. It will seem that sheer accountability will demand that they be allowed to fail. Some will argue that this should happen.

But we are not talking about a single car company or an individual bank. Newspapers like The *New York Times* may fail. The Department of Energy may be organized out of existence. Old courts may be folded into new ones. The big picture, however, remains.

How we see and relate to the world around us is the issue. And even though there may well be higher planes of consciousness in store, as some have argued, people will still need to shape their world through familiar processes.

The Worst It Could Be

Whenever one discusses a situation spinning out of control, there is the danger that it will stay that way and get worse. It is certainly possible that all the "snap-back" inherent in human beings and institutions will only "snap" this time.

If the system breaks entirely as a result of Disclosure, this is what it might look like:

The economy could shatter into a global depression. The governments of the major financial powers could be so completely discredited on the issue that no one will want to grant them the power to intervene in a way that might fix things. Depression mixed with fear is a potent drink to swallow. It leads to repression, long-term military rule, and fascism.

Seeing the world come apart could also have a devastating psychological effect on humanity. Many pundits and psychologists throughout the years—in comments and reports—have speculated that the interaction of a superior and inferior civilization could lead to the collapse of the weaker one. If our natural human resiliency is suppressed by faltering economies and violent reaction, we could fall into a vicious downward spiral that simply cannot be stopped.

The bottom could be the unhinging of our world, the loss of the industrial base needed to run a technological society, and a descent into a kind of global madness. Our civilization could collapse as completely as did the Aztecs or Incas.

Writer and historian Will Durant said, "A great civilization is not conquered from without until it has destroyed itself from within." Whether one thinks that humanity will recover and grow from the experience of Disclosure depends not just on what the Others are here for, which is an external consideration, but how strong one views the civilization that humankind has built.

We are not naive on that score. The world exists in a precarious place today, primarily as a result of our own choices. The pessimists have much evidence from which to argue their case.

Although we believe the immediate impact of Disclosure will be very difficult those first years and perhaps beyond, we do not believe—short of news that the Others actively mean us harm—that this collapse is a certainty. Instead, the world could easily see a re-birth. In the last century, we have adapted to so much fundamental change that widening our perspective to include the vast universe should ultimately be seen as a beginning and not an end.

Vignette #5:
Encrypted Field Report

✧✦✧

PERSONAL AND CONFIDENTAL

June 3

Jim,

After the fatalities at the South Parkway roadblock, if we don't get this martial law thing framed right, we're sunk. People are so stirred up, when they see a guy with a gun and a uniform it gives them someone to take it out on. It's like they see our own people as an occupying force, but they're Americans!

Sounds like Congress is going to approve the Bring Them Home Act, but if we bring half the overseas forces home, they need to stay commissioned and on the streets here in our cities, and when they hit the streets, people need to see them as being there to help.

The fact that aliens are hiding out somewhere does not give somebody the right to boost a new refrigerator, and if you ask people straight up, that's what they'll tell you. Period.

So why is there still looting after more than two weeks? Because people feel like the federal government is MIA, like Baghdad or Katrina, and they're right, because Washington doesn't want to come on too strong because people are understandably furious since finding out the people in charge are just a lying sack of bureaucrats.

The real problem is the states, which haven't figured out that the basic service they have to provide now is not education or even jobs, but security.

If the state Governors don't step up fast, then somebody else will. And I'm not talking about aliens, but these petty thieves, gangs, organized crime, and God knows who else. The local police do not have the firepower to take on some of these whackos who are out there armed to the teeth with war surplus explosives and trash-talking Armageddon. The feds need to quietly let every state know that if they want resources, they got them. After the incident in Ohio where they broke into an Armory and got away with it, you know these dead-enders are planning all kinds of new hits on targets that are a lot softer than they ought to be.

Imagine if these ETs are watching us and we can't stop fighting with ourselves? That scares the hell out of me.

Mick

Chapter 6

The [New] Age of Aquarius: Turn On, Tune In, Drop Out.

If the masses started to accept UFOs, it would profoundly affect their attitudes towards life, politics, everything. It would threaten the status quo. Whenever people come to realize that there are larger considerations than their own petty little lives, they are ripe to make radical changes on a personal level, which would eventually lead to a political revolution in society as a whole.

—John Lennon, radio interview, 1975

Day One will unleash the same primal social forces triggered by the assassination of President Kennedy and the Vietnam War during the 1960s. Insecurity will rule. People will see once again that governments cannot be trusted and that powerful conspiracies really do exist.

The older generation will interpret Disclosure through establishment perceptions. They will see only how it challenges the world they knew. Younger people will embrace a new way of looking at our world and other worlds. Because of this split, the first decade After Disclosure will come closest in tone and texture to the 1960s as any decade since. Whether you think that is good news or bad, be ready. The elements are already in place.

One big difference from the 1960s, of course, is that more technology will be in place. Ideas will spread faster, morph faster, disappear faster. All of this will contribute to a new generation gap, a new counter-culture. Protests will be common, as large, unhinged segments of the population turn away from the *status quo* and experiment with new ideas. Music will carry political messages. Social experimentation will take center stage. Although some will cling to the old trappings that brought them comfort, others will throw them aside and seek a brand new day.

Friend or foe, the presence of other intelligent beings will make people consider humanity's place in the universe. Life may still consist of work, daily routine, and the final flickering out of our loved ones and then ourselves, but our days on Earth may also be elevated by wonder and awe. Possibly even a sense of destiny.

For others, it will create existential dread. Because fear and panic will probably predominate at the beginning, there may be a lingering, dampening effect on the human spirit for a time. Whether or not the Others pose a direct threat to humankind, their acknowledged presence will still precipitate an indirect negative effect on our institutions, particularly those dealing with wealth and power. That will make life hard for a while, and cheerful dispositions may be greatly in demand.

Naturally, what happens after Disclosure will depend greatly on what is actually disclosed. If the news is catastrophic, terrifying, or unfathomable, then all bets are off. Most of the following possibilities (but not all), deal with the type of Disclosure that can be intuited from our own research and observations. Namely, that we will learn a massive cover-up has been underway for years, that "Others" exist, and that we are still coming to terms with what it all means.

Shock and awe will predominate for some time. Some will argue that the so-called Disclosure is itself a cover-up, just another form of mind-control. This belief will be supported by the fact that the political leadership will be concerned above all else with managing the information, withholding what it can and spinning the rest. This obviously includes lying. People will continue to need to make their voices heard loudly if they want positive change and, above all, the truth. Others will simply want to be a part of the great shift. They will claim to have seen UFOs or to have been abducted. Some will be telling the truth, some will have been mistaken, and others simply will be piling on in a new version of stolen valor.

There will be finger-pointing and accusations of collaboration that will turn neighbor against neighbor. This could be aggravated if it is confirmed that one or more species of the Others exist in human or near-human form, or can take on that form through some manner of manipulation.

Finally, we will learn that, in the name of protecting the population, actions were taken that are disturbing, illegal, and dangerous.

Will these revelations alter life? Certainly they will bring great change, but not necessarily in every way. After all, people from all over the globe have learned about their governments committing war crimes, assassinations, and gross deception, and still those citizens carry on with their business.

Daily Life

The grinding "Great Panic" of the first year A.D. will not prevent people from trying to return to some sense of the normal. The operative word here is "trying." It will not be an immediate snap-back, and the situation will vary from city to city, nation to nation. Disruption will continue, from sustained power brown-outs, to transportation delays, to canceled events and meetings.

Rude awakenings await the fussy kind of person who gets angry over a dropped cell phone call while driving to his favorite restaurant. Things will not work perfectly for a while.

Roads may be easier to navigate because fewer cars are on them, in turn due to disruptions, shortages, perhaps even the rationing of gasoline. When ambulances have a full tank of gas, they might set records reaching the scene. A few weddings may be postponed, but just as many others may be scheduled by lovers who fear a cosmic Armageddon. Why not meet your death in holy matrimony?

In this period of adjustment, the new normal will be about learning to live with uncertainty. "Sure things" will be less sure. All of this will occur

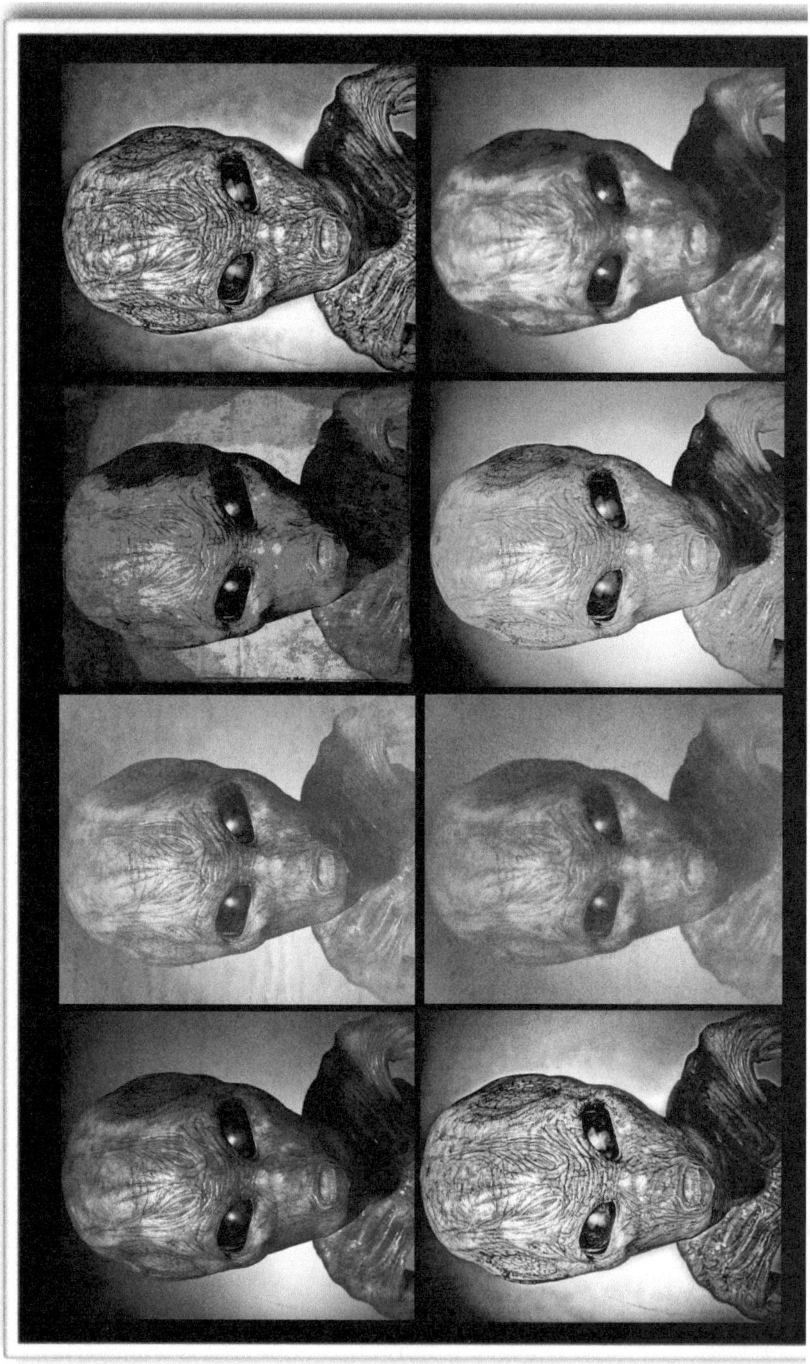

Expressing ourselves. We must come to grips emotionally with the speed and impact of the changes. Image by Masteresfx.

even in the absence of a counter-move by the Others. Whether they are openly seen or not, their presence will permeate everything. If they do react in some fashion, reactions will intensify even more.

With time, however, people will long for their old ways. Human resiliency will play its part, but so will the lack of options. Staying home and watching endless television will not be an option everyone can embrace. People will continue to need to work, lest the power plants fail, satellites become inactive, and wi-fi stops working. Even during the great disruption of Disclosure, people will still need to emerge, in one form or another, from their electronic caves into the sunlight.

Restaurants that closed to give employees time with their families, and then stayed closed because they could not get the proper foodstuffs, will try to re-open but with limited menus. The trend toward consuming locally grown food will accelerate. More restaurants will begin growing some of their own food and spices.

When cars break down, we need someone to repair them, and when they are not repairable, we expect someone to sell us a new one. The people who sell them will need the banks to offer credit. Automotive dealerships that had armed security for months A.D. will soon find customers showing up again. These customers will either want big, secure cars and SUVs that can go anywhere, or they will want cheap, fast, gas-efficient ones. Buyers will care less about color choices or chrome wheels. Companies will experiment with new car designs that incorporate names related to space news, perhaps Andromeda, Universe, or Satellite.

Family Still Matters

Strange as the new world may seem, bursting with situations altered from what they were before, the essential basics will still have to operate in our lives. Even Germany and Japan came back to life after the devastation of World War II. Life finds a way.

Whereas much of the adjusting will be happening around the world as seen on the screens of our computers, phones, and televisions, the most important changes will occur in people's homes.

Bruce Sallan, author of a parenting column, *A Dad's Point of View*, will probably be one of the voices advising us amid the blanket of media that will descend. To parents wondering how they should talk to their children, he emphasizes as much honesty as the child can handle. "It is alright to be scared," Sallan emphasized. The important thing is to learn everything possible and be prepared to answer your child's questions as honestly as you can. But pay special attention to your child's state of mind. There are already plenty of children waking up from nightmares in the middle of the night, Sallan reminds us, and this will undoubtedly intensify after Disclosure. The accounts of kidnapping by aliens will terrify adults and children alike. There will be parents who seek to minimize this and to tell their children that nothing really has changed, because to their knowledge most families have not had vivid UFO encounters or abduction experiences.

However, other families *have* had experiences, and once Disclosure happens, virtually all of the people who have kept their sightings and experiences tucked away out of public view will be able to have them acknowledged. Honesty, therefore, should be the best family policy.[1]

Education

Along with family, one of the great regulators of the return to normalcy will be school. Parents will still wake up, still feed their children, and still send them to school, so that they themselves can get to work, get paid, and keep the lights on. In even the smallest towns, school is the community gathering place. Keeping kids in the classrooms will be a priority.

Imagine the first day back, A.D. In the teacher's lounge, many teachers will wonder if so much of what they have previously taught is either wrong, or about to seem basic, simplistic, and outdated. Most textbooks will need to be re-written.

In the classrooms, students will feel the uncertainty infecting their instructors, but they will also sense the excitement of living through a monumental re-evaluation of what passes for knowledge during a turning point in human history. Initially, schools will focus on reassuring young children that their world is not about to end, that they are safe. Many of those preaching calm will doubt their own words.

Assuming the days go on with no catastrophic attack from the skies, the mood will change from one of projecting calm to a new phase. If ever a "teaching moment" is to be thrust into the world headlines, the moment of Disclosure will be it. All of the books in public libraries and bookstores that have been relegated to the "Metaphysical" section will fly off the shelves. This will be confusing in its own right, given that the disinformation campaign throughout the years has fed one fallacy after another into the dialogue. Ironically, at the same time that so many textbooks become outdated, so too will many of the books about UFOs and aliens.

Even as they are working with their students, teachers will realize that they had been living in a kind of fiction. Their previously accepted knowledge will be subject to critical analysis. In the A.D. world, the teachers will be as much students as the children they teach, swimming in the deep waters of a new paradigm, trying to find solid ground.

No More Falsehoods or Derisions

Initially, the academic world will receive harsh criticism. For years, there has been more evidence supporting the reality of UFOs than there has been for speculative scientific theories about black holes and dark matter. Yet professors and researchers refused to consider that evidence, preferring the safety of more comfortable topics. But like the media, the academic community will quickly forgive itself. Its members will fall over themselves to fund, research, and study the impact of Disclosure. Some careers will shatter like so much broken glass. Others will be made overnight. This will be a new academic gold mine.

Universities were incubators of change in the 1960s, places where traditional liberal arts disciplines were undergoing rapid transformation. This will happen again as Disclosure redefines and rejuvenates each of them.

History and Political Science

History books will need a top-to-bottom rewrite as we assemble a new chronology of our civilization. In particular this will mean everything from the Second World War onward, but also possibly a significant portion of our ancient history.

It will be a sobering moment when educators admit that much of what they knew was wrong. Textbooks will be missing more than a few pages about the world's clandestine history and the lies that were told to keep it contained. As the structure of UFO secrecy is subjected to hard analysis, it will become necessary to reinterpret most of modern political history.

Consider the work facing a presidential historian if a few of the following stories turn out to be true.

- President Dwight Eisenhower's famous Farewell Speech of 1961 issued a warning about the growing power of the "Military-Industrial Complex." Was Ike also speaking about the breakaway civilization that was being created to capture, profit from, and hide UFO reality? Was he briefed on Roswell after his election as president, as the Majestic-12 documents claim? And if those documents are authentic, why and how were they leaked in the 1980s? Did Eisenhower really meet with extraterrestrials in the mid-1950s?
- President Kennedy, on a flight to Berlin, is alleged to have said that he told Marilyn Monroe about the reality of UFOs. Indeed, might we have cause to re-examine the death of Marilyn Monroe, or reinterpret the assassination of JFK in that context? Recently, a videotaped interview surfaced from the late Colonel Philip Corso, the coauthor of *The Day After Roswell*, in which he claimed to have briefed Attorney General Robert Kennedy about UFOs. If the Kennedy brothers knew about ET reality at the same time they were fighting the power of the CIA, did they harbor their own disclosure plans?[2]
- President Nixon, based on two sources, took his friend Jackie Gleason to see alien bodies at Homestead Air Force Base while in Florida in 1973. Could there be an ET connection to the resignation of Richard Nixon? Could it have anything to do with the 18 minutes of silence on the infamous Watergate tapes? Events that seem like conspiratorial fantasy in a world without UFOs might seem credible in a world where their reality is confirmed.

In the A.D. world, the preceding questions may be fruitful or not. But it is guaranteed that there will be many new and intriguing questions to emerge, burning bright in the media, then settling into academia for further investigation and integration into the historical record.

Political science—the study of the political institutions of the world and about the nature of power—will be hit hard by Disclosure. How could it be that political scientists have missed something as powerful (and expensive) as the UFO coverup? How could political scientists have ignored the hundreds of known cases of military jets being scrambled to intercept UFOs?

Society will see how the discipline of political science had become an ideological prop for the National Security State, part of a revolving door system whereby government insiders, once they leave their jobs in Washington, become hired to teach at prestigious universities. In the A.D. world, people will see them as complementing the intelligence community and private money groups that have been managing the UFO secret.

The upside will be the advent of many young political science scholars who will dedicate themselves to understanding and dissecting the true structure of power in our world. They will take no prisoners in this endeavor to understand the criminal nature of so much of contemporary governance.

Economics

Although traders, industrialists, and entrepreneurs work to keep the economic engine of the global economy running, the academicians will watch them, studying how the economy has been hit hard in the short-term, and deep in the long-term. The numbers comparing life before and after Disclosure will be an unending source of reports, papers, and dissertations.

Of greater significance will be the new field of black budget economics. Consider Deep Throat's advice to Watergate reporters Bob Woodward and Carl Bernstein to "follow the money," then consider economists applying this advice to the entire UFO cover-up. At one conference after another, economic scholars will discuss and analyze how it was possible to siphon away billions upon billions of dollars in public and illegal funds.

Entire careers will be devoted to this pursuit. Scholars will be forced to realize that not all of the black budget monies derived solely from tax dollars. Sophisticated studies will be published detailing the relationship between intelligence communities and such illegal activities as drug trafficking and financial fraud.

Psychology

The study of the human mind will need to keep pace with the emerging facts. After the requisite soul searching and recriminations about how the psychological community dropped the ball regarding potentially millions of abduction victims, allowing them to believe that they were victims of some form of mental defect, the field will be primed for a rejuvenation.

One area of concern will be the field of human memory. How, for instance, has it been possible to manage human memory in the aftermath of the abduction experience? True, many memories leaked through after the experience, but most did so incompletely, and so many never did until many years had passed. This is an area in which the classified literature is undoubtedly vastly ahead of the "topsiders."

There will also be a resurgence in the study of the phenomenon of social control. What is it about the human brain that enabled billions of human beings, from the slow-witted to the brilliant, to become duped by a propaganda system of UFO denial? Why could they not see that the Emperor was, indeed, wearing nothing at all?

At the same time, the ongoing adjustment to the reality of Disclosure should spawn study after study trying to make sense of how people coped with the initial shock, and then the transition going forward. College courses will be constructed around the Great Panic of Year One, focusing on the human desire A.D. to hoard all manner of items for reasons that were unclear even to the hoarders.

The great prize for psychologists will come when enough information becomes available to begin comparative psychological studies of humans and the Others. Presumably, at some point, they will have access to information about how these Others think and live. When they do, we will inevitably learn new truths about the nature of ourselves.

Anthropology

The study of comparative human cultures has long been relegated to the sidelines of the liberal arts, but will be energized by the emergence of "exoanthropology." No longer forced to focus solely on the possibilities of what it means to be human, anthropologists, similar to psychologists, will be looking at the human being by way of comparison with the Others. As in the field of psychology, many new insights will emerge about such things as human social interactions, organization, hierarchy, aggression, and collaboration.

There is probably much that the men and women who have been working secretly for the Breakaway Group already know about the Others. Much of this may be integrated into the academic environment, facilitated and controlled to a large extent by these hidden scientists. This will be an area of great sensitivity, and black-world scientists will not readily participate. When they do, their sources of information will be scrutinized carefully. This topic is important, as governments around the world will want accurate information on the Others. If there are multiple groups of Others, trying to define the hows and whys of their own interactions may be critical to our own survival.

Archeology

For years, establishment archeology has ignored evidence of advanced technology in the remnants of ancient cultures. The construction and features of the Great Pyramid of Giza, the Peru's plains of Nazca, Stonehenge, the famous Central American crystal skulls, and many more anomalies have been excluded from the debate in modern archeology. Professional archeologists do not deny these artifacts; they merely explain them as fundamentally conventional (as in the case of the Pyramid, Stonehenge, and Nazca) or declare them as of unproven authenticity (as with the crystal skulls).

Scientists who are quietly interested in these matters can hardly expect to publish papers about them. Orthodoxy, not diversity, rules this field. Dispute the dominant theories, and you fail to get published. Failure to get published translates into a loss of funding, credibility, and ultimately one's livelihood.

Once the existence of the Others has been acknowledged, the game changes. Suddenly, what is now dismissed as "forbidden archeology" becomes mainstream, even cutting-edge. Undoubtedly, some of the alleged evidence of alien intervention will turn out to be dead ends, but will all of it? It will be the job of archeologists worldwide, most of whom work in universities, to sort out what is true and what is not.

Disclosure of the truth about the presence of Others on planet Earth will hit archeology like a 9-plus Richter magnitude earthquake. It will open that field up to a fresh analysis of the ancient origins of the human race. One in which we may discover—and begin to fill—a gaping hole in our ancient history.

Literature, Philosophy, and the Arts

Although clearly distinct from each other, philosophy and literature are both essentially studies in human wisdom. Philosophy, after all, means "love of wisdom," and there is no question that the world's great literature is fundamentally about reaching deeper levels of wisdom regarding humankind's place in the universe.

Disclosure will shake the academic communities of these disciplines, forcing its members to confront the often meaningless and irrelevant discussions to which so much contemporary literary criticism and academic philosophical analysis has now devolved. There is nothing like the shock of such a life-changing event such as Disclosure to force one to start looking at the big picture in one's life and realize how much time one has wasted.

What will be left for these disciplines are their foundations, which are based on some of the deepest reflections that human beings have ever made about themselves and the universe. When confronting the reality of another species that may pose a substantial threat to one's ego, if not one's very existence, what humanity will need is inspiration. People will need strengthening of the spirit. They will need the example of the best that our species has offered, and this is readily available through the great books of our civilization.

We will rediscover the power, solace, inspiration, and spur to greatness bequeathed to us by such writers as Tolstoy, Goethe, Shakespeare,

Milton, Yeats, Marcus Aurelius, and countless others. The same holds for the tradition of fine arts and music, including such geniuses as Bach, Mozart, Beethoven, Chopin, or within the great tradition of jazz, or the exquisite traditions of music from the Indian subcontinent, of China, of the Near East and Africa. Then there is the human artistic tradition, too overwhelming to summarize. Our species has been nothing if not continually inventive in the fine arts, finding new ways of expressing who we are, what we are, and where we are in the cosmos.

Do the Others have philosophy? Literature? If they do, what are these like? What do they think of our contributions? It is mind-expanding simply to consider the topic.

Our past writers, philosophers, musicians, and artists have given us perhaps the greatest gift for life A.D. They are reminders of who we are. And of the inherent greatness and divinity that resides within the human being. Thus, the great souls of the past will be rediscovered. They will be needed to support and inspire those of us living in the most demanding period imaginable.

Those thinkers and artists will also inspire the greatest outpouring of deep reflection and profundity of the human condition yet achieved. On the shoulder of giants will stand those, After Disclosure, who will see farther, clearer.

Popular Culture

Some people do not read Shakespeare or listen to Mozart. They swim in the waters of popular culture, a milieu encompassing movie stars in drug rehab, artists organizing charity concerts, and every new film, song, and artist arriving on the scene. All of that will be affected, changed, and re-formed by Disclosure in ways about which we can only speculate, because pop culture always arises from the moment in unpredictable manifestations.

After Disclosure, humanity will experience a cultural explosion that will rival or surpass the Renaissance. The revelation that we are not alone will supercharge the Zeitgeist. Artists the world over will need to express themselves on this subject, to interpret it for their audiences. Painters will turn to their canvasses, writers will struggle to tell the story in new ways, and even comedians will find fresh new jokes.

From Twitter to Facebook to YouTube, the Internet will be ablaze. The numbers of Websites spawned by Disclosure will dwarf anything before. People will need to communicate their feelings and discuss their fears, and therefore the social networks will vibrate with activity.

Reliably, if it happens within the next decade, Bruce Springsteen will have a new song about it, and it will be the most downloaded song on iTunes. Old protest songs may be dusted off, given new lyrics, and find a second life.

Almost certainly, too, there will be a revival in the use of hallucinogenic drugs. After Disclosure, users of such drugs will try to "break on through to the other side," in this case, the other side being a place where they will claim to find the other entities inhabiting our world. Whether the drugs are psychedelic standbys such as LSD, or mescaline or emerging ones like Salvia Divinorum, Ayahuasca, Dimethyltryptamine (DMT), or something newly developed in a laboratory, one or more will be embraced for the counter-culture's new vision-quest. The idea of the party drug scene will shrink back, and the idea of seeking enlightenment through drugs will be in favor again.

Meanwhile, the media will never be as happy as it will be AD. Even seemingly distant relatives of the news, such as *Entertainment Tonight*, will find their own spin. Everything that affects the world, like 9/11 or the Arab Spring, also affects celebrities. News will want to cover how the rich and famous are handling Disclosure, because the celebrities will act as surrogates for the audience. If they admit to being scared, the audience will know that "it's okay" for them to feel the same way. This will translate to red-carpet interviews where celebrities wear gray ribbons and talk earnestly about reaching out in peace to the Others.

An entirely new form of celebrity will be created. From among those who have had some form of abduction or contact experience with the Others, a few of them will be famous or modestly famous for one reason or another after Disclosure. We may see an entire group of B- and C-level celebrities who are vaulted forward into the public's awareness, simply because they will be able to talk openly about their experiences.

But the biggest emerging celebrity will be someone in the lineage of Carl Sagan and Neil Degrasse Tyson, a scientist who has a tremendous ability to connect with an audience. Unlike Sagan and Tyson, however, this sci-lebrity will fully and completely embrace the technological wonder that allowed the Others to come from their home to ours. On the other hand, for every newly minted celebrity who speaks in a careful, measured manner about how the world is changing, there will be new versions of Nancy Grace, Keith Olbermann, or Glenn Beck.

This Revolution Will Be Televised

Adapting to change is what television does best. As a relentless purveyor of culture, it mercilessly tosses aside what is not working and casts about for something else that will work. Then it produces that form of programming for as long as people will watch it, eventually tossing aside the genre, star, or series until it needs to be called into duty again, albeit with a "new" twist.

As our digital age continues to transform itself, people have gained many new options for watching their news and entertainment. Even so, television—namely, serialized episodes of news, non-fiction, reality, drama, and comedy—will still exist in some form after Disclosure, and it will adapt. Indeed, ratings will probably be exceptional.

There has never been a twist as new, invigorating, potent, and compelling as Disclosure. So long as the Others do not detonate magnetic pulse weapons worldwide, depriving us of our technology and knocking us back to the Stone Age, television will love this brave new world.

For decades television shows have been attempting to prove or debunk UFOs. Most of those will become instantly obsolete and will never air again, at least in their original form. New programming will be needed. Veteran Hollywood producer Rob Kirk predicts that networks will scramble immediately to re-purpose those old episodes. They will still have plenty of excellent interviews and eyewitness reports that can be salvaged.

The narration will be re-written to remove the tone of skepticism and incredulity that these shows have often had as their point of view. A few new interviews, a couple of all-nighters re-writing all the voice-overs, and new programming that looks tailor-made for AD will be on the air, almost immediately.

However, that is patch-work compared to what will come. Depending on the type of Disclosure that comes to us on Day One, there may be photos, videos, lab reports, secret warehouses, and unclassified documents. It may very well be a treasure trove of raw material. As the news divisions scramble, no one will be better prepared to turn this around quickly than a Hollywood reality producer. Deals between production companies and networks will be struck so fast in the days immediately AD that there will be no time for Business Affairs lawyers even to write a deal memo. These will be virtual "handshake" deals, struck and consummated over text messages, e-mails and cell phone calls. Entire shows will be delivered and aired in these early days before the paperwork catches up. This will be a boon to the existing companies, as networks will want instantly to call and hire teams they have worked with before.

There will be requests coming out of Hollywood to embed camera crews into government or private enterprise groups that are on the leading-edge of contact issues. If it turns out that there is a fast-response crash retrieval team somewhere in the breakaway civilization, networks will demand access to it for their own purposes. Imagine how addictively watchable *The Deadliest Catch* became for audiences. What if, instead of fish, aliens are invoked?

As an example of what we might expect, imagine a new show called *Above and Below*. In this series, almost anything goes, but its stock in trade is an aerial point-of-view, seeing the world below from a POV of a flying saucer. This is used as a transitional device to go into the world below, the massive underground base and tunnel system that has been created over the decades.

The series would be a vehicle to take audiences into previously classified labs. If there are any live EBEs that have been acknowledged, access to the units that manage them medically, as well as the security attached to them, will be deemed of paramount importance. The best example from today's landscape would be a demand to go to "S-4" (just south of Area 51) with an all-access pass and see what is going on there. If it turns up empty and abandoned, expect loud cries of "foul." However, that is non-fiction programming. In TV parlance, this means serialized documentaries, no matter how hyped or inflated they may be. The other side of the coin is so-called "reality" programming, which, as viewers mostly realize, is not especially real at all.

Reality producers will not miss a single beat to inject Disclosure into their series. Any series in production—featuring anything from survivors on an island, to competitors locked in a house, to suitors vying for spouses—will keep the cameras rolling. This will give us moments where the latest celebutantes cry and rage over their reactions to the news.

Although it may seem to trivialize the news that is breaking around us minute-by-minute AD, the truth is it will provide a service that should not be discounted. These kind of contrived shows still feature real people, or at least people who are more real than an actor on a sitcom. Audiences identify with their problems, share their anxieties and pain, rejoice in their triumphs. They will be looking to these same people, whether we like it or not, to see how they respond and, by extension, how they themselves should respond. Producers who script the scenarios for these reality shows will incorporate reactions from what they see on the news, their friends and family, and their own feelings. They will then create situations for the players, contestants, and celebrities to react to Disclosure. For example, *The Greatest Loser* may be about trying to lose weight, but the immediate post-Disclosure shows will feature players who struggle not to over-eat to calm their fears about the Others and the potential fate of the world.

Yet even as existing shows bend and twist to add Disclosure as just another "challenge" for their contestants, writers, producers, directors, and executives will be assessing what should come next and to get it on-the-air before their competition beats them to the punch. This process is going to yield some shows themed specifically around contact that are likely to be stranger than we can even predict now.

Within months, the tsunami of Disclosure will hit scripted programming. Television dramas and comedies will also work through the impact of AD in waves, just like their non-fiction and reality brothers and sisters. Existing shows will incorporate it immediately into their scripts, if at all possible. For example, an episode of the *C.S.I.* franchise may, depending on the facts that are learned, deal with human mutilations by the Others. Some shows may be constrained because of their period settings, but some, perhaps *Mad Men*, might slip in a line from a character about the police officer in Socorro, New Mexico, who thought he saw a flying saucer and its alien occupants out in the desert.

A standard three-camera sitcom, however, could insert content into the next script up, and put it on the air almost immediately. Humor will be tricky, but it won't be long before people demand to laugh, no matter what the news about the Others turns out to be.

Oddly, writers who once specialized in ripped-from-the-headlines movies of the week, a genre now nearly extinct, will be the ones who have immediately acceptable skills.

As an example of new dramatic series in the AD world, imagine an hour-long drama, *Breakaway*, that allows viewers to experience the pre-Disclosure world of secrecy through the eyes of real characters whose life stories have been optioned for their underlying rights. If *Mad Men* can find success with characters from another time living their lives against the backdrop of a New York advertising agency, then it seems likely that viewers can similarly experience the cover-up in order to understand how we got to where we are.

Then again, in television programming, anything can happen.

The Next Generation of Movie Aliens

What will the new models of alien/human contact look like in Hollywood films? It's a challenging question, particularly because the one thing we know for certain about this contact, based on where we are now, is that it has happened by stealth, hiding for decades in the shadows of public discourse.

Unless these Others appear with hundreds or thousands of Motherships in the skies, an entire genre of films dealing with hostile alien invasions such as *Independence Day* will probably be wiped out. A potentially more interesting template may be the kind springing from films such as *Alien Nation* and *District 9*. Less firepower, more nuance.

The world, even the world as interpreted through fantastic storytelling, will have to adjust to this new reality. Because, in the new world, fact will have caught up to fiction.

The Man Who Puts the Extra in Extra-Terrestrial

Todd Masters is a special effects creator who has offices in both Hollywood and Vancouver, B.C. For two decades, Masters has made his living designing all kinds of creature effects for film and television projects. Ask Masters how many versions of an alien gray he has helped create and he just laughs. He created the original *Dark Skies* grays, and multiple other iterations of alien life, including those from *The Day the Earth Stood Still*, *Invasion*, *The Arrival*, and even *The Last Mimzy*.

Masters knows that his life will change after Disclosure. For starters, he and his team of creature designers have always made alien beings the old-fashioned way, creating them based on experiences and living organisms that exist here on Earth now and in the past, then interpreting them "to the furthest reaches of the mind." He says that, similar to everyone else, he will be glued to the television news coverage on Day One, but that even as he is watching, he will also be directing design teams to base a new generation of physical and digital creations on the emerging reality. Even if all he has to go on at first is a black-and-white photo of a dead alien from decades ago, that will be enough to begin.

The hitch in the work flow, however, is that the demand for his company's services will be fundamentally changed.

Currently, his buyers want fantastic eye-popping creatures. They want to see movies that are "what-ifs," whether they be about alien parasites or never-before-seen werewolves. After Disclosure, Masters thinks that non-fiction will eclipse fiction, at least for a while, and that audiences will want stories based on fact. He thinks that many films that would have been dismissed as too "sci-fi" in the past will now be greenlit to production as true stories.

Filmmakers Thrust into the Future

James Cameron's *Avatar*, a massive success today, may immediately be seen as a hopelessly naive, antique artifact of the last days of official denial. That is, his portrayal of humans as the marauding bad guys may be inverted if we learn that human culture has been subverted by an alien presence. If so, it will not end the desire to hear stories, but merely change which ones have the greatest resonance. It could potentially tarnish or damage Cameron's career, given his heavy-handed "bad human, good alien" storytelling.

We have already discussed Steven Spielberg, but here we can add that, given the suspicions through the years that he has been part of a government plan to acclimate the public to the reality of ET, one can imagine that he will jump into the fray.

Disclosure will not end Steven Spielberg's fascination with aliens. Rather, it will send him off on the journey of his lifetime. He may abandon whatever project he is currently working on and begin on what may be his seminal work. The man who has given so many windows into contact can hardly turn his back on the field when his dream of knowing the truth finally comes true. Nor will the movie-going public accept passivity from him. They will have seen him on television as a regular commentator in the immediate aftermath of the confirmation of contact, opining on what it all means simply because—by virtue of having tried to make sense of it through his own prism of film—he will be considered an expert. And compared to the average human being on the planet who has only given the subject passing thought, he will be one.

A Comic Book Perspective

Many have already thought about this world of AD because they have read widely in the world of comic books. After all, alien invaders, predators, and warriors have always been a staple of storytelling in these pulpy pages.

The aliens of *Marvel Comics* tend to be more spiritual, blurring the line between God and extraterrestrial. Characters such as Galacticus and the Silver Surfer possess vast cosmic abilities that make Earth's superheroes look like insects.

In DC Comics, the concept of the alien is more about the heroes. Superman and Martian Manhunter, for example, are given great powers by virtue of coming to Earth to live.

Beau DeMayo, a self-described "comic book nerd," has read them all. Perhaps most important about aliens in the Marvel Universe, he points out, is that they are responsible for the evolution of human life on Earth, an idea supported by many who believe in ETs. The DC Universe is also interesting, DeMayo points out, as it takes a "community approach to its aliens." In its pages are organizations similar to the Federation in Star Trek, or intergalactic police forces comprised of many aliens.

Both the DC and Marvel universes share one common theme: To rise to their full potential, aliens must discover and embrace the essence of humanity. "Being human," for example, is the way Superman seeks to check the potential abuse of his powers that he might otherwise indulge in. The Green Lantern is the best of the Lantern Corps, because of his human will and spirit. Even the Norse God Thor, whose Asgardian past is now being played as rooted in extraterrestrial origin, must live among humans to be humbled and grow to be a better man. Because the focus is always on the discovery of the hero's humanity despite his or her off-world heritage, it could be seen as creating a strange prejudice against aliens.

Comic readers will also not have a problem accepting it if the reality turns out to be that there are multiple races of the Others interacting with us. Whereas films tend to see the human-alien interaction as binary—us and them—comic books see the universe as us and them, and them, and them. With hundreds of alien races in those fantasy universes, humanity is portrayed as just another race. However, we are not completely knocked off our pedestal, because all life in the universe is connected. Usually, too, all roads lead back to Earth in some fashion.

Stan Lee's Point-of-View

Stan Lee's name is almost synonymous with comic books. He was the man in charge of Marvel's creative output during its heady rise to fame during the 1960s. Almost all the characters being turned into movies these days—Iron Man, Hulk, Spider-Man, Captain America, Thor, X-Men, the Avengers—were created, co-created, or re-invented by Lee during his days as the company's patriarch. Through the years, Lee has given a great deal of thought to aliens. "I always try to go against the grain and use them as the starting point for the story and try to twist it," says Lee. "If they're introduced to us as being good, then they're actually bad. If we're told to fear them, then they're probably here to help us."

As for real ETs, in contrast to the comic book variety, Lee thinks they are "out there" for sure, and maybe even over here. "There must be other intelligent life in the universe—living, sentient beings," he said. "Whether they have come here in UFOs or not, I don't know. But I figure there must be something to them because so many people have seen them."

Indeed, Lee had personal testimony to that effect. His "right-hand man" at Marvel was his operations director and artist Sol Brodsky. Lee describes him as being very "level-headed," so he was shocked to hear from Brodsky about a car trip he had just made to Las Vegas. "When we were driving, I think we saw a flying saucer," Lee quotes Brodsky as telling him. "It was fast, it didn't have any wings, stopped right over our car, hovered, then zipped away faster than anything I'd ever seen." Both men wondered if it was a government test of an experimental aircraft, but Brodsky believed it was more than that. In the aftermath, Lee developed his own theory that flying saucers were not from other planets but from the future.

On the subject of a panicked population, Lee has played it both ways through the years as a writer, doing what suits the story and his telling of it. Personally, he believes Disclosure would stimulate an "incredible amount" of curiosity from the public, that people would be "intensely interested" in the news. He predicts panic only if the aliens are portrayed as dangerous and hostile. Otherwise, he feels that people will accept them and continue on with their lives. In his view, the group that should feel panic most would be the people who have kept the secret—because the rest of us are going to feel anger and annoyance regarding their decision to withhold information.

What would happen to the aliens of Lee's imagination, as well as to that of other comic book writers, once we know aliens are real, and we have confirmed photographs of them? Lee thinks that comic writers will adapt and assimilate quickly. They will soon be telling stories starring the Others, trying to help their readers work out their own feeling about them.

Contact as a Laughing Matter

The revelation of first contact with an alien intelligence is a serious matter. Still, like almost everything else in the world, it will be treated by someone as the inspiration for a joke. Whether it is a riff on "To Serve Man" being a cookbook, to an alien fixation with probing and crop circles, Disclosure may well usher in boom times for joke-telling.

Chris Rush is a New York comedian and an original contributor to the *National Lampoon* series. When he spoke with the authors, he was in the final preparation for a one-man comedy show called *Reality: The Myth*. He is a devoted "verbal cartooner" who revels in the art of the ad-lib and could see himself immersed in the coverage of Disclosure. Then, he would get himself down to a comedy stage, armed with three or four premises, and let loose.[3]

✧✦✧

> Maybe they won't be little gray guys with Jiffy-Lube and anal probes. Maybe they will be advanced cow-like creatures who have come to our Earth to arrest Ronald McDonald for war crimes. Or maybe their IQ level compared to ours would be like a human trying to talk to yogurt—armed and violent yogurt. So maybe they will sterilize the Earth, turn the Moon into a gigantic mothball and store their winter clothes there. Even so, you're still gonna have some [idiot] with a shotgun on the New Jersey turnpike aiming at them.

✧✦✧

One of the reasons Rush thinks people will need to laugh is that the most potent comedy comes from things that, underneath, are scary to the audience. He thinks Disclosure will create a climate where people need to laugh more than ever.

Rush was friends with comedy great George Carlin, and the two had spoken at length about the nature of reality. As Rush notes, "The UFO thing just naturally falls in there." In their discussions, Carlin expressed his opinion that the "planet's owners" have known about the Others for a long time, but have not confessed their knowledge because they never felt they could control what would happen if they did. Carlin thought that knowledge of how complex the universe is and how other life has come here would "put us in our place and make us think." Also, that "the *them* and *us* thing here on Earth might disappear."

Visions from the Future

Every artist in the world—whether they be American or Chinese or Iranian—will have something to say about humanity's changed circumstances. Trying to imagine this explosion of content is nearly impossible, given that there will be hundreds of millions of minds trying to express it when the time comes. By way of example only, here are a few possible turns in this coming story:

- A traveling museum containing exhibits of alien artifacts and bodies that will generate lines like the earlier King Tut exhibit, times 10.
- Competing stadium rallies, pro and con for increased contact, will force singers, actors, and politicians to choose sides.
- More than a thousand new books about contact will be available for purchase within two years AD. Entire sections of libraries, real and virtual, will be devoted to the topic.
- Apple will release a new laptop/tablet computer hybrid, incorporating design elements from recovered alien wreckage and our own technology, known as the iFusion.

As it always does, art will draw from life. In many cases, it will create new forms of commerce around its expression. All this is unpredictable, except that it will surprise us.

But what art will the Others bring? Will we get to see their culture as they have seen ours? Or is it possible that among their great works of art is humanity itself?

The Next Great Health Care Debate

Consider the state of biotechnology today, independent of any interference or assistance from the Others. Humans stand on the verge of dramatic breakthroughs in genetic engineering, synthetic biology, anti-aging drugs, stem-cell treatments, body implants, and regenerative medicine. By 2020, it is likely that the human genome will be understood, meaning that the ability to manipulate human DNA will be vastly greater than it is today. This means that a genetic transformation or beneficial remodeling of humanity will be possible. A more frightening thought is that it portends the possible temptation for a genetic transformation of some humans into a kind of Master Race.

What if the Others already began this process?

Abduction reports suggest that our reproductive systems and DNA are of interest to them. There is belief among many researchers that some form of hybrid species has been the end goal. There has also been ample speculation that the Others have manipulated the human genome in our ancient past. We may be their creation, or been biologically influenced by them.

If it turns out that the Others have played God with our biology, it would shake us as much as the basic confirmation that we are not alone. It not only would make us feel less unique; it would shatter any perception of equality we might have with them.

The debate would then move to motive. We would look for evidence—in abductee reports, DNA study, the revised historical record, and from the Breakaway Group—as to what the Others hoped to get from this. Do they think of us as their children and are simply trying to make us better and healthier? Or do they think of us as livestock, put here to populate the planet for their return and colonization?

If anyone wants a scenario for panic in the streets, it will come from this. This discussion may not start immediately on Day One. It may take years, as new information is released and discovered.

Although the shock from such a revelation would be deep, its effect may be greater still on our current debate about using genetic tampering to create everything from clones to healthier humans. If we have already been manipulated, one might argue that it removes a key obstacle to further tampering. Some will undoubtedly argue that it is better for humans to manipulate their own genes than to have another species do it for them. Our own scientists, now armed with public support, may work to accelerate human evolution in order to make us stronger to a dangerous interloper from elsewhere.

Conversely, it may turn out that the knowledge and help of the Others will enable humankind to live longer and healthier lives.

Whatever the motivation, if Disclosure creates scientific conditions where human DNA can be altered without a great morality debate to hold it back, our children or our children's children may grow up in a world where they have been given a bonus allotment of years. This might give the individual much more time to experience the glories of being alive but, for society, it may be a mixed blessing. Our population is already testing the carrying capacity of the Earth. If we live longer and die less, Earth's resources may simply exhaust that much faster.

There is no doubt that the state of medicine today is changing rapidly and great advancements are coming, contact or not.

Dr. Jeffrey Galpin specializes in Infectious Disease Medicine, Molecular Biology, and AIDS research, and was the principal investigator who applied the first gene therapy for HIV/AIDS. He also contracted polio when he was eight years old, something that changed his life, and gives him pause to consider what an advanced intelligence could offer us, if they wanted to. He held out hope that "there would be a sharing of intellectual properties between our civilizations." This could lead to better treatments and preventative measures for our most feared illnesses. Still, humanity needs to beware of such gifts. The molecular genetics of life is tied to and dependent upon the universal clock of aging and death. All manipulations, therefore, will have consequences.

Such changes could affect the economy, expanding the number of productive years that people would want to be in the work force and lengthening the years they would live in retirement. If such gains come with a need to have our bodies tinkered with like a car getting a replacement part, some of us will sign on and others will not.

Ultimately, besides simple life expansion, the Others could conceivably help us achieve immortality by mapping the chemistry of the human brain like a hard drive, and facilitating its implantation into a new cloned body that is younger, healthier, and yet still the same person. Sort of.

Still, nothing is more likely to fan the flames of paranoia and hostility more than the thought that the Others have been messing with our bodies, for whatever reasons. This returns us to our premise that the decade after Disclosure will borrow some inspiration from the 1960s.

The Next Generation

Today, as our world is observed and acted upon by unknown intelligences, humanity is mostly asleep at the wheel. Disclosure will rouse many of us. That deeply felt shock, the presence of Others, will cause great masses of people to question their values, to question how they had been living their lives. The knowledge that there is another species operating here on Earth, a species that lives and thinks in ways that may well be beyond what humans generally reach, will be sobering and liberating at the same time.

Imagine that billions of people, upon considering the presence of beings that are exceptionally intelligent and maybe telepathic, possessed of magical technology, and possessing a cosmology of far greater sophistication than our own, are here now. Many will ask a basic question: *Have I been wasting my life?*

This feeling, aggravated by political assassination and misguided war, is what triggered the change that started in the United States and spread globally as the 1950s gave way to the 1960s.

Reliving the Sixties. Peace, love, and understanding won't be any easier to find this time. Photo courtesy of Jacom Stephens, iStockphoto.

Wherever we are going as a society, as a world, we will not arrive there on the Day of Disclosure, nor even 10 years later. The changes inherent in such a mind-expanding way of seeing life will create ripples of hope and fear for many years. It may be unclear for decades which emotion will prevail.

We remain optimists. Eventually, humanity will find its way home. New ways will take root, and life will go on.

Most change—to become firmly entrenched—requires the arrival of a new generation that no longer remembers the old ways. This will be true of Disclosure.

This time around, perhaps the new incarnation of the 1960s really will usher in a time of peace, love, and understanding.

Vignette #6:

Need to Know

✧✦✧

RALLY FOR UFO TRUTH NOW

What: Citizens Rally @ U.N.
When: June 23
Where: New York City, Outside United Nations
Time: 2pm
Other: This gathering has not received proper permits from the city. Officials have vowed to make arrests. Come at your own risk.
Contact: endufosecrecy@gmail.com

****

NEED-TO-KNOW
Song Lyrics

I'm ready to be told
Time for secrets to unfold
It's our time to come of age
Time for truth to turn the page
Wanna be inside the dark
Live within a question mark
Be a friend or foe
Tell me now
Need to know
You say we must wait our turn
You say too much to learn
You say cover-up is fine
It's your plan, not mine
You say it will blow my mind
You say it will change Mankind
You say things'll fall apart
No more fear, that's from my heart
We say, Now is the time
We say, This is the plan
We say, we need to know

Chapter 7

Paradigm Shift: Our New Place in the Universe

The greatest obstacle to discovering the shape of the Earth, the continents, and the oceans was not ignorance but the illusion of knowledge.

—Daniel J. Boorstin

There are times in human history when new information and new revelations can transform the world. Ideas that had been held as timeless truths can shatter overnight. In our world, Disclosure will be that trigger. It will usher in a time comparable to the era of Copernicus and Galileo, when humankind first realized that the universe did not revolve around the Earth.

The word *paradigm* was coined by the philosopher of science, Thomas Kuhn, in his 1962 study, *The Structure of Scientific Revolutions*. He used it to describe a coherent theory of reality. When scientists obtain data that fails to conform to the dominant paradigm, the data are considered anomalies and normally discarded. Kuhn agreed that sometimes this is reasonable to do, but when too many anomalies litter a paradigm, something is wrong. Every now and then, a great thinker comes along who sees the world differently. This new vision makes sense of the anomalies and incorporates them into a larger, more complete, more accurate paradigm. Newton was such a thinker, said Kuhn. So was Einstein.

In this chapter, we discuss how the impact of Disclosure will affect the dominant paradigms in scientific thinking, as well as that other great interpreter of reality, religion.

Five centuries ago, it was the religious institutions that resisted the paradigm shift. The issue was whether the universe was Earth-centered or Sun-centered. The Polish astronomer, Nicolas Copernicus, was so fearful of Church reprisals to his great work on this subject, *De revolutionibus orbium coelestium*, that it was published only after he died in 1543. It was an important theological issue, because the Catholic Church had taken a stand on the matter. The Church maintained that, as God had made humankind the centerpiece of his Creation, mankind's world was at the center of the universe. Science, however, made it clear that this was not so.

Incidentally, the issue of extraterrestrial life was raised at around the same time, and received even greater resistance. The Italian scientist and free-thinker, Giordano Bruno, had the audacity to believe that the stars were in fact like Earth's own Sun (he was the first known person to argue this). He believed in the existence of other worlds and of other beings created by God. In other words, Bruno said that there were extraterrestrials in our universe and that they, too, were God's children. His reward was to be imprisoned for seven years, then burned alive for heresy in the year 1600.

During most of the ensuing centuries, Christianity in general has been silent on the matter of extraterrestrial life. Since the modern UFO era began, however, we have seen interesting developments on the matter. Christianity is a large umbrella, encompassing an impressive number of branches and sects, and its adherents have expressed every position on ET life and UFOs one can imagine.

Today, the greatest blind-spot regarding Disclosure belongs to the scientific community. Despite the evidence, it has steadfastly ignored the UFO mystery. Indeed, establishment science has hampered the search for truth by joining the chorus of naysayers who have made the experiencers of extraordinary events feel shunned, ridiculed, and possibly insane.

The situation regarding religion is different, if for no other reason than there is such a variety of them around the world. People's spiritual beliefs may have certain things in common, such as the existence of a reality beyond the physical one of our five senses, but beyond that, almost anything goes.

Yet we should distinguish the science and religion from their institutions. Science, despite its institutional shortsightedness and conformity, is ultimately based on empirical observation and testing. That is why so many scientific conclusions, no matter how firmly believed, are called "theories" (Einstein's Theory of Relativity and Darwin's Theory of Evolution). As the philosopher of science Bertrand Russell pointed out, scientific conclusions are always provisional. They are subject to change when new evidence is presented. This may be an emotional drawback for those who demand certainty in their lives, but Russell argued that it is an advantage over the long term.[1]

Religious truth, on the other hand, at least when it is based on revealed statements from Holy Books, is not so easily subject to modification. As a result, we may expect certain of those religions to push back when confronted with a reality as shattering as Disclosure. Many of their adherents will undoubtedly see this unbending quality as a strength, a firm shelter within the raging storm around them. Even so, there is reason to believe that many of the world religions will show the ability to adapt.

The End of Religion?

Many analysts have concluded that the announcement of intelligent life in the universe would destroy traditional religious faith. They point out that many of Earth's religions continue to be heavily anthropomorphic, seeing humanity as the center of God's plan. The announcement (or arrival) of sentient beings, therefore, would be too much for them to bear.

Other analysts, such as astrobiologist Paul Davies, theorize that visiting aliens might have discarded theology and religious practice "as primitive superstition," and would persuade humanity to do likewise. Or, "if they retained a spiritual aspect to their existence, we would have to concede that it was likely to have developed to a degree far ahead of our own."[2]

These assumptions seem to have become a mantra in the Search for Extra-Terrestrial Intelligence (SETI) community and elsewhere, repeated so often that it feels as though they were established fact.

No Fear

In 1994, researcher Victoria Alexander conducted a survey of clergy from Protestant, Catholic, and Jewish congregations that asked, "Would you agree that 'official confirmation' of the discovery of an advanced, technologically superior extraterrestrial civilization would have severe negative effects on the country's moral, social, and religious foundations?" She concluded that ministers did not feel this would threaten their faith or that of their congregations. Religions would not collapse.[3]

Eight years later, in 2002, a Roper Poll similarly asked, "Would an announcement of extraterrestrial Intelligence precipitate a religious crisis?" Not only was the answer overwhelmingly "no," it actually rose with age. Ninety-three percent of respondents over age 65 said it would not be a big deal. Roper concluded that "very few" Americans thought that an official government announcement on extraterrestrials would cause them to question their religious beliefs.[4]

In early 2010, another survey examined the issue, this time with respondents from around the world. The results put another nail in the coffin of the SETI claims of religious berserkers running amok over Disclosure.

The survey was designed by Ted Peters, a professor at the Pacific Lutheran Theological Seminary in Berkeley, California, and was called *The Peters ETI Religious Crisis Survey*. With his colleague Julie Froehlig, Peters interviewed 1,300 respondents, including believers from Roman Catholicism, mainline Protestantism, evangelical Protestantism, Orthodox Christianity, Mormonism, Judaism, Islam, Hinduism, and Buddhism. Atheists and agnostics were also included. The survey tested this hypothesis: "Upon confirmation of contact between Earth and an extraterrestrial civilization of intelligent beings, the long established religious traditions of Earth would confront a crisis of belief and perhaps even collapse."[5]

Here are some of the responses they received.

- "Finding ETI, I believe, would be a profound and wonderful event."
- "Extraterrestrial religious beliefs and traditions will differ, perhaps greatly in some ways. However, they live in the same universe with the same God, and a similar array of religious responses and developments would likely have developed on their world."
- "Nothing would make me lose my faith. God can reach them if they exist."
- "I believe that Christ became incarnate (human) in order to redeem humanity and atone for the original sin of Adam and Eve. Could there be a world of extraterrestrials? Maybe. It doesn't change what Christ did."

The authors concluded: "Religious persons, for the most part, do not fear contact."

A small minority did not believe in extraterrestrials. These respondents, in what can be described as the "rare Earth" camp, believe life on Earth to be so rare that a second creation of life is unlikely to have occurred elsewhere. Even this belief, however, does not necessarily make people fragile. One evangelical Protestant remarked, "I don't think they are out there. But if they are, that's cool."

The only respondents who predicted the collapse of religious belief systems were self-described atheists and agnostics. Believers expected to carry on with their lives. Many even expected some form of Disclosure within their lifetimes.

The acknowledgment of Others demands that we look at our universe as larger, more crowded, and less Earth-centered than we have in the past. That, by itself, is not a fatal blow to any institution.

The Vatican Moves Toward Disclosure

The world's largest church seems to be positioning itself to be at the forefront of Disclosure. The Vatican has long maintained several major astronomical observatories and a collection of radio telescopes. In recent years, its hierarchy has stated, in one form or another, that we have company. Perhaps they know something is afoot, or suspect its inevitability.

Until his death in 2008, Monsignor Corrado Balducci, long-time friend of Pope John Paul II, and the Vatican's leading exorcist, had stated his personal opinion many times about the reality of extraterrestrial life. "There must be something between us and the angels," he told an interviewer. "If there are other beings, they are surely more evolved than we are.... It is illogical and a bit arrogant to believe that we are the only intelligent beings in God's creation." Balducci believed that Jesus died for these beings, just as he did for humanity. "He is called King of the universe," emphasized the Monsignor. "Never underestimate the great mercy or compassion of God." Balducci was not speaking in purely theoretical terms. He stated more than once his belief that contact between humans and extraterrestrials was real.[6]

The Vatican's astronomers have also expressed their belief in extraterrestrial life. In 2005, Vatican astronomer Guy Consolmagno concluded that chances are better than ever that humankind is facing a future discovery of extraterrestrial intelligence.[7] In 2008, Vatican chief astronomer Father Jose Gabril Funes granted an interview to the *L'Osservatore Romano* newspaper that made headlines around the world. Father Funes stated his opinion that intelligent life may exist elsewhere in the universe, and that such a notion "doesn't contradict our faith."[8] The same year, the Reverend Christopher Corbally, the vice director of the Vatican Observatory, said, "How wonderful it would be to have other life beyond our own world because it would show how God's creation just flows out without abandon."[9]

It is doubtful that all of these Vatican authorities would speak so openly if they felt they were in conflict with official doctrine. Quietly, a policy appears to have been decided upon.

Christians and Aliens

Some Evangelical Christians have placed the Bible squarely into the middle of the UFO issue. They have no problem believing UFOs are real, and some even welcome the idea of extraterrestrial visitors. One respondent of the Peters Religious Crisis survey wrote, "From an evangelical Christian perspective, the word of God was written for us on Earth to reveal the Creator. Why should we repudiate the idea that God may have created other civilizations to bring him glory in the same way?"

Yet this viewpoint is a minority among Biblically-based Christians. The Bible makes no reference to other worlds. Such Christians who do believe in UFOs usually interpret them as demonic, not as extraterrestrial. One respondent of the Peters survey spoke for many Christians when he stated, "I personally believe that Satan, the enemy of Jesus, will attempt to deceive the world into believing he is an ET and many will fall for it."

Charles (Chuck) Missler is one of the world's leading Christian ufologists. He is a graduate of the United States Naval Academy and Air Force flight training, and holds a Master's Degree in Engineering from UCLA. He also knows as much about UFOs as most non-Christian ufologists. He is well-informed about their history, the cover-up, and specific cases. He knows about the testimony from astronauts, radar controllers, and jet pilots. He simply explains UFOs and aliens through the lens of Biblical interpretation as inter-dimensional beings that have a physical reality.

In his book, *Alien Encounters* (coauthored with Mark Eastman), Missler argued that what we call UFOs are not aliens from another planet, but demonic entities described in the Bible. Read the *Book of Genesis* and you will find this passage: "And it came to pass, when men began to multiply on the face of the Earth, and daughters were born unto them, that the Sons of God saw the daughters of men, that they were fair, and they took them wives of all that they chose."[10]

The offspring of these encounters were known as the "Nephilim" or "Fallen Ones." Some ufologists interpret this passage as interbreeding between humans and extraterrestrials posing as "the Sons of God." Missler replies that the truth is the other way around: what people think to be aliens are actually "the Fallen Ones." They are not from another planet, but have been here all along. They oppose the will of God and seek to undermine God's creation, humankind.

That UFOs often appear to be physical and are even tracked by the world's militaries does not alter this. Such entities, according to Christian ufologists, can be completely physical, and there is nothing stopping them from appearing to use technology. During abduction experiences, they also manifest in physical form, yet this remains a form of spiritual attack.

Christian ufologist Dr. Michael Heiser describes these as most likely "an inter-dimensional (that is, spiritual) reality…one that can manifest in truly physical form, and not beings from another planet."[11]

There is also a Christian school of thought in ufology that claims abductions can be fought with prayer, specifically by invoking the name of Jesus Christ.[12] Not surprisingly, this has been rebuked by non-Christian abduction researchers, and is questionable by a review of abduction literature. One of the most famous of all abductees, Betty Andreasson Luca, was a devout Christian who experienced multiple abductions spanning most of her life. She also certainly did not interpret her experiences as demonic.

In the post-Disclosure world, many Christians will see the Others as demonic beings. To them, the Bible is not a matter of interpretation or conjecture, but the unerring word of God for all time. Christian author and former television producer Coleman Luck recalled that the New Testament speaks of a "great deception" to take place during the "End Times." At that time, the Anti-Christ will be appear and will deceive most Christians away from their faith. He added that "an essential part of that deception will have to do with what appears to be alien contact." Beings claiming to be extraterrestrials will seem to prove that Jesus was not the savior of mankind. "Ultimately," Luck concluded, "that lie will be overthrown."[13]

It is a clear that most evangelicals will interpret the "Others" according to strongly held Biblical-based beliefs. In this context, some of the most relevant passages in the Bible will be:

"For our wrestling is not against flesh and blood, but against the principalities, against the powers, against the world-rulers of this darkness, against the spiritual hosts of wickedness in the heavenly places."[14] This is from Ephesians, a letter from the Apostle Paul, and one of the earliest Christian documents. What Paul appears to be saying here is that humanity's great struggle is against spirits that are literally "in the heavens." In the same letter, he refers to Satan as "the prince of the Power of the Air" and "the prince of the aerial host."[15]

Another passage from Paul, this one from Thessalonians, will resonate with Christians in the post-Disclosure world, as it speaks of the arrival of

"Satan with all power and signs and lying wonders."[16] Might the shock and awe of a more technologically advanced civilization be interpreted in this way?

Another passage, this one from Matthew, will surely be read in Churches around the world: "For there shall arise false Christs, and false prophets, and shall show great signs and wonders; insomuch that, if it were possible, they shall deceive the very elect."[17]

Ultimately, many Christians will interpret a Disclosure announcement in light of the *Book of Revelation*, which discusses the Second Coming of Christ being preceded by natural disasters, famines, the arrival of the Anti-Christ, and a war in the heavens.[18] During the Cold War, it was easy for Christians to interpret this last as a nuclear exchange between the United States and Soviet Union. However, the announcement of extraterrestrials could provide just as much fodder for interpretation. What this means is that Christians will be wary, at the very least, of a major Disclosure statement. They may well take on a more serious opposition as matters develop, expecting that the battle of Armageddon is at hand.

People do not change overnight. For better as well as for worse, during times of stress, during periods of great uncertainty and even fear, believers will hold more closely than ever to their faith. One key article of faith among Christians is that God will not allow his creation, humankind, to be possessed by dark, Luciferian forces. Instead, it remains within the power of all souls to accept God and reject Satan.

If the Christians are right about how they interpret the UFO phenomenon, it is hoped that the rest of humanity will thank them for their stand against a demonic presence masking as extraterrestrials. If they are wrong, or even incomplete, in their analysis, they will be seen as obstructionist or even dangerous, refusing to see the truth that stares them in the face.

Disclosure may not resolve this matter. The dispute may continue for a long time.

Other Faiths, Easier Transitions

Some faiths appear positioned to accept the reality of "Others" arriving or living on Planet Earth.

Belief in extraterrestrial life is integral to members of the Church of Latter Day Saints. In Chapter One of the Mormon *Book of Moses*, we find this explicit statement: "And worlds without number have I created; and I also created them for mine own purpose; and by the Son I created them, which is mine Only Begotten. And the first man of all men have I called Adam, which is many. But only an account of this Earth, and the inhabitants thereof, give I unto you."[19]

God tells Moses that there are other worlds and other peoples. These other worlds are God's business, and need not concern Moses or people on Earth. Yet Mormons do believe that they will have interaction with extraterrestrials after their death. Similar to other Christians, and like people of other faiths, Mormons see themselves as children of God. Unlike other versions of Christianity, however, they believe they will *become* God—who, according to their belief, was once a man. Members of the Latter Day Saints believe they are Gods in training, so to speak, who will rule a world with its own population in their next incarnation. How this might affect their attitude toward extraterrestrial or interdimensional entities that are here on Earth would certainly be interesting.[20]

Islam, with 1.5 billion adherents, is the world's second most-practiced religion (after combining all the various Christian faiths). It does not have a strong position on the existence of extraterrestrial life; belief one way or the other is not related to the fundamentals of its creed. But neither does the religion provide any roadblocks toward accepting an extraterrestrial or interdimensional reality. One respondent of the Peters survey stated, "Islamically, we do believe that God created other planets similar to Earth." Another wrote, "Only arrogance and pride would make one think that Allah made this vast universe only for us to observe."

The texts of the Koran give support to these positions. "All praise belongs to God," states Islam's holy book, "Lord of all the worlds." One commentator on this verse continues: "Worlds of Matter and Force, worlds of Spirits and Angels, worlds of Beauty and Goodness, worlds of Right and Law—worlds that we can imagine or understand and worlds which we cannot comprehend even in our imagination."[21]

The Islamic scholar Mirza Tahir Ahmad quotes another verse in the Holy Koran discussing the creation of "the heavens and the Earth, and of whatever living creatures He has spread forth in both...."[22] Islamic scholars have long commented on the extraterrestrial implications of this verse. During the 1930s, Abdullah Yusuf Ali commented, "It is reasonable to suppose that Life in some form or another is scattered through some of the millions of heavenly bodies scattered through space."[23]

Passages such as these will certainly hearten Muslims in the face of the acknowledged presence of Others on our world, whether they be extraterrestrial, interdimensional, or anything else. Allah rules over all, and may introduce them to humanity at His discretion.

The post-Disclosure world will also prompt many Islamic scholars to re-examine the nature of the jinn, commonly translated into English as *genie*. The jinn are frequently mentioned in the Koran as creatures occupying a parallel world to that of humankind. Along with humans and angels, they are one of the three sentient creations of God. Interestingly, only humans and jinn have free will. The jinn live in their own communities and, similar to humans, can be good or evil. The Koran mentions that they are made of "smokeless flame." In other words, a source of heat or light.

Unlike Christianity, where the devil is a fallen angel (Lucifer, or "light bearer") who had rebelled against God, the Islamic devil is a jinn named Iblis. He was granted the privilege to live among angels, then rebelled against God, and ever since—like his Christian counterpart—has continued to lead humans astray, which he will do until the Day of Judgment.

We can easily see, then, how other beings that become known to humans in the world AD, might be interpreted as fallen angels by Christians, or as jinn by Muslims. In the case of Muslim believers, however, the attitude may well be less antagonistic than those of Christians, because some jinn are said to be good. Furthermore, according to Islamic belief, while the jinn Iblis may be a deceiver, he has no power to mislead true believers in God.

Although Judaism has little to say about the idea of extraterrestrial life, the religion, similar to Islam, should have little difficulty in assimilating it.

According to the Talmud, there are at least 18,000 other worlds, although little else is said about them, including whether or not they are physical or spiritual. One kabbalistic book, the "Sefer HaBrit," even mentions a planet called Meroz, where extraterrestrial creatures exist.

Buddhists, too, will have no problem assimilating the new reality. Buddhism has always understood that there are beings throughout the universe. This was taught by Siddhartha Gautama, the Buddha, more than 2,500 years ago. One Buddhist response to the Peters survey was that "ETs would be, essentially, no different than other sentient beings, i.e., they would have Buddha Nature and would be subject to karmic consequences of their actions." Another wrote: "As a Mahayana Buddhist, with a worldview that includes in scriptures Buddhas and bodhisattvas from many different world systems, such news would not be shattering theologically, though of course institutions and practices might reverberate."

The same reactions can be expected from adherents of Hinduism, which also holds to the idea of multiple worlds and their relationships with each other. In addition to these material worlds, there is also the unlimited spiritual world, where all purified living entities live with a perfect conception about life and reality. Indeed, spiritually evolved humans have received guidance and help from these entities of the spiritual world.

New Religions

Given the sheer diversity in worldwide religions, there will be no single religious response to Disclosure. Some already agree with the premise, others are moving in that direction, others have never considered it, some embrace the Others as divine emissaries, and some assail them as the work of the devil himself.

No matter what the disposition of the many religious institutions, standing pat will not be viable. Change will be a bumpy ride, more so for some faiths than others. In the end, most of the world's faiths will expand their message. God will be seen to rule over all life in the universe, although undoubtedly some faiths will continue to claim that humankind has a special place in God's plan.

Religion has never been a static human endeavor. We have seen Christianity and Judaism compete for loyalty, and we have seen Christianity fracture into its many permutations. Other faiths, too—such as Hinduism, Buddhism, and Islam—have gone through their own historical changes.

Undoubtedly, new religions will be formed in the post-Disclosure world, influenced by who the Others are and what we learn of them. They will also be influenced by some of the adept and facile minds that spring to take advantage of the instability.

At least one of these religions will explode into the public consciousness with the right message at the right time. It is possible that the top religion of the future is one you have not yet heard of.

The Universal Order

As with all our examples, the claim is not that this particular chain of events will occur. Rather, by outlining one specific possibility, it is easier to understand the post-Disclosure dynamics that will be at work.

Imagine that the Disclosure is murky rather than clear. Authorities only confirm some form of visitation by intelligent non-human beings. Yet, we are not in any tangible contact with them, our knowledge of them is ambiguous, and they seem uninterested in communicating with us. Such a shadow world is perfectly suited for the creation of a new religion.

In this scenario, we focus on a congregational minister in Albuquerque, New Mexico, who uses Disclosure to vault into prominence. The minister, we can call him Reverend Harper, seizes the initiative on the first Sunday following the Disclosure announcement with a stirring speech from the pulpit. Rather than denounce these mysterious beings as being Satan's army, he announces that he has been called by God to reach out, bringing them to Christian religion if they are not already devoted to Christ.

Reverend Harper puts his congregation to work 24/7. They build a website and send out an email prayer. The message of his email prayer is simple: Harper has received word from God to reach out to these Others and let them know that they are loved and welcome in the greater Kingdom of Heaven. Within days, Harper's site has received millions of hits and crashed servers. As the first week after Disclosure draws to a close, Harper has been interviewed by the major broadcast and cable networks and been quoted in major newspapers and magazines.

The publicity has caused groups to spring up in cities around the United States and elsewhere, all signing on to Harper's agenda. Throughout this media blitz, his message has continually refined itself. His small church in Albuquerque has a new sign out front proclaiming itself "The Congregation of the Universal Order."

Next Sunday, Harper's sermon is covered live and streamed around the world. That night it is posted on YouTube to million of views. Ready or not, Reverend Harper, the Universal Order and his extraterrestrial connection, has gone viral. He also realizes he needs something more to keep people interested.

Now Harper announces that he is starting a prayer chain to contact the Others directly and speak to them about their feelings about the deity and to communicate to them the love that people of faith have to share. He points out that governments have had more than 60 years to communicate and have failed miserably. It is time now for God to be consulted. Harper says that when the membership of "The Universal Order" reaches 10 million, the prayer chain will focus its holy energy into an attempt to contact the mind and spirit of the Others in the service of the Almighty. They will extend the hand of friendship and ask them to join in common cause to find the greater Glory of God throughout the universe.

It takes two days to hit the 10 million number. At noon the following day, again to massive news coverage, Harper bows his head in prayer as the news cameras record millions of other people world-wide doing so. From Albuquerque to New York to Paris to Beijing to Mexico City, heads bow with him. It is the largest prayer chain ever attempted.

All eyes and cameras turn to Harper to see how he interprets the results. The man who less than two weeks earlier was a mid-level minister with no career prospects now has the ear of the world. He says he has been humbled by the experience and realizes he has been called by God to be his messenger. Harper confirms that, indeed, the Others have spoken directly to him. He has been given a vision to build a church in the middle of the New Mexico desert. It will be large enough to accommodate a hundred thousand people. It is here, he says, that the Others will reveal themselves.

As the days go forward, Harper's vision appears to have a price tag in excess of million dollars. His critics argue that there is no way to verify any communication with this other intelligence. Harper's answer is that the time for soldiers, lawyers, and bureaucrats to handle this affair has passed. Now it is time for men and women of faith to take the lead. Within weeks, ground is broken on property less than 75 miles from Roswell, New Mexico.

Within a year of Disclosure, the Congregation of the Universal Order holds its first services in the new church. One hundred thousand people have seats in the enclosed stadium-like affair, at least that many others are in RVs on the campgrounds surrounding the area, and nearly a billion people worldwide take part, in real time, as the Reverend Harper, the new Prophet of Contact and Channeler of the Universal Order, walks to the microphone. He turns his eyes toward the heavens and says, "We are here Brothers and Sisters. Are you listening?"

The Nature of God

While it may be useful to learn about free energy, an extraterrestrial United Planets, or to peruse the *Encyclopedia Galactica*, it may not be the first thing on our minds when we begin to engage in honest contact with the Others. If people could ask one single question, many would want to know how these Others conceive of God, followed closely by their attitude toward the afterlife. Energy, flying cars, and genetic manipulation will come further down the list.

Certainly, we may learn something new about God. Either these Others believe in some form of deity or they do not. If they do, it may be possible to compare ideas. If they do not, they may have their reasons, just as many of us have ours. It could lead to a spirited debate among humans, if not with the Others.

Most likely, what they think about religion will be related to the other great institution through which we interpret reality: science.

Science

The first great question that Disclosure will raise for scientists will be: How did the Others manage to get here?

Did they cross the incredible distances of the universe to get to us? If so, we would need to ask why most reputable scientists declared such a thing to be impossible. It will either mean that the laws of physics do not operate the way they think they do, or they have closed their collective minds to things that obviously were possible. Have the Others always been here in some manner? Did they traverse dimensions or even time? If so, it still means that scientists have collectively lived with their heads in the sand.

Beneath these issues, deeper trouble will be brewing. The shock experienced by all other sectors of society will be amplified among professional scientists.

Recall the 1961 Brookings Report. It concluded that, of all groups within society, scientists and engineers might be most shocked by the discovery of superior creatures, "since these professions are most clearly associated with mastery of nature." Although non-religious people tend to believe that Disclosure would traumatize the faithful, it may well be that men and women of science will be most deeply troubled, at least initially. For during times of crisis, faith may be all a person has to rebuild their life. The scientist's faith in "mastery of nature" will surely be humbled, if not broken, by the Others.

They will also be subject to profound public scorn. For years, scientists had arrogantly ridiculed legitimate inquiries into UFOs, dismissing virtually all contact evidence as hoaxes. The ineptitude of the scientific establishment in detecting such an obvious presence will be of profound significance.

With their record of failure and lack of intellectual rigor so badly exposed, people will begin to study the relationship of science to the national security structure of power. Not in generalities, but in specifics. That will inevitably lead to the clandestine world, the world of secrets, and the breakaway civilization that has grown within its secure confines.

At this point the public will hit upon some answers, one of which is that a portion of the scientific community has known about these things all along. It is just that their work was classified for decades. And the rest of the scientific establishment bought into the "deny and ridicule" concept so deeply that they were forced to simply ignore inconvenient facts for fear of losing grants, prestige and promotion.

Even in the pre-Disclosure world, independent analysts have concluded that too much of America's scientific and innovative talent is dominated by national security restrictions and requirements. A 2009 report from the National Research Council argued that "national security controls on science and technology are broken and should be restructured." Such controls, stated the report, initiated to protect U.S. technological secrets and advantages during the Cold War, have become obsolete, and now hamper America's global competitiveness.[24]

Disclosure will bite the world of secrecy in its proverbial rear end, and there will be calls around the world to investigate the structure of innumerable scientific establishments.

There will be two other areas of immediate concern and blowback to the post-Disclosure scientific community. One will be the previously mentioned Search for Extra Terrestrial Intelligence (SETI). The other will be the NASA space program.

Disclosure of UFO and ET reality means not only have classified elements of the scientific community known about it, but that the SETI program has been nothing other than a diversion. NASA's controversy will be worse. Most likely, there will be admissions that NASA astronauts were silenced regarding UFO data and sightings, as has been frequently argued. Moreover, what if it also turns out that NASA had concealed anomalies on the surfaces of the moon and Mars, also something that has been argued for years. The result would be an angry public and a call for a complete housecleaning.[25]

What the public will learn—along with many unsuspecting scientists themselves—is that the management of the scientific community for national security purposes has been a matter of policy, overseen at the highest levels of national security.

Many important re-evaluations will be underway. One of them will concern the late Dr. Carl Sagan.

Keeping the faith? We may finally reconcile science and religion. Observing the Milky Way using the laser guide star facility at Yepun, August, 2010. Photo by Yuri Beletsky (ESO) via Wikimedia Commons.

Carl Sagan: They're Everywhere But Here

Carl Sagan took America by storm during the 1970s and 1980s and became, practically speaking, America's public Scientist-in-Chief. He first entered millions of living rooms as the affable scientist who appeared regularly on *The Tonight Show with Johnny Carson*. The Cornell University professor had a passion for astronomy and a gift of making complex ideas easy to understand.

Sagan's celebrity increased with the release of the PBS *Cosmos* series in 1980, when he became famous for his phrase "billions and billions" to describe galaxies, stars, and planets. He pioneered the science of exobiology and promoted SETI through the use of radio telescopes to listen for signals from space.

As an investigative reporter for PBS, specializing in space science, Bryce Zabel met Carl Sagan several times in 1981. *Cosmos* was still airing on the network, and the unmanned *Voyager* spacecraft was approaching the planet Saturn.

Sagan gave a live, on-air interview as the pictures came in and were assembled by the Jet Propulsion Laboratory in Pasadena. He was effusive about what a great moment it was for humanity. He talked passionately about how this first step beyond Earth would someday lead to manned adventures further into space. He was positive that the universe, because of the sheer number of habitable planets and what he saw as the "bias" toward life, would be teeming with intelligent beings.

After the show, Zabel asked Sagan if given his feelings about a universe filled with life and humankind's imminent expansion beyond our own Earth—he felt that some of those life-forms could have already come here to see us? Might this explain reports of UFOs? Sagan reacted strongly and negatively, citing his famous phrase, "Extraordinary claims require extraordinary evidence."

In a half-hour parking lot debate, an annoyed Sagan made his case. He argued that the chances of extraterrestrial spacecraft visiting Earth were vanishingly small. His explanation for all the UFO sightings hit the basic points. Most were misidentifications of natural phenomena, he said. The rest were from lonely people who created hoaxes in order to feel important.

What about all the police officers and pilots? Sagan shrugged and said not one of them ever got a good photo of what they saw. No extraordinary proof meant it could not be taken seriously. Sagan did allow that the Cold War might have had a part to play in the UFO mystery. Some sightings could be of classified technology, and this most likely explained the suppression of some UFO.

His bottom line could not be moved. He stressed as strongly as he could that, in his view, there was no strong evidence that aliens were visiting the Earth either in the past or present. Then he got in his car and drove away.

Throughout his career, Carl Sagan continued to advocate for the Search for Extra Terrestrial Intelligence. He even wrote *Contact*, a novel on the subject that was adapted into a film. He clearly described his own feelings when, in the novel, the director of Central Intelligence (DCI) explained to a cabinet meeting, "There had been more than a million UFO sightings reported worldwide…and not one of them seemed on good evidence to be connected with an extraterrestrial visitation." Fifteen years later, in his final book, *Demon-Haunted World*, Sagan wrote, "There are reliably reported cases that are unexotic, and exotic cases that are unreliable."

Sagan's twin insistence that the universe was full of intelligent lifeforms, yet none could ever reach Earth, seemed wildly illogical for a man so open to the idea that intelligent life was thriving throughout the cosmos. This is especially odd, given his contention that we were a young civilization and that most others were likely to be many years beyond us.

One of Sagan's classmates at the University of Chicago, Stanton Friedman, a nuclear physicist-turned-UFO researcher (and the man who broke the Roswell case), called Sagan out publicly on his dismissive stance. "Every large scale scientific study of flying saucers has produced a significant number of cases which not only cannot be identified," argued Friedman, "but which clearly indicate that some so-called flying saucers are manufactured objects behaving in ways that we Earthlings cannot yet duplicate with our manufactured objects."[26]

Why would a man of Sagan's brilliance waste his professional lifeenergy within such a close-minded and contradictory belief system? Why shut your mind to the one thing you most want to discover? It made no sense during Sagan's life, and it makes less today. What could explain such behavior from a man who fervently believed in alien life and seemed committed to finding it?

There is one answer—speculation only—found in fiction. In 1997, just four months after Carl Sagan's death at the age of 62, the penultimate episode of the NBC UFO series *Dark Skies* gave Sagan his own fitting tribute. In that episode, the debunker hired by Majestic-12 to confound the public with radio telescopes searching for signals from space while simultaneously discrediting all UFO reports was none other than Carl Sagan.

The cover-up authorities had given him a choice as to whether or not he could learn the truth. Once he did so, however, he would never be able to speak about it publicly. Just as Harvard astronomer Donald Menzel had done before him in the 1950s and 1960s, he would have to deflect people from the truth. Or he could insist on his right to speak freely—but then the real truth would be withheld from him.

In the TV episode, the Carl Sagan character selected Door #1. Perhaps the real Carl Sagan made the same decision. In the topsy-turvy world of official denial, it is reasonable and possible that some day, in the not-so-distant future, a Freedom of Information Act request will uncover a document that shows Carl Sagan was in on the cover-up. For people who respect his vision and intellect, it would make a great deal more sense.

Whatever his motivation, however, the legacy of Carl Sagan will be tarnished. He will be seen either as blindly refusing to believe extraterrestrial life could actually be here now, or as willfully hiding that fact from humanity.

Sagan Was Not Alone

Carl Sagan was hardly the only scientist relentlessly hostile to the idea that alien life could be interacting with humanity here on Earth. If anything, the more we have learned about the probability of intelligent life elsewhere, the more the stridently skeptical the scientific community has become on this point.

With a few exceptions, astronomers and astrophysicists today have accepted Sagan's skewed view that the universe probably abounds with life, and none of it has ever reached us. Even when Stephen Hawking made waves by arguing that aliens might be hostile, he never entertained the possibility that UFOs might be real, and those beings flying them might be the very aliens he was worried about. Even U.K. Royal Astronomer Lord Rees, while firmly favoring the likelihood of extraterrestrial life in a landmark March 30, 2010 lecture, could not resist ending it with a dig against

UFO belief. "If the aliens had made the tremendous technological effort to come here across inter-stellar space," he opined with obvious amusement, "what a pity they only made a few corn circles and went away again and what a pity they only met a few well-known cranks."[27]

His statement proved two things. First, as noted earlier, the policy of "deny and ridicule" has worked so well that most of society's established authorities now do the work of the secret-keepers without prodding. More importantly, it proved that when Disclosure actually does come, the scientific community will be filled with prominent members who not only did not get it, but never looked for it. What can one say of Lord Rees and his colleagues, learned men and women, whose scientific curiosity missed the greatest story of our time, whose scientific method included ridicule of decent observers who actually were correct?

Fortunately, however, scientists are not the same as science itself.

New Frontiers

The Disclosure of a non-human intelligence interacting with humanity and planet Earth will shock and discredit the scientific community's old guard, but it will also rejuvenate and spur our science to an unprecedented degree. Some of this may depend on whether or not the Others decide to be helpful, and some of it may depend on what secrets can be pried out of the Breakaway Group. However, it is probable that, barring any support from either of those (who have, after all, been secretive all along), there will still be important breakthroughs in a number of areas of current scientific endeavor.

- ✧ **Genetic manipulation.** What else can we learn about genetics? Assuming we gain access to alien physiology and genetics, we may gain great insights into ways of improving human health, increasing mental capacity, understanding what controls cellular and organ regeneration, and extending the human life span.
- ✧ **Fighting diseases.** Will we learn of an effective vaccine or cure for HIV, diabetes, cancer, or any number of other debilitating diseases? If we do, this could lead to vastly increasing the human life span.

- ✧ **Understanding biological evolution.** Do complex organisms evolve solely by means of natural selection, or are there other processes that come into play? It may be that having access to data regarding complex, intelligent, non-human life forms that evolved elsewhere, or else were genetically modified in some manner, could contribute toward solving this question, which many biologists consider to be among the greatest mysteries of their field, and has nagged at them for years.[28]
- ✧ **Understanding consciousness and memory.** There are a plethora of knotty questions wrapped inside of these, but the issue comes down to what is the human mind, and can Disclosure spur us into new avenues and answers? It is very likely that a deeper understanding and analysis of the abduction phenomenon can help in this regard. Somehow, human memory can be manipulated to a degree beyond what most of us consider feasible. Much of this is chemical, and much is electrical. But what else? What is the part of our brains, our minds, that enables us to have consciousness of ourselves, of our existence, of our "identity?"

These would be some of the questions in the area of biology. Certainly, physics would receive a major nudge.

- ✧ *What causes gravity?* We know that the universe has four forces: gravity, electromagnetism, the "strong" force, and the "weak" force. But gravity is the least understood of the four, and contemporary physics does not explain how it works. Some physicists think it might involve tiny, massless particles called gravitons that emanate from gravitational fields. The craft we have come to term "UFOs" may be using a form of electrogravitics. It is possible that Disclosure can enable us better to understand gravity. If so, we may stand a fair chance at arriving at a genuine "theory of everything," otherwise known as "a universal field theory."
- ✧ *Where is the rest of the universe?* Only four percent of the matter and energy in the universe has been found. The other 96 percent, termed dark matter and dark energy, remains elusive. It is possible that understanding how the anti-gravitic field propulsion systems of alien craft may lead us to breakthroughs in this arena as well. Or perhaps the ETs or Breakaway Group might decide to tell the rest of us, if they know.

There are a few other areas that warrant an expanded treatment.

In Search of Holy Grails

Any technology that has allowed interstellar or interdimensional travel has probably harnessed a basic source of energy available in the universe. The question is: Will it be shared with us to our benefit, or used against us?

As we have noted, our oil-based economy is unlikely to survive for the next 100 years. If ETs have learned how to utilize an unlimited energy source of the universe, then it may very well be that power is literally all around us, and it is free. Of course, we might assume that somehow, the human power structure will find a way to make people pay for it. This could be a major political battle of the future. (See Chapter 8 for more details.)

For now, the best that our current paradigm of scientific thinking has offered us is that we need to become more efficient and conserve more. Breakthroughs are not discussed or apparently anticipated. Within our current, conventional technology, an interesting invention known as "the Bloom Box" offers some intriguing possibilities. The Bloom Box is described as a solid oxide fuel cell using liquid or gaseous fossil or bio fuel to generate electricity on demand. It is essentially a small box that can power a home. Oxygen is fed to it on one side, and fuel on the other. The two combine within the cell to create a chemical reaction that produces electricity. There is no burning or combustion, and no need for power lines. The box is said to be highly efficient, but its exact operation is still not widely understood. Although it is clean, it still relies on hydrocarbons, for example, fossil fuels.[29]

Another source of energy, widely used in our world today, may receive a boost from Disclosure. This is the Sun. After all, the Earth receives 86,000 trillion watts, or terawatts, of solar radiation energy on a constant basis. This is more than 6,000 times the amount of energy used by all humans on Earth each year. It ought to be enough for quite some time, assuming we develop a way of utilizing it. However, although this is attractive, it is hard to imagine using solar power to fly from Los Angeles to Tokyo, at least without other radical breakthroughs.[30] Nor does it seem likely that flying saucers operate on solar energy. Still, it is possible that important developments can be achieved, some of which might receive a boost from what we learn of UFOs or the beings operating them.

Moving into more exotic solutions, we arrive at Zero-Point Energy (ZPE). It is called "zero point" because it is energy that exists at zero degrees Kelvin; in other words, without any thermal energy. For this reason ZPE is often referred to as the vacuum energy, as it is associated with the vacuum of empty space. That is, ZPE exists everywhere. An easy way to visualize it is to imagine an ocean from high above, and then at the surface level. Far above, it looks placid, calm, and flat. But in a rowboat in the middle of the Pacific, you would see tall waves and constant, powerful activity.

This is something like the fabric of reality. Imagine an atom, then an infinitesimal portion of that, and then another infinitesimal portion of that. At that incredibly small portion of reality, there is a great deal going on. Matter and anti-matter seem to "pop" into our reality and annihilate each other. There is a tiny release of energy at that level, and capturing it has become a Holy Grail for a few visionaries. If it can be extracted and used, one could see its application for interstellar travel, as well as for possibly anything else; it is truly "free" energy. Do the operators of UFO craft employ ZPE? Maybe.

It may also be that the operators of UFOs—both "ours" and "theirs"—use clean nuclear fusion. This form of power generation is often discussed in the open literature, but is something the general public knows little about. It is another Holy Grail.

Current nuclear power plants use a process known as fission, which tears atoms apart, releasing energy and radioactive by-products. Fusion is different. It occurs inside every star, and has been replicated by humankind in the form of the hydrogen bomb. A nuclear fusion reactor would duplicate this process, but in a controlled way. It involves fusing together two "heavy" hydrogen atoms, known as deuterium and tritium, to produce helium—inert and harmless—and vast amounts of energy. Electric cars, to name merely the first and most obvious transformation, would become nearly universal.

We have yet to produce clean, controlled fusion, at least in the open, non-classified world. But researchers continue to work on this problem, and many believe it can be achieved. If so, we would vastly reduce our dependency on petroleum, make energy clean and relatively cheap, and profoundly change our world.

No matter what the breakthrough may be, we cannot expect immediate transformations to take place. For energy to be widely utilized, it must be widely distributed. This requires changes in the "built environment," or in other words, within a society's infrastructure. One energy analyst described the problem by way of an analogy from 18th-century Britain, when coal was already understood to be a vastly better source of energy than wood. Yet, wood remained dominant all through that century. The reason was that the economy, technology, and distribution systems were set up for wood. Coal extraction techniques had not become efficient enough. By the 19th century, the built environment had caught up and could meet the challenge of transitioning to coal. Even in the 21st century, such things can take time.[31]

No matter what the long-term solution to our energy needs may turn out to be, there is a likelihood that Disclosure will clear a path toward it. After all, whatever these craft are using for power, it is something that enables them to hover indefinitely and accelerate instantly, all in silence. This is an extraordinary amount of power. It is something we do not currently use, and that is what matters. We can be sure that the scientific community will be jumping over itself to understand everything about it.

Computing

With or without Disclosure, humankind is on a trajectory. Certain events may speed it up, others may impede it, but the destination is clear. That is a world in which computing goes vastly beyond our current levels, creating a world so different that we struggle to visualize it. This is why many computer science professionals used the term *Singularity* to describe it. Just as the singularity of a black hole is a unique phenomenon in physics, beyond the ability of our physical laws to predict, so too is the world that lies before us in regard to computing, nanotechnology, artificial intelligence, and biotechnology. In particular, the Singularity signifies the moment when machine intelligence exceeds biological human intelligence, becomes sentient, and becomes the driving force of our civilization.

The relationship of Disclosure to Singularity has never before been raised. In doing so here, we are opening a new discussion and expect that any hypothesis suggested now may need to be refined, revised, or even rejected with the passage of time.

Anyone who feels that UFOs are a bit "far out" for their normal intellectual fare may want to consider what our near future is probably going to look like. Ray Kurzweil, arguably the most prominent of the futurists writing about artificial intelligence, foresees machine intelligence surpassing human intelligence during the first half of the 21st century. Among AI experts, this appears to be a mid-range estimate, possibly a bit early. Generally, most predictions for the advent of Singularity are between 2030 and 2080, although a few push the date into the 22nd century.

It may not be a world in which machines replace people—the vision of which is seen in such apocalyptic movies as *The Terminator*, *The Matrix*, *I Robot*, and others. According to the experts, humans will also be modified and plugged-in, making old-fashioned, unenhanced *homo sapiens* a thing of the past. Nanotechnology may have a major role to play. Imagine a nanochip the size of a human brain cell, designed to duplicate all the functions of that brain cell. Such chips are currently thought to be possible. Now imagine that it functions more efficiently than your brain cell, and imagine that a certain percentage of your frontal lobe is supplemented by these nanochips, giving you an IQ of 200 or more. What's more, you would have telepathic connectivity to the World Wide Web, and also to other people.

Though this may be possible, it gets even stranger.

Consider developments in genetics and biotechnology. During the first decade of the 21st century, the human genome was finally mapped in its entirety. This is important, but this incredibly complex genome is only beginning to be understood by scientists. Within the next few decades, it will be better understood and mastered. Inevitably, attempts will be made to enhance it in one way or another—if not for the masses then for the few. Such enhancements might include "switching off" the gene for aging. Others might enable greater physical strength, greater intelligence, or even abilities to interact with other dimensions of reality—what some would call "the spiritual realm." The possibilities are almost too awesome for contemplation.

Nanotechnology is about to become a major industry. Defined as "the engineering of functional systems at the molecular scale," it has also been described by the U.S. National Science Foundation as "the next industrial revolution," enabling microscopic implants that kill cancerous cells, a box the size of a sugar cube containing the entire contents of the Library of Congress, or materials lighter than steel with ten times the strength.[32]

The potential of nanotechnology goes far beyond these examples. Think about "nanofactories" similar to the replicator device featured in the television series, *Star Trek: The Next Generation*. Packed with miniature chemical processors, computing, and robotics, a nanofactory would produce items quickly, cleanly, and cheaply, directly from blueprints. It might also proliferate exponentially, as nanofactories make more nanofactories. Such a device would be making "the building of products…as cheap as the copying of files."[33]

What this all means is that, with or without Disclosure, with or without the aid of the Others, human society is going to look very, very different than it does today. Consider how the continually increasing connectivity will change our world. During the late 1980s, the rudiments of the Internet were coming into place. By the mid-1990s, the World Wide Web, complete with graphical user interface, was a fact, but still in its infancy. By 2000 the web was ubiquitous. Still, the revolution continued. YouTube arrived in 2005, roughly when cell phones became true hand-held personal devices with digital cameras, music libraries, full web access, and more. What level of global connectivity will exist in 2030? 2050? 2100? How intelligent will our "devices" be? How small?

We all know this abstractly, intellectually. But to use a loaded word, the world will be utterly alien, with or without real aliens being acknowledged. Here is the world as it may well look during the second half of the 21st century.

- Computers that exceed human intelligence in many or most key areas.
- Genetically modified human beings with a variety of implants.
- Human-machine cognitive interfacing to create the possibility of a truly cybernetic organism.
- Computers embedded everywhere.
- Microscopic "nanobots" that can be programmed with intelligence (or perhaps by a computer intelligence) to compile or decompile at will into any shape or structure imaginable.
- Holograms and virtual reality everywhere.
- The advent of quantum computing, an event that may be a profound leap into a new world of computing, vastly beyond our current level.
- Lifespans that may go on for a long, long time.

What we are talking about is essentially a new species of human and most certainly a new level of intelligence, possibly orders of magnitude beyond what we experience today. Perhaps human nature will not change all that much, but then again perhaps it will. It may also be that only some humans stand to benefit from such perks, and may set themselves up as a true Master Race, genetically modifying and enhancing themselves to their heart's content, while also modifying the "rabble" to suit their specifications. After all, humans have done it to farm animals for 10,000 years. The coming world may be paradise, or it may be hell, depending on who you are.

This is a realm of speculation that will probably have more than one mistake and several dead-ends. Yet, as of this writing, these are outcomes that, strange as they may seem to some, are possible to envision. Only time will tell.

Disclosure and the Singularity

Because predicting the future requires a combination of imagination and extrapolation, there are several ways that this techno-utopia or techno-dystopia may relate to Disclosure. It depends upon when Disclosure occurs, and it depends on when the Singularity occurs.

If Disclosure occurs first, it will likely speed up the coming of the Singularity. After all, while shocking the scientific community and psyche to the core, Disclosure will nonetheless spur it to an unprecedented degree. Computer science will undoubtedly be one of the key areas of study, if for no other reason than to deal with possible defense implications.

One thing to consider is how the approach of the Singularity will affect Disclosure. For the closer we approach the Singularity, the more likely that Disclosure will occur. As the power of the computer becomes overwhelming, as the interconnectivity of our world becomes ever more pronounced, as our ability to detect other intelligences continues to broaden and deepen, it becomes ever more likely that something will give. The unknowns are when it will happen and what will trigger it.

If the Singularity occurs sooner, so will Disclosure. If, as some of the Singularity "optimists" would have it, that event is likely to occur in or around 2030, then Disclosure will probably arrive a year or two before—barring, of course, the accidental mass sighting or some other unforeseen act—say, a surprise statement by a powerful figure. If, however, the Singularity is slower to arrive, for instance 2080 or 2090, this will make Disclosure predictions a little more interesting, and certainly more difficult.

All we can say is that time does not stand still, and the world of tomorrow will not resemble the world of today. Somewhere along the line between now and the post-Singularity world will be a moment when the sum total of intelligence and computing power in human civilization will see the obviousness of an advanced non-human presence here on Earth. Exactly where that moment will be along the line is impossible to know, but that we will cross it is undeniable.

Religion and Science: New Paradigms from an Old Conflict

One of the most fascinating results of Disclosure will be a new relationship between religion and science. The two modes of thought have been uneasy bedfellows since the modern age of science began four centuries ago, and in fact the basic conflict extends back more than 2,000 years to the ancient Greeks.

Two elements of the conflict must be distinguished. The first concerns what philosophers would term *epistemology*—that is, how do we know what we know? What constitutes valid evidence for knowledge?

Accounting for certain variations and distinctions among them, religions usually claim to acquire their knowledge by revelation. The assumption is that an important element of reality is normally hidden from humanity, but can be revealed at certain times. These revelations often come as flashes of insight appearing to a single person. The source of the revelation is usually understood to be divine. Such revelations are not usually debatable; believers are meant to accept them without argument. After all, how could God be wrong?

Such an attitude toward truth is unacceptable to a scientist, who is constrained to adhere to a certain method—the scientific method. This means, above all, collecting data through observation and experimentation, then formulating and testing a hypothesis. Such testing must also be repeatable. Someone else must be able to be duplicate the test. This is a critical point. The hypothesis, in order to be valid, must be testable, or to use the word that scientists themselves use, it must be "falsifiable." Simply put, the hypothesis may be true, or it may be false. But if you can test it to find out one way or the other, then at least it is falsifiable.

It is unlikely that Disclosure will alter this distinction between scientific and religious thought. These are two systems of thinking that are fundamentally different. They comprise a basic philosophical divide. And yet, this does not mean they cannot coexist. Many of our best scientists possess a faith in God. Dr. Francis Collins, director of the Human Genome Project, said eloquently that "reason alone cannot prove the existence of God. Faith is reason plus revelation." To do this, one must think with the spirit as well as the mind. "You have to hear the music, not just read the notes on the page. Ultimately, a leap of faith is required."[34]

Disclosure and the God Hypothesis

There is another element to the conflict of Religion vs. Science. To describe it, we need to speak in more general, approximate terms. Yet, the conflict is real. It is about something that religious thinkers believe in, and something about which most scientists remain agnostic or even doubtful.

Parting the heavens. The Big Picture begins to emerge. Photo courtesy of NASA/STSci.

We are talking about the existence of a spiritual realm, the existence of God, and all that goes along with it. In other words, will Disclosure will offer us proof for this belief, or at least strong supporting evidence?

Within UFO research literature, there is no shortage of claims that the "aliens" possess their own spiritual orientation. People who recall abduction experiences have occasionally commented that the beings took them to pray. Indeed, it seems possible that these beings themselves exist in what we might loosely call the spiritual realm.

What if these beings claim to be the "divinities" worshiped by early human societies, or that they created us? Even if they made no such claims, what if many people gain that impression? Five thousand years ago, the ancient Sumerians wrote about their gods, calling them the Anunnaki. What if some of these beings are interpreted as such? What if they have something provocative to say about Jesus Christ, Mohammed, or other important spiritual beings of human history? In other words, what if Jesus or Mohammed or Buddha are seen as one of "them?" Events like these would spark intense reaction by people everywhere. Some would believe the claims; others would call them deceptions. Even barring something so spectacular, it is conceivable that the Others may have insights into other dimensions, insights that people come to accept.

Throughout the history of modern ufology, there have always been "nuts and bolts" researchers who have taken a strictly materialist point of view of these other beings. The assumption is that the Others are flesh-and-blood entities, probably from another planet somewhere else in the universe, and have come here to investigate us. However, not everyone agrees. For sure, the UFO phenomenon has often been strange, and has suggested various non-materialist aspects. Telepathy seems to be involved. Time sometimes seems to be manipulated in some way that we cannot yet understand. And there are many people who claim to receive channeled or telepathic communications from ET beings. None of this proves that the Others are spiritual entities of some sort, but it may be that this is sometimes the case.

Ultimately, we may learn that the concept of "mind over matter" is not only valid, but true. Admittedly, this is a definite *if*, but *if* the Others can demonstrate that all humans possess inherent spiritual gifts that have been denied throughout much of our history, *if* we as a species learn to awaken that part of us which may be dormant, *if* we learn to "see" reality from a broader, deeper perspective than we have previously seen, clearly that would change religion, and it could well change science, too. In that case, for humanity would then have upgraded its operating system. In such a situation, much of the old software would probably be upgraded, too. This does not mean rejecting old beliefs and values, which seems unlikely. It would be more like expanding our circle of understanding to incorporate new realities.

Our eyes would see more, our minds would grasp more, our hearts would feel more. No thinking person can deny at least the possibility of our ability to attain such a state. The question is, will knowledge of the Others spark such an awakening? After all these years and all these debates, where lives have been lost and ruined on both sides, it is possible that somehow the Others will be instrumental in bringing about something we have yet to do ourselves: fuse spirituality and science.

If so, then our current debates between religion and science will seem pedantic and irrelevant to people a century from now. If they are lucky, they will have graduated to the next grade level in the grand school of God's universe.

Vignette #7:

Network Memo

✧✦✧

From: Shiloh Ray <s.ray@netburbank.com>
Subject: Re: Thursday Meeting
Date: November 16, 2021
9:23:02 AM PDT
To: Robb Canwood <robb.c@netburbank.com>

Hey, Robb! Did you see the numbers for *Above and Below?!* They were bigger in week two than the first week w/o the lead-in or the promo on the big show. We have a monster on our hands. Just make sure that they know they can't miss a production deadline—if they're having trouble with access, let me know. I like tunnels, they're great, but if we can get an alien in one of them, I know that's asking a lot, but just keep your eyes open, okay? Maybe you see something in the shadows, and you go searching....

Also, I had a chance to look at these pages on the *Breakaway* pilot last night. I think we gotta pull the trigger on this one, too. We're gonna sell this as a true story, so tell them to stick to only what they've read from a good source and to use our consultant. We're paying him for his story, we might as well use him.

Shiloh

Chapter 8

Exopolitics Rising: Moving from First Contact to Informed Contact

Divide and rule,
a sound motto.
Unite and lead,
a better one.

—Johann Wolfgang von Goethe

Whether or not the Others choose to engage with us in the A.D. world, we will begin to engage with them. At that point, questions will abound: Who will speak for humanity? What issues will be on our agenda? Where, how, and when will formal contact take place? What will our world be like? How will Disclosure change *us*?

The answers will be determined the same way humans deal with other problems: the practice of politics. In countries around the globe, from China to Israel to the United Kingdom, this process is often nasty, and the other side is often characterized as evil, stupid, or both. When practiced between nations, outcomes can be positive and cooperative, or aggressive and violent, ranging from the eradication of smallpox to global war. When practiced between humans and another intelligent life form, one can only imagine the outcome—which is what we will do in this penultimate chapter.

The Politics of Exopolitics

Throughout the years, the UFO phenomenon has prompted the creation of new terms and concepts:

- ✧ Ufology, as the study of the UFO phenomenon
- ✧ CE1, CE2, CE3, CE4, and CE5, to describe levels of "close encounters"
- ✧ Disclosure, as the effort to end UFO secrecy.

In the 21st century, another term, *exopolitics*, coined by researcher and writer Alfred Webre, has come into use.

Stephen Bassett, head of the Paradigm Research Group (PRG), which has advocated for UFO Disclosure since the 1990s, defines exopolitics as "the art or science of government as concerned with creating and maintaining governmental policy toward extraterrestrial-related phenomena and extraterrestrial beings." The Exopolitics Institute, headed by Michael Salla, PhD, describes it as "an interdisciplinary scientific field, with its roots in the political sciences, that focuses on research, education and public policy with regard to the actors, institutions and processes, associated with extraterrestrial life, as well as the wide range of implications this entails through public advocacy and newly emerging paradigms."

In other words, exopolitics involves the politics of "us" and "them." Considering all the problems associated with human-to-human politics, imagine what mistakes have been made or could still be made in any relationships with Others.

In human-to-human politics, people never agree for long; factions and in-fighting are the norm. The same is true for exopolitics. The bottom line is how we assess ourselves, and how we assess the Others. If we cannot agree on the former, how can we possibly agree on the latter? In our world today, it is a fantasy to think people can agree on that point. Throughout the history of ufology, there have been researchers who have emphasized the dangers posed by these other beings, and probably just as many who have focused on their benevolence. In exopolitics as in national politics, you have Conservatives versus Liberals.

Most of the voices today who explicitly identify with exopolitics fall into the Liberal camp. In the first place, by advocating for UFO Disclosure, they implicitly oppose the secret-keepers in the clandestine world. Secondly, the very act of considering how to engage beings from elsewhere in a political relationship implies a belief in common ground. Third, contemporary proponents of exopolitics often (although not always) characterize the Others as highly evolved spiritual beings who are concerned for humanity's positive development. If this is true, then we surely would want to move this process along. If there are technological secrets being held by the clandestine world in the form of clean and cheap energy, then we have yet another reason why Disclosure is desirable.

This is the turf staked out by "The Disclosure Project," headed by Dr. Steven Greer. Since the 1990s, this group has periodically called for "open, secrecy-free [Congressional] hearings on the UFO/Extraterrestrial presence on and around Earth." In addition, it calls for revealing secrets about "advanced energy and propulsion systems that, when publicly released, will provide solutions to global environmental challenges."[1] Greer argues that there are many witnesses who can testify about the reality of such covert programs and technologies, although they are afraid to come forward without help. His group also wants legislation to ban space-based weapons, focusing on a vision of space-based exploration that brings all Earth cultures together.

Greer's attitude toward extraterrestrials, described earlier in this book, is to embrace and welcome them. Depending on how one assesses them, his program can be characterized as visionary, utopian, or dangerous.

In essentials, the same can be said for the Exopolitics Institute, headed by Dr. Michael Salla. Its philosophy is very inclusive, promoting "citizen diplomacy initiatives" for peaceful interactions with extraterrestrial civilizations that are monitoring humanity. It also supports "whistle-blowers" or even private citizens who claim to have physically interacted with extraterrestrials, or had access to covert military-corporate programs involving extraterrestrial technologies.[2]

Both of these groups offer hope that a post-Disclosure world will be a better place. Certainly, one would be hard-pressed to disagree with their desire to challenge the global military-intelligence-industrial complex. Basically, to give peace a chance.

If these other beings turn out to be rapacious, destructive, or otherwise a threat, as speculated earlier in this book, the argument for secrecy might well be a strong one. Why cause panic if we are helpless anyway? Under such circumstances, naturally, we would be less inclined to want to engage them in any sort of constructive political process. To such researchers who believe this is the case, the very idea of exopolitics is foolish at best, suicidal at worst.

And yet, it could be counter-argued that, even under these conditions, exopolitics is a reality. "They" are here, and are interacting with us. Even if the relationship is one of hostility, politics inevitably enters the process at some point. Von Clausewitz, the great theoretician of modern warfare, famously described war as "the continuation of policy by other means."

Perhaps our exopolitics would benefit from fewer strongly held positions about the nature of the Others. It seems likely, anyway, that the truth lies somewhere between the extremities.

Stephen Bassett's Paradigm Research Group (PRG) avoids discussion of the matter altogether. Instead, Bassett's message is simple: the "truth embargo" needs to end first, and all other issues can be sorted out later. His activism has resulted in numerous annual "X-Conferences" near Washington, D.C., organizing fax campaigns on Washington, and trying to pull the world together website by website. In 2011, PRG organized a World Disclosure Day on July 8, and later in the year gathered more than 17,000 signatures for a Disclosure Petition to the White House "to formally acknowledge an extraterrestrial presence engaging the human race." The White House policy to all petitions is to offer a formal reply once the signatories exceed 5,000.

Regarding the petition, the White House did issue a predictable statement on November 4, 2011: "The U.S. government has no evidence that any life exists outside our planet, or that an extraterrestrial presence has contacted or engaged any member of the human race. In addition, there is no credible information to suggest that any evidence is being hidden from the public's eye."[3] Any other answer would certainly have brought a storm of unwelcome publicity to the White House, especially in the lead-up to an election season. Still, PRG can claim credit for being the first civilian organization to elicit a formal policy position on UFOs from the White House, and has positioned itself to continue beating the drum and engaging the media on this issue.

Throughout the years, PRG's efforts have resulted in hits and misses. Yet Bassett has been an active and forceful proponent of Disclosure, having promoted a strong movement throughout Europe and elsewhere. As of mid-2011, there were active exopolitical websites in more than 20 countries.[4] Beyond that, he has encouraged others to imagine what a post-Disclosure world will look like. "It is not whether there is an extraterrestrial intelligence engaging the planet, it is what are we going to do about it?"[5]

Exopolitics is an idea whose time has come. Because Others are already here, then by definition exopolitics is being practiced. The fact that it is not yet being conducted openly makes no difference as to its reality. Some humans are already making decisions based on UFOs operating within the Earth's environment. In fact, the political dialogue between Us and Them may be strained, nearly incomprehensible, and potentially dangerous. But it has been underway for a long time, and it is happening now as you read this book.

The First Exopoliticians

Given the situation of military minds of the 1940s grappling with something beyond any previous experience, we can appreciate their sense of urgency, their scramble to understand the truth, and their need to try to catch up technologically.

Such a situation would require the utmost secrecy, not only from one's national rivals, and not only from one's population, but also—perhaps most important—from the Others themselves.

The first exopolitical decision to be made was to keep things hidden. That dictated countless other decisions that followed, the accumulation of which created a secret world. With the same hubris that allowed pharaohs to build colossal monuments, these men built a new world. They populated it with their trusted fellow-travelers, and resourced it with money and assets that were siphoned from the public they convinced themselves they were serving.

In time, the structure of secrecy among the human players had become other-worldly. Probably by the 1970s, they had largely moved beyond formal governmental channels of control, although government funding and military security continued to be useful. Enough breakthroughs had been made, even by then, to distance them from the civilization they had set out to defend. Home-made flying saucers? It is possible that they even had those, along with a secret space program and more.

Changing our POV. Seeing the Earth with new eyes. "Moonbase Clarke" by Kimmo Isokoski, used with permission.

But there is more to this breakaway civilization than mere possession of flying saucers. Recall that the NSA in 1965 was 35 years ahead of the consumer world in its computing technology. May we assume that it and other deep-black agencies are at least a few decades ahead of the world right now in a variety of key technologies? If our mainstream scientists are predicting major breakthroughs in computing, artificial intelligence, nanotech, and biotechnology by around mid-century, what is the likelihood that the classified world will achieve them sooner? What is the chance that key breakthroughs in those fields have already been made? And yet there is more to a breakaway civilization than even these developments. There is the matter of physical separateness.

Separate, Not Equal

Everyone has heard of Area 51 as a location where the human response to the Others is said to be carried out. It is by no means the only such place. There are other bases, as well as warehouses and levels in normal military and civilian locations, that belong to the breakaway civilization.

It is entirely possible that the passage of time has allowed the separateness to include deep underground facilities. In other words, Earth may be home to an underground community that is "off the grid." A lot of good research on this has been done, most notably by the investigator Dr. Richard Sauder, who has demonstrated that the U.S. national security establishment made plans to go very deep underground no later than the 1960s. He also made it clear that for years, the technology has existed to go deep. Finally, he has exposed leaks from insiders giving information about massive, deep, clandestine bases and tunnels that traverse beneath our feet in almost labyrinthian fashion.[6]

If deep underground bases seem chimerical, consider the likelihood of bases deep beneath the seabeds of our world. That is, beneath the oceans themselves. Lest one dismiss this as mere fantasy, consider that the technology has existed for many years to make this a reality. There are, of course, several known examples of tunnels that go for miles beneath the ocean floor. The Channel Tunnel, or Chunnel, connecting Britain to France, is the most famous of them. Likewise, the technology to extract oxygen from the ocean has existed for more than 50 years—it is through this technology that nuclear submarines can stay submerged for months at a time. If you have enough oxygen and a source of power—for instance, a small, portable nuclear or geothermal generator—you have enough to get started on a large base that can be rather comfortable below the ocean floor.[7]

In addition to Sauder's well-documented research, there are other tantalizing links to the underground world.

One, for example, concerns an assistant secretary to a branch of the armed forces in a new Republican administration. This person told a family friend that he had been "briefed" for some eight weeks at an underground facility outside of Washington. Asked the purpose of the briefing, this highly placed man, who went on to become a cabinet secretary, said, "There is intelligent life in the universe. It's here. And I've seen it."

The man said that the information he had been given caused him to cry himself to sleep for a number of nights. The reason, he told his shocked listener, was that he had children. "This is not the kind of world I thought they'd grow up in."[8]

What kinds of things are going on that require months-long briefings in underground facilities and cause grown men to cry? The cabinet secretary told the family friend that aliens were just the "tip of the iceberg" in terms of mind-blowing revelations.

It is clear, then, that large underground facilities not only are real, but are connected in some way with the reality of ETs or "Others" here on Earth.

We should ask ourselves: Who are the people who briefed the incoming cabinet member on the nature of the Others? Presumably, these would be the representatives of Majestic, or whatever the organization is being called now. That they can traumatize a worldly, intelligent professional with dramatic new information about the nature of reality reinforces the idea that we are, indeed, talking about a breakaway civilization.

The combination of secrecy, money, new technologies, new types of encounters, and physical separateness make up for a different state of mind that exists among such a group.

After all, perhaps the key feature that defines a distinct civilization is its belief system—its paradigm, in the fullest sense of that word. That is, the sum total of beliefs concerning one's place in the universe, as well as one's knowledge of other civilizations. Here, too, the world of Majestic appears to have developed something entirely different from the rest of us. After all, it is a world that may have its own space program, a vastly more powerful computing and artificial intelligence, biotechnology that may be off the charts by our standards. With all this, it could well be in some form of contact with intelligent non-human groups. One can only wonder at the changes in worldview that would be launched by such regular contact. In all likelihood, it is a world in which the fabric of reality is understood in a way that we have not begun to grasp. Its members may see themselves as so far removed from the rest of us that they have given up on the possibility of bringing us to their level. They may not even see the rest of humanity as "fully" human.

Unlocking the Door

This Breakaway Group is a key component in any post-Disclosure exopolitical equation. It ought to be a major priority of a U.S. president, along with other national leaders, to gain control over it. The question is, will any occupant of the Oval Office have the courage to try?

The answer depends not only on the ambitions of the president, but his or her ability to manage and influence the key levers of power within the government. No President can do this alone.

A glaring reality of our era is that the law is not being followed regarding presidential control over the UFO situation. Some apparently are briefed on the matter, others not.

One inside source has told the authors of his "professional knowledge" that Presidents Reagan and Bush (senior) were briefed on UFOs and extraterrestrials, and is near certainty that President Carter had also been briefed. He was less certain about President Clinton, and felt confident that President George W. Bush had not been briefed. Another well-placed individual said that President Obama had been briefed on the bare essentials of the UFO/ET reality, but that he had no influence over policy. The distinct impression was made that the briefing was not mandatory. It was given, the insider said, "out of respect" for the president's office.[9]

Yet another story related to the authors, given by a retired officer from one of the U.S. military services, underscores the lack of power held by the U.S. President on this matter. An elderly man lay on his deathbed, speaking in a secured medical facility to the officer, who was accompanied by a security detail. Long before, the dying man had handled alien wreckage and seen alien bodies. The officer interviewed the man for some time, comparing notes. The bodies the man had seen were definitely not human: they were short, had large heads, and had fairly human-looking eyes—not the black, insect-like eyes attributed to the "Grays."

Near the end of their meeting, the officer opined that it was a shame the man's story could not be revealed, that it was a matter of importance to the world. The man replied that he could never talk, that he had taken a life-long secrecy oath. Yes, but wouldn't it be wonderful, said the officer, if the man were released from his oath, say, by an executive order from the president?

The dying man's answer was startling and instructive: "It would take a hell of a lot more than an Executive Order from the president to release me from my oath."

When asked by one of the authors what this meant, the officer replied that, obviously, it meant someone else was in charge. When asked if this meant an international control group, something like the Bilderbergers, was in charge, his answer was, "Yes, something like that."[10]

John Podesta, a senior advisor to President Clinton and the transition chief for the Obama Administration, has been outspoken on the need for openness on the matter of UFOs, while implicitly acknowledging the lack of presidential authority on the matter. At the National Press Club in 2007, he said, "I think it's time to open the books on questions that have remained in the dark on the question of UFOs. It's time to find out what the truth really is that's out there. We ought to do it because it is right. We ought to do it because the American people, quite frankly, can handle the truth, and we ought to do it because it is the law."[11]

Whether justified or not, the UFO phenomenon has prompted the creation of a sprawling, illegal, extra-constitutional structure, beyond the control of the highest elected official in the land and beyond the oversight of the citizen's elected representatives.

This unlawful structure no doubt explains why the record on presidential briefing appears to be so spotty. If the president is aware of the illegal nature of the cover-up, as the sworn chief executive of the country, his oath would demand action. Therefore, knowing the bare essentials sounds like a useful compromise. The President knows that the challenge is real, but is assured that competent people are on the job. The less he knows about specifics, the greater his plausible deniability.

All indications are that congressional representatives are not briefed on this matter. How can prominent elected officials worldwide—the people entrusted by citizens around the world to run their governments—be so in the dark about this great secret? The answer lies with the secret-keepers themselves who appear to believe that revealing the presence of extraterrestrials is too dangerous a step, and that elected officials represent the ultimate security risk.

When Disclosure finally moves from impossible to inevitable, politics will take the most prominent seat at the table.

Politically Incorrect

The first problem of one's "exopolitics" is deciding what to think of the Others. This will depend on the evidence that has been provided about them, and possibly whether any of them are discussed in a Disclosure statement. No doubt, one's exopolitics will also be tied in some way to their current political beliefs, whether these be liberal, conservative, radical, or anything else.

Let us speculate that Disclosure is forced (say, by an undeniable mass sighting), but no extraterrestrials are produced, and none come forward. This will cause no small headache for the ruling groups, to say nothing for the rest of us.

In that case, even the existence of the Others will be treated politically. Everything else is treated that way, from immigration to national defense; it will be the same for Disclosure. First, the President will be advised on what to do and how to do it. The advice will probably boil down to this:

✧✦✧

> "Mister President, if you decide that we need to be forthcoming on this issue, then we will need to act quickly. If our opponents get a clear picture of what is going on, they may go public before we do. If they do, you will look like part of the problem. They will taint you with the decades of lies, and you will forever be on the defensive. Say the word and we will discretely prepare your announcement—coordinating with the allies will be the toughest part—but we'll use a cover story to divert attention. Then you just go out there and lay it out. We need you to come across as open, but more than just a little bit pissed off. You need to place yourself on the side of the people and promise them more information. It's like the campaign, sir, you have to run against the Establishment."

✧✦✧

The Pottery Barn rule also applies here: You break it, you bought it. Whichever party controls the presidency will own Disclosure, an unpredictable place to be. But once the decision has been made in the White House, the only viable option for the party in power will be to jump all over it, then hope that the opposition is confused enough to be slow off the marks.

In the United States, there will be a national coming together, a closing of ranks. The party in power will reach out to the opposition in the spirit of bipartisanship, and the outsiders will have to play along. But as the days turn to weeks and the weeks into months, the disruptions and difficulties will become policy issues. The opposition leadership will then be free to embrace the President's goals, but not his methods. He and his party will be accused of incompetence and partisanship. Whichever party is in power will be accused by the opposition of acting too slowly, or too fast, or too strongly, or not strongly enough.

Beyond the policy implementation aspect, it is interesting to consider whether the two major parties in the United States will have an exopolitical "attitude" that forms with time in the world after Disclosure.

One might imagine the Democratic party tending toward inclusion. We may hear statements implying that the Others are innocent until proven guilty. They may tend to press for conciliatory gestures on the part of the nations of the Earth, and messages of peace. They—or more accurately, their constituents—will more likely see the glass as half full. They may even press for the United Nations to grow in strength and become the leading voice speaking for the Earth.

Defining the future. The rules constantly change and so does the game. A vote taking place at the United Nations Security Council. Photo courtesy of UN Photo/Mark Garten

The Republican party, in contrast, will move toward security first. They will invoke President Ronald Reagan's famous phrase from Cold War missile negotiations, "Trust, but verify." They will argue that gestures need to be made from a position of strength, given that the Others have shown such a consistent interest in human military capabilities since the 1940s.

They will certainly not trust the United Nations to speak for anyone, let alone the United States. It is to be remembered, also, that a substantial portion of Republican Party strength draws from Bible-belt Christians, who will be likely to see the Others as demonic.

Disclosure will accomplish something in American politics that has happened only rarely. Very likely, there will be a credible, capable third party arising from the chaos of the moment. Perhaps even a fourth and fifth. Disclosure will shatter the old political paradigm.

One new party finding support might be called the Aquarius party. Its agenda will be that the Others should be embraced. They will not be hardened political types, but a collection of New Age believers who see this new reality as confirmation that the Age of Aquarius is here, if only we embrace it.

Another party may favor an Earth-First approach. Its members would argue that the Others are irrelevant. They have not attacked, nor have they revealed themselves since their arrival. Humanity's problems are vast and deepening, they will say, and we must solve them ourselves. Expecting help from extraterrestrials is wishful thinking and unlikely to happen. Their slogan will be "Power to the People," and by people, they will mean humans.

There will also be those who see the Others as the beginning of end times. This is the Armageddon group, populated by doomsday thinkers, evangelicals, and survivalists. They will have much to say because many of them will have been waiting their entire lives for something this devastating. Some of them may start within the Republican Party, but they may well bolt if they feel the Republicans are not responsive enough to their beliefs.

If one thinks of the American political system as a spectrum of belief, the Disclosure world will look like this, going from pro- to con- regarding the arrival and disclosure of the Others:

AQUARIUS

DEMOCRAT

REPUBLICAN

EARTH FIRST

ARMAGEDDON

The success or failure of these new competitors for the American voters will depend on who can convert their passion into competition in the political arena. Armageddon believers may have the most passion, but some may not stay active if they think the world is ending. Earth Firsters may find themselves absorbed into the Republicans in the same way that the latter have tried to harness the Teaparty movement of 2010, or it could go the other way around, with the Republicans collapsing into the new party. The Democrats will try to appeal to Aquarians as being sympathetic to their cause but still "solid" regarding traditional national security.

It will be a political free-for-all. The winners may still be the Republican and Democratic parties, but even if they survive the battle, they will be changed by the fight to stay in power.

In nation after nation around the globe, great changes will be played out as the political deck is shuffled. The volatility of the situation is more easily seen in light of the Arab Spring of 2011.

Indeed, the Arab world will become further inflamed by Disclosure. The democratic uprisings that swept across that political landscape showed deep dissatisfaction among the people. The rest of the world discovered, much to its collective surprise, that a new generation of Arabs want a greater voice, and not necessarily one influenced by sharia law. Arab youth of today, like youth elsewhere, have grown up with the Web. Arab women are also finding their voice. We are seeing an entire culture that had been dominated for generations by a tightly authoritarian political and cultural system now, in the age of the Internet, showing cracks. Matters will become more volatile still with a growing belief that the traditional cultural patterns need to be revised. This is aside from the pandemonium likely to occur because of uncertainties in the petroleum market, up until now the main source of income to much of the Arab world. As was once said of the American Revolution, it will feel like "the world is turned upside down."

Elsewhere in the AD world, dictatorships will fall to populist uprisings while some multi-party systems may face calls for dictatorships. Change will be in the air.

Amid such turmoil that is likely within the domestic politics of so many nations, the ultimate political battle must be waged internationally. How will these many nations come together to blend their voices into a single message for the Others? Is that even possible?

Before discussing this, we need to understand the specific troubles that will be faced by the United States, for years the leading force behind the cover-up, and most probably the source of most of our knowledge of the Others.

Reclaiming Legitimate Power

The United States lacks the global power it had during the Cold War. Yet it remains, at least militarily, the world's most powerful country, and in many ways still the global agenda-setter. Many nations will view the United States with increased skepticism if its role in the UFO cover-up is established clearly. Still, its military power will be seen as the best shield possible against an outside threat, although some nations might see it as unnecessarily provocative.

In a nation founded on principles of popular sovereignty, in which Lincoln's phrase, "A government of the people, by the people, for the people," carries deep emotional resonance, it is no small matter that in the world AD, the president acts not just with Americans in mind, but the citizens of the entire planet. Many of the important issues at stake in today's world will be amplified post-Disclosure:

- Will we live in a world that promotes human freedom, or will we live in a global police state?
- In a world that is already a global village and interweaves further each day, who will make the most important decisions affecting the lives of ordinary people?
- Will we have a public culture in which truth is readily available, and in which citizens can make informed decisions about their world?
- How can Disclosure help the human-built infrastructure support our ever-increasing population with its ever-stronger thirst for energy?

✧ Can Disclosure save the natural global ecosystem from collapsing due to excessive human pressures?

Change is coming; the only question is what it will look like. That battle is being fought now; it will still be in progress when Disclosure occurs. Then, that radical act of openness on an issue of such magnitude will energize and ultimately transform the debate.

All modern presidents have been elected with the support of the wealthy and powerful, all of whom have strong interests in the promotion of an international order that they themselves dominate. This puts the Disclosure president in the middle of this battle—entirely separate from the issue of the Others and their agenda. He or she must decide what side to choose.

The first option will be to embrace the status quo of power, and to continue to navigate the ship of state through the rough waters with as little disruption as possible. Recall that for Disclosure even to happen, the powers-that-be will have had to make a decision that the cost of maintaining the cover-up was greater than the cost of letting it go. Letting go of the cover-up, however, will not mean letting go of power. Having given the president the information, and thus the go-ahead, they will now want him or her to help them re-assemble the system in a way that continues to grant them control.

The second option is to embrace change. It would mean using the act of Disclosure as a personal release from duty to the puppet-masters. It would mean working for reasoned, humanitarian policies to bring about a peaceful transition and a courageous confrontation of the truth.

Will the world get another Millard Fillmore, or a new Abraham Lincoln?

The Disclosure president will already know that he has thrown the dice and bet his presidency on this single announcement. He will have had company, of course. Many other world leaders will have thrown their own reputations into the fire of Disclosure, but it is the American President to whom the world will look.

His advisors will carry messages from the power elite that the world is so troubled now that the President must keep the peace at all costs. As the expression goes, he must "dance with the one who brought him."

It will be a powerful argument. No president will want the world to come completely unhinged on his shift; better to play it safe. Yet the A.D. world has no safe course of action. Knowing this, the Disclosure President may choose another way. He may choose to go to war. Not with the Others, but with the Breakaway Group.

In that eventuality, he would actively work to reclaim full constitutional authority in the name of the people. This does not mean seizing power in the form of a dictatorship, but it does mean enforce his authority over the runaway black budget, and particularly over the Majestic operation insofar as it utilizes the resources of the U.S. military and U.S. tax dollars, and insofar as it operates on U.S. territory.

In the disruption that follows Disclosure, if the president were to assume this level of power, he would understand that his life would be in danger. Yet, perhaps in a moment of quiet while sitting in the Oval Office, reflecting on the actions of those who came before him, he may decide that the risk is worth it because the times demand it. The opportunity to set things right may not return for a long time.

He may survey the political landscape and realize that the dynamic has shifted and that he has more legitimate power than the secret-keepers. There would be allies. They will include the people—not only U.S. citizens, but citizens from every country on Earth. And he would see the posturing on Capitol Hill, the investigation committees being formed, and the subpoenas being issued.

He might sit up at night with a trusted advisor, and together they may war-game the pros and the cons of his next move. They will agree on a plan of action. The Attorney General will be brought in to make sure the language is clear, legal, and above misinterpretation. A single loyal executive secretary would be brought in before daylight to type up the statement. It would be released in the morning before any time for leaks or attempts to interfere.

✧✦✧

> "By Executive Order, the President of the United States releases all individuals from black-world, ET-related secrecy oaths. In the accompanying statement, the President points out that it is the contention of the Attorney General that the oaths that kept the secret all these years have been superseded by the act of Disclosure. He is now calling on the men and women who were part of the cover-up to come forward as a patriotic act of cleansing and to deliver their sworn testimony before the Truth and Reconciliation Committee. Those that do will be granted immunity from charges, so long as they tell the entire truth. He orders the FBI, the DHS and the CIA to coordinate protection for all witnesses and their families who wish to cooperate wherever they are worldwide."

✧✦✧

This may strike you as a rosy scenario. After all, the Disclosure president may be as co-opted and corrupted as most of his predecessors, but it may not matter. Primal forces of people power will be unleashed, and the end result may still be that the Breakaway Group's days will be numbered.

In terms of the global situation, no matter what the actions of the U.S. President, there will still be a power vacuum. If the U.S. Disclosure President is strong, that is to say actively involved in a struggle to reassert the power of the American people to control their own government, he will be tied up in battle at home. If he is weak, he will be damaged by the fact that his own country will be seen as the prime architect of the many decades of subterfuge.

Elsewhere, other nations will be roiling with their own issues. The political leadership of many countries—France, England, Russia, and so on—may find that they, too, were duped by the Breakaway Group which was, at its peak, one of most highly functioning global organizations ever created. Other countries may want to ignore Disclosure, but find themselves struggling with its collateral damage of economic dislocation. No one will have emerged unscathed.

We cannot forget the Others in this equation. Whether or not they reveal themselves more openly, they will remain a focus of attention. Exopolitics demands that the nearly 200 nations in the world learn how to act and react to these changed circumstances in a coherent and effective manner.

Currently, exopolitical activists accept, as an article of faith, that the one piece of enduringly good news about any public revelation and acceptance—whether these Others are benign or nefarious—is that their presence will serve to unite the people of Earth as never before. Nationalism will suffer as we see ourselves as Earthlings first, and distinct nationalities second. An international problem needs an international solution, they say. It will be necessary to establish open, international, collaboration on a full array of political, scientific, social, economic, cultural, and religious issues.

Having this degree of international cooperation will be pointless if humanity responds in an uncoordinated fashion. What if, after all, we are dealing with a real threat? Coordination will be essential. What if, even barring a dire immediate threat, we wish to transition to a new energy paradigm? In such a case, uncoordinated action can have severe and negative consequences.

Another Way to Look at It

The elephant in the room AD is none other than the United Nations. After Disclosure, the U.N. will be very active and receive much attention. Resolutions will be passed and committees formed. There will be more work than ever to consider, a shifting trail of facts, and discussions about the correct course of action. But the announcement that the Earth has visitors will not suddenly transform the United Nations into a gathering place for the brotherhood of man. Instead, the unprecedented level of stress upon it will lead to the realization that it is not up to the task at hand.

The greatest issue to split the United Nations will not be the Others and the difficult debate about what should be done. Instead, it will be a simple definition of what the U.N. is meant to be in the changed conditions. There will be impassioned debates about how powerful the organization should be. No one will agree. Meanwhile, the problems will grow and this international gridlock will occasion despair around the globe.

Then, one of the members will act. Although the country we are about to suggest is an example only, to provide a scenario, the point is that it will be a non-traditional outreach by a country not normally associated with global leadership.

Imagine the country is Brazil. During the years of cover-up, this country had its own thriving group of UFO investigators and a military that tried to grapple with the problem. In 1957, four years before the Betty and Barney Hill case in the United States, the abduction of Antonio Villa Boas occurred there. In 1958, the Trindade Island UFO photos were taken off its coast. In 1986, as many as 20 UFOs were seen and tracked over Brazil by ground radar and at least six airplanes in a case that was widely publicized. In 1996, an alleged crash of a UFO took place there, near a small town called Varginha.

Brazil also happens to be the fifth-largest country by geographical area and population. When, in our hypothetical scenario, it invites representatives from China, Russia, and the United States to discuss the lack of coordinated response to the Others, these nations respond in the affirmative. When the four leaders emerge from the talks, they announce formal invitations to key countries to join them in Sao Paulo to continue the discussion.

The President of Brazil is suddenly the man of the hour, and his country is the place. The leaders say they are not challenging the United Nations, they are simply moving past it, looking for a fresh start, acting out of a desperate need, expressed worldwide, to stop the fighting and get some work done.

They form a group, announced in Brazil as the *Alianca planetaria externas*, or the Planetary Alliance External. The world's media immediately shortens it to PAX, which everyone likes, because it means "peace" in Latin.

PAX begins monthly meetings in Sao Paulo. The first thing members agree on is that the purpose of their meetings is not to surrender their national sovereignty. Their constituents back home, having seen the failure at the U.N., seem to agree.

The Past Actually *Is* Prologue

Our world today is in a situation analogous to that faced by the young United States of America more than two centuries ago. The American colonists had fought for independence from the monarchy of Great Britain, and the concept of liberty was central to all political discourse. The idea of instituting a new monarchy was discarded in favor of the more radical idea of a republic, something that had only succeeded in the past on a limited, small scale, and which only once had existed over a large area: ancient Rome.

A basic problem was, how to ensure sufficient freedom for the 13 newly independent states, while keeping them strong enough to provide for self-defense. In other words, what was the balance between centralization and decentralization?

The first answer was to decentralize. This was the early United States under the Articles of Confederation. Immediately, problems arose because the young nation was already far more knitted together than people realized. The central government had almost no power; it had no president (only a Congress), and even lacked the power to tax (having to request funds from the states). Each state set its own currency and tariff policy, so that if one state instituted high tariffs, these would be negated by a neighboring state that eliminated them, which in fact happened. The situation was untenable for the long term, especially for such a large nation as the young United States. There were calls to create a system with stronger centralized powers.

Such calls were anathema to many of the patriots who had fought for independence. Why did we bother, they said, if we are to replace one king with another? Centralized, concentrated power, then as now, was fiercely distrusted. The solution was an ingenious compromise: a federalized system with checks and balances. The central government was strengthened considerably and still answerable to the people. The states retained considerable (although less) independence of action. And finally, the piece that enabled the anti-Federalists to live with the compromise: The Bill of Rights, which codified the basic, inalienable rights that each citizen would forever possess. The new solution was not perfect (it retained the institution of slavery, for instance), but it created a structure with great flexibility and durability.

Now, in the 21st century, our world continues to move away from a system of independent nations. Corporations engulf the globe, spanning nations, answerable only to shareholder value. Today, they are like feudal barons who have divided up the world's resources. National laws are subverted by their power, and international political structures are too weak to stop them. This is the current structure of the "New World Order." It does not have to be this way, though. The advent of Disclosure can prompt the promotion of a federalized, global system of governance that is not under corporate domination, which in fact submits them to enforceable laws, and which also has an enforceable global "Bill of Rights."

No system of "One World" government will work. Nationalism is still too strong and it still has its advantages. But the arrival of the Others guarantees that the status quo is also unacceptable. It demands a new vision, and a pragmatic global system that will eventually replace the faltering United Nations, just as the United Nations replaced the faltering League of Nations.

Creating a stable, flexible, and fair international system will require an exceptional degree of vision, pragmatism, ethics, dedication, persistence, and courage. We do not know if it will happen. However, we know this: it is surely possible, and it is what should be done. For an equitable future for humanity, it must be done.

Some of the issues that ought to come up early in the deliberations of a globalized, federalized system, should be:

- How to research and implement the many solutions inherent in UFO technology to the problems facing our society today, and how to ensure that these are safely managed for the greater good of all.

- ✧ How to transition human society safely away from its petroleum-based global economy.
- ✧ How to reign in and manage the culture of runaway secrecy.
- ✧ How, generally speaking, to meet the challenge posed by the Others.

In short, this process would oversee the transformation of our civilization.

Although we present a positive path for world leaders, a path that we believe has a good chance of being a benefit to humanity, we must not delude ourselves. Post-Disclosure matters may continue to develop according to the trends of the past many decades.

This is the trend of growing international corporate power, of centralized state power, of ever-greater regulation of citizens, and of even more intrusion into the private lives of people via electronic surveillance (both in public places like metropolitan areas and inside your computer). It is the trend toward a permanent state of "Code Yellow" within the United States. It is a trend to distract and control populations from the reality of the world around them. It is, therefore, a trend to siphon power from the public realm to the private realm, reserved only for those few who possess the resources and manage the levers of power in order to maintain themselves in their positions.

If it turns out that there are energy solutions in UFO technology, as it surely appears, then it is equally likely that some of those solutions could be adapted for weaponry. It would be of paramount importance to prevent a free-energy device that can heat a house indefinitely from being converted into a bomb that could wipe out a nation. Ensuring safety over this process might involve controls and surveillance measures that have already begun with the Homeland Security revolution following 9/11. This will no doubt meet with a great deal of resistance.

Other issues would also be tricky, but ultimately resolvable. What if, within a generation or two after Disclosure, the rest of the world gets the ability to do what the Breakaway Group is alleged to be doing now, traveling potentially off-world in exotic craft to places that are energy-sufficient, which have oxygen below-ground, and so on? Would the powers of the Earth at that time allow people simply to go off around the solar system, colonizing at will? In fact, they might, but then again maybe not. We may see a variation of the activities and struggles that occurred during Europe's age of expansion and colonization, perhaps with new declarations of independence, as well.

This struggle will not be resolved overnight. It will take years, decades, generations, centuries.

Besides the basic political issues, there will be other key concerns: world poverty, climate change, pollution, possible extinction of our species, and many others. These will also be on the table.

Big Brother Versus Big Other

In the post-AD world, our exopolitics will not be fully in our control. It seems clear that the other intelligences—the Others—will be in the picture. The three main possibilities are:

1. **Constructive engagement.** If they admit their presence openly, we can begin a formal process of interaction. We should make it clear that they have no right to interfere. Our planet, our society, and our lives are at stake. We must control our destiny.
2. **Benign Neglect.** This seems to be the current policy. They interfere, at least covertly, and we ignore it. This way of doing business is going to wear very thin, post-Disclosure. It is one thing to debate whether something is happening and take no action because it is unclear what to do. But if something is happening, and you know it, and they know you know it, then interfere-and-ignore simply is at odds with our human nature. Still, if humanity is not in a position to do anything about it, that may be a long-term result.
3. **Hostile Convergence.** Undeniably, the most frightening option. Namely, that at least some of our visitors mean us harm, whether it be phasing out the human species as we know it, or some other form of control and manipulation. If this is so, as we said earlier, humans will resist when cornered.

The mind reels at the implications of some of the other wildcards of contact if they come to pass, and how they would affect and possibly destroy progress toward a reasonable future for humanity in the shadow of Disclosure. The most disturbing one may involve the infiltration of our society by the Others.

What if it comes out that some people in our society are actually not *of* us, but who are *with* the Others?

Is this so difficult to believe? If the the Others understand the trajectory of humanity's technological development, they would probably know full well that within another few generations, humanity might pose some genuine problems for them to contend with. They might decide that when this happens, the "right" people are governing the world. Wouldn't it be logical for them to have their "people" working on the inside, so to speak, managing the human hierarchy?

Even aside from the issue of control, abduction researchers such as Budd Hopkins, David Jacobs, and others have concluded that an important component of the abduction phenomenon includes creating a hybrid species. Presumably these hybrids at some point might be living among us.

If the Grays are a kind of biological artificial intelligence designed and built for space travel, then their arrival on Earth, a planet with a different atmosphere and gravity than their own, would pose dangers to them. Perhaps the mission statement embedded in each Gray is to create a life-form using the indigenous body of the prevailing intelligent species. Maybe that is why it has taken so long—generations—to accomplish.

What would our reaction be if we learned that something like this had occurred? In other words, if we learned that "they" in effect had taken over control of our all-too-human infrastructure? Or if they had managed us all along, throughout our history? There would probably be many people who might throw up their hands and say, "Fine. Whatever. Let them run the world." But not everyone would feel so generous. A political firestorm would be in the making. There might just be a long-term political movement that attempts to determine who the "infiltrators" are. We might experience an alien-hunting McCarthy-era.

This could quickly get very dangerous, both for reasons of public vigilantism, as well as for the reaction it might engender from the Others. Still, in the event that our society and culture *are* under subversive attack, many would argue that humanity needs to get a handle on the matter now and deal with civil liberties later.

Already, without reference to the threat of "Others," humanity has started down the road of citizen control. Consider the Internet, for example. It is not simply nations such as China, Iran, Saudi Arabia, and North Korea that seek to control access to the Internet. Nations such as Australia, the United Kingdom, the United States, and other societies with long traditions of freedom have been passing laws to intrude upon and restrict Internet access, and have been putting out feelers to see just how far they can go.[12]

Within the United States, various cocktails of laws have been passed during the Clinton, Bush, and Obama administrations to enable government surveillance of citizen Internet activity. Starting in 2005, news reports began to assert that the NSA was conducting warrantless spying on phone and email communications of people inside the United States, and that it was secretly collecting phone call records of millions of Americans. They were doing this from data provided by major telecommunications companies such as AT&T. Despite several legal challenges, the program continues to exist under the Obama administration.[13]

Developments like this are merely the tip of the iceberg. The legal revolution undergone in post-9/11 America has been formidable, but really only codified the changes that had long been taking place. Rather like a debutante, 9/11 prompted the "coming out party" of the National Security State.

All things being equal, liberty-loving people world-wide would agree that this is a bad thing. And though it is not easy to find passion to defend the secret-keepers of the Breakaway Group, we have not been allowed to know all the facts they have. If they have knowledge that causes them to believe humanity is in the midst of a silent invasion, then their ramping up of security, surveillance, and military power could feasibly be defended. If that is so, however, it virtually guarantees that the most intense debate AD, in a political sense, will mirror the 9/11 post-mortem, especially if there is a rush to security followed by a longing for freedom.

Suddenly, in a silent invasion scenario, martial law seems very plausible. If superior beings from somewhere else have come here, and their designs on us do not involve blowing up the planet as they do in the movies, but taking it over without a fight, then Disclosure will set powerful forces into motion. As both Lincoln and Roosevelt did to win their respective wars, the Disclosure president may lead the charge to fight back first and sort out the damage later.

Again, we come face-to-face with the great unknown in the debate over Disclosure. The people most complicit in the cover-up know things that we do not. After seven decades, we certainly should hope they have a better idea than we do. If, however, after all their advantages of money and security, they do not know any more than the rest of us, we should fire them for incompetence if we can.

Imagine what the top-level of the Breakaway Group may know by now. It is entirely possible that the Others have been here, interacting with the Earth and humanity for eons. Throughout all of human history, our species would have had no ability to deal with them in any way approaching parity. Surely, they could easily avoid detection if they wished.

Recall that our amazing, magical technology is all recent. Consider what it meant to belong to a small agricultural or nomadic community anywhere on Earth a mere 300 years ago. At that time, the total human population was one-tenth what it is today. There were no telephones, no automobiles, no locomotives, not even bicycles. There were people and horses and carts and sailing ships. Most people lived their lives within a small geographic area, interacting with the same people in the same small village for their entire lives. Most could not read or write, and there were still entire cultures that had no writing at all. In such a situation, anyone who saw a craft or object from one of the intelligent groups that were here on Earth had virtually no options. Amazing sightings might be discussed with family members or friends, and perhaps become passed along as local legends. That would be about it. For millennia, this is how it had been.

Then everything changed. Human population began the sharp increase that continues to this day—in 2011 we surpassed seven billion. Science took hold of our civilization and transformed us in ways scarcely imaginable to previous generations. Within the blink of a cosmic eye, humanity went from being a society of horses pulling carts to one in which we now stand at the brink of quantum computing, advanced AI, nanotech, and biotech. We are about to re-invent ourselves as a society, as a civilization, as a species. Our means of detecting and recording UFOs is vastly better than it ever was, and this will only improve.

Is there any possibility that these Others would not know this? If they have been here all along, they know of our development. They see us now, poised and ready to leap into their world. Perhaps not as equals, no. But as scientific progress is not a linear thing, it is just possible that we are on the verge of transformation that is not quantitative, but qualitative. Something utterly different, more substantial, more formidable.

Yes, they must know this. We must ask ourselves: What is their attitude toward this?

They might have taken only a passing interest in humanity for many ages, while they went about their business, here on Earth and perhaps elsewhere. Perhaps our recent development as a scientific species was something they did not anticipate, or perhaps it has been something they have been waiting for.

Of course, if they have been here for a long time, humanity is possibly a long-standing project. Have we been modified by them? Have they managed us in some way throughout our history? If so, did they guide us to an understanding of science? Did they influence our religions and spiritual beliefs? And if so (considering the violence inspired by so many religions) did they do so maliciously, or with an intent to help?

Or could it be that, despite the suggestive hints left by ancient drawings, carvings, artifacts, and architecture, that the Others are indeed only recent arrivals? If so, did they arrive when they realized we were on the scientific fast-track?

The answers to these questions, if we ever get them, will influence how we respond to them. If we get no answer, we will surely develop countless think tanks to study and debate the possibilities.

In such an event, what might those think tanks conclude? They would study the available UFO evidence, just as many researchers did before them. Judging from the sightings, possible abduction experiences, and other encounters with what may have been some of these beings, they would be left in some confusion.

For instance, why have the Others alternately hidden and revealed themselves through the years? The majority of UFO sightings, after all, have not been over major populated areas, or seen by large numbers of people—but some have. Are the Others being coy in some manner? Are they trying to get our attention? Why show up so blatantly in certain places, such as the lower Hudson Valley in the early 1980s, or the collapsing Soviet Union in the late 1980s, or Phoenix in 1997, or Stephenville, Texas in 2008, or China in 2010 and 2011? Are they nudging us? Slowly making themselves more and more obviously known? If so, the conclusion might be that they have been preparing us all these years for contact.

Then there are the crop circles. Although there are claims that the formations go back many decades, even centuries, reliable reports started in the 1970s. At that time, most were simple affairs. By 1990, however, they had attained an awe-inspiring complexity, size, and precision that defies common sense. Despite the proliferation of hoaxers, there appear to be distinguishable differences between the "real" and the "fake" circles, including biological oddities at the nodes of the stalks in genuine crop circle formations, the perfection of the creations themselves, the astonishing size of some of them, and the speed with which the genuine circles are made—typically overnight, and several apparently in the middle of the day with no one seeing the culprit.

Some have speculated that the circles are a clandestine human operation. Perhaps they were "scrolled" from a geosynchronous satellite using precision microwave technology. If so, then why? Is some black-budget operation playing a head-game with humanity in the fields of southwestern England and central Ohio, making people believe that aliens are creating mathematical and artistic masterpieces in our corn fields? Or that some secret team of Leonardo da Vincis continues to evade being caught? For, no matter who is making them, these formations are among the great artistic creations of our era.

We should hope that the Others are behind them. If so, they are probably trying to nudge us into a realization of a higher intelligence. This would surely be a good thing.

Author/abductee Whitley Strieber has written nearly a dozen books on the subject, and claims to have experienced ongoing abductions. He has felt personal contact with the Others, (or the Visitors, as he has called them), and believes that their agenda may involve a warning about an impending apocalypse here on Earth. Other abductees, too, have often claimed they have been exposed to images of environmental disaster.

If these people are to be believed, the Others are warning us about the danger to our planet through nuclear proliferation and ecological meltdown. And while, as silent invaders, they may not have changed our ways, an open Disclosure of their presence may lead relatively quickly to an emerging global consensus about saving the Earth, realizing how precious it is.

But the extreme variety of UFO sightings, the many types of vehicles seen, the various types of "aliens" themselves, will lead to a major problem for future think tanks. It is probably a current problem inside Majestic. This is how to fill out the "scorecard" of just who is who.

The maddening aspect of a post-Disclosure world is that we may not be much further along in knowing just who we are dealing with than we are today. Frankly, what is most unsettling is that there is no guarantee that Majestic does, either.

There are so many possibilities to contemplate, so it is easy to lose oneself in speculation. Still, if we observe the phenomenon not as scientists demanding proof, but rather as intelligence specialists trying to assemble the most likely scenario, we might conclude that there are multiple groups with (probably) multiple agendas, here to visit Earth, perhaps live on Earth, and to observe humanity at this particular juncture in history. We may well be, at the dawn of the new millennium, the greatest show in this sector of the galaxy.

Our Universe, Our Planet, Ourselves

Disclosure is the ultimate wake-up call. Recognizing that other intelligences find our world and ourselves of interest will have a powerful impact on our consciousness.

Open knowledge of them will simultaneously turn us inward and outward. For exopolitics is not only about our relations with the Others, it about how we organize among ourselves in relation to *them*.

People will begin to grasp that, compared to our differences with the Others, the differences among ourselves in terms of race, sex, nationality, and religion are insignificant. This realization will create a new political opportunity. A global consensus will emerge about saving the Earth. We will realize more fully, more painfully, how glorious and precious our beautiful blue world is. Perhaps this is the true message from the Others. But even if not, it will be our own realization.

This new way of looking at ourselves may enable us to save the planet from environmental disaster, as we find ourselves able to work together to stop ecological ravages and the massive loss of species diversity. We may even stop our own extinction.

At the same time, humanity will look outward. Whatever our assessment of these other beings, whether they be hostile, benevolent, indifferent, or some combination of the three, we will recognize a connection with forms of life beyond our world. It will be a key moment in the history of human consciousness. "If we ever establish contact with extraterrestrial life, it will reveal to us our true place in the universe," wrote author Isaac Asimov. "And with that comes the beginning of wisdom."

Some of us will begin to advocate for spreading the human race beyond this cradle of life into the vast universe, probably using alien technology as an impetus. It will be the ultimate exopolitical act to devote our resources to building these craft.

In success, a future generation of exopoliticians may save our home only to make it possible for some of us to leave it.

Vignette #8:

Poll Results: Emerging Views After Disclosure

OpinionDynamics

Abstract: Emerging Views after Disclosure

Poll Question:

Since the public disclosure of the presence of extraterrestrial life here on Earth, describe your level of confidence in the United States government to handle the matter correctly.

A.D. + One Week

39%	Not Sure
23%	Confident
17%	Skeptical
12%	Extremely Confident
09%	Extremely Skeptical

A.D. + One Year

32%	Extremely Skeptical
27%	Skeptical
21%	Confident
15%	Not Sure
05%	Extremely Confident

A.D. + Ten Years

30%	Skeptical
25%	Confident
17%	Extremely Confident
15%	Extremely Skeptical
13%	Not Sure

ANALYSIS

The initial shock of Disclosure was followed in the first 12 months with a tremendous degree of skepticism regarding the government. In the span of 12 years, the number of people who are skeptical appears to be nearly identical with those expressing confidence. This may be evidence that the government is slowly reclaiming some marginal degree of citizen confidence.

Chapter 9

Open Letters: Inside/Outside

Courage is resistance to fear,
mastery of fear—not absence of fear.

—Mark Twain

No event in the history of civilization will shock more than the realization that we have company in the universe, and that Others are involved with us. It is not simply the greatest story in human history; it may be *the* story of human history. We can only hope that as this reality unfolds, we will also come to realize, as will the Others, that humans are one-of-a-kind, worthwhile, and have something to contribute in the overall scheme of things.

We do not subscribe to the view, often espoused as a joke, that Earth is some backwater, out-of-the-way planet in the middle of nowhere, and that we would be of no interest to other life forms.

Whether or not the universe is "teeming" with life, any expression of it—particularly one with intelligence—is bound to be of interest to other intelligences. The Earth is bursting with an astonishing variety of life, and humanity is a unique and often-contradictory life-form. Indeed, there is plenty to recommend this planet and its inhabitants for visitations by curious Others.

Let us, for one final time, return to the famous Brookings Institute report, because even in 1960 there was hope that learning "we are not alone" might be good news.

The knowledge that life existed in other parts of the universe might lead to a greater unity of men on Earth, based of the oneness of man or on the age-old assumption that any stranger is threatening. Much would depend on what, if anything, was communicated between man and the other beings. The fact that such beings existed might become simply one of the facts of life, but probably not one calling for action.

The lack of urgency in this statement was predicated on the likelihood that first contact would be long-distance, not in our face. The authors of the report assumed that any communication between humans and Others would be punctuated by years of silence, due to the distance of the stars and the limitations of radio communication. They did not consider that we had already attracted visits to our world.

To us, that is the ultimate call to action. We have written three "open letters" as we conclude this book.

1. First, to the unelected people who keep this secret contained to this very day.
2. Second, to the Others who have created the situation in which we find ourselves.
3. Third, to those of us who believe we can handle the truth and are prepared to help make that day happen. That is, quite possibly, to you.

To The Keepers of the Secret

We know who you are. We have saved this last chapter for you.

You might have been called Majestic-12, or MJ-12, or Majic at one time or another. Perhaps you still are. Perhaps you are the same group that was once labeled the "Silence Group." Maybe you are a private enterprise group, living part-time in our world, and the rest of the time in your own society—the one we have labeled here as the Breakaway Group.

It does not matter. You know the outlines of the truth, and you have spent untold fortunes delaying the day when you share it with the world. You must think about that responsibility you have taken upon your shoulders. You must wonder occasionally if perhaps the time has come to lighten the burden.

We know that at least a few of you are reading this book, or you have assigned someone to read it and summarize it. This is not our ego talking; given that the phenomenon is real and the secret is being kept, it is obvious that someone's job must be to understand the issues relating to Disclosure, to gauge the public's evolving attitude, and to calibrate contingencies.

Although some believe that you are preparing the world for gradual Disclosure, we are skeptical. You probably have done some analysis of what A.D. will look like, an analysis that resides in deeply classified "contingency plans." In our analysis, you seem to be in no hurry to use them. However, you should be.

We have written this book to help prepare the world for Disclosure, knowing full well that such a duty should never have fallen to people like us, but rather to elected government officials. You created the vacuum; we merely stepped into it. You have read eight other chapters to reach this one. Some of it may have struck you as naive, and some of it may have made your blood run cold, knowing that we know what you do with your lives, even if we do not know exactly who you are. You would not be human if you did not feel some guilt over how far this situation has gone, and for so long.

Do you really believe that only you have the right to know this information? Is it your view that by blinding the rest of humanity to this reality, the world's problems will be easier to solve? Or is there something else at work here, something about power, even a misplaced sense of entitlement and birthright?

There must be some of you who are ready for this next step, some who understand that whatever the original motivations for the secrecy, it is long past time to deal with it. Time only makes the problem harder to manage.

We sympathize to some extent with your situation. If the positions were reversed, it is possible we might have acted as you have. Because we do not know all that you know, we can only speculate.

Inside your group, the inside joke may be that you can't be "a little bit" forthcoming on this issue any more than a woman can be "a little bit" pregnant. But that may not be entirely true. At least initially, the public may accept the notion that some information must remain classified for national security reasons, and that other information is being shared with other countries as a comprehensive plan is worked out. Eventually, partial disclosure will lead to full Disclosure—yes—but as this road is traveled, there will be time for people to grasp one concept at a time before moving on to the next. Disclosure can come in stages, and in fact that is realistically the only way it can proceed. It has to start somewhere, however.

The decision to move ahead will come from within, or it will come from without. If within, it will be because some of you concede that the time has come for reasons that are either self-serving or pragmatic. If it comes without, it will be because events dictate no other choice. You must sense that current inaction guarantees eventual compulsion. If you wait until forced, the public will judge you more harshly than if you step forward now, into the light of openness, and speak the truth. It will be easier to spin a voluntary Disclosure than a forced one.

A great divide separates the world of today from the world of your fathers and grandfathers. That world, shaken by wars both hot and cold, was judged unable to withstand the shock that Disclosure would bring. This world has seen deep into the vastness of our universe with powerful technology and, instinctively, we all know that we are not alone. You will not destroy us by confirming the basic fact. We will hear the truth, absorb it, and move forward with our lives, changed as they might be. The details are another matter, but they should be worked out with representatives of the people rather than an unelected, secret society. Pass the baton.

You have had a lifetime to assess the situation privately. Now is the time to discuss it publicly. In every time, there is a season, and the season of openness is upon us. Public opinion has shifted through the years to where this next act is inevitable.

Moving beyond. As we explore the universe, history begins again. "Double Star Station" by Kimmo Isokoski, used with permission.

Have you developed new technologies that put humanity on a better footing with the Others? Why keep it to yourselves, hidden away for a war that may not come? Share it with the world, unleash it for the betterment of humankind. If the technology you have come across still bewilders your best scientific minds, then bring it into the light. Let the millions of scientists around the world add their effort and understanding to the problem.

Mostly, you need to understand that we already know. Not the details that you have, to be sure, but the macro idea of contact. By coming clean, you will allow us to take control of our governments again, to reach out to other leadership around the world, and to move forward in uniting the Earth.

This is happening, anyway. Every public relations expert on the planet—including those in the very military that spawned your group—knows that the best outcome in today's world comes in getting ahead of the story. Assuming you are interested in controlling the spin of this reality, you cannot successfully spin from behind, only from the lead.

Take a stand, come forward, admit your mistakes, and claim your victories. Give us the truth that we deserve, the truth as you know it.

Many of you will still have a place—based on your own expertise—in the world as it re-forms A.D. Some of you will need to retire and step aside. A few, probably not so many, may face penalties. But all of you stand before God as you know God, and before your fellow humans, with a dark stain of lies across your souls.

The truth will set you free.

To the Others ✦✦✦

We know less about you than you do about us. On that basis, establishing anything like an open relationship with you is not especially practical. Based on the history of your actions, you want it this way.

And yet you of all beings must know that time will not stop. Our civilization, our species, is on a trajectory. The day will come when we find you, openly, without question. We believe that day is coming soon, whether it be five years, 20 years, or even a century more, it is as inevitable as day follows night.

It may be that, knowing this eventuality cannot be stopped, you have elected to control us in some way, to manipulate us. If this is so, you play a dangerous game. You have seen how quickly the human race can learn, how quickly it can transform itself. If you are seeking to control us, particularly if this is for your benefit at our expense, then your plan will eventually backfire. For the day will come when we learn of this deception. At that point, things may become difficult for you.

It may also be that you support us, this world, and all the life that lives here. Naturally, we would like that to be so, and we know that some researchers have found reasons to believe it. If this is the case, however, we must ask you why you stand by while Earth, so magnificent, so precious, continues to slide into chaos and disaster. We do not look for a savior; we know that, having created this mess, we must clean it up. But it strikes us as odd that, if you are in fact benefactors, you seem to be standing by as helplessly as the great masses of humanity.

Perhaps you look on us and our world as a kind of zoo. Maybe it even amuses you as you observe the spectacle that is humanity. We are something like a trapeze artist on a high wire. If we reach the other side of the wire, our society will be even more fascinating, more challenging, than ever before.

And yet we may fall. If we do, if our infrastructure suffers a significant collapse, that could change things, at least for a while. Is this why you are here—to see whether or not humanity will successfully move to the next level of civilization? Or, have we simply evolved enough that we are now intruding on your reality more and more, and are becoming a positive nuisance?

Whatever the answer, we can assure you that the day will come when we know it. Our species may seem ignorant and blind, and it is true that for most of our history it has been so. But it will not always be so. Things are changing. The day will come when you are forced to deal with us in some manner more substantial, more mature, than you have hitherto.

To Those of Us Coming Out of the Dark ✦✦✦

The very fact that you read this book says something about you. Whether or not you gave the matter any previous thought, you are now an activist in the Disclosure movement.

The struggle to end UFO secrecy has been going on since the 1940s. To our older readers, we encourage you to join this struggle because the history of the world during your lifetime demonstrates its necessity. You know in your heart that change is overdue. To our younger readers, born into the throes of a world in transformation, we ask you to be visionaries. We ask you to incorporate your own worldview of the Earth as a small, blue planet that needs healing with another, grand, view: that knowing we are not alone will create its own positive change in our lives.

The first step in effecting this change is to acknowledge what Eleanor Roosevelt said, "No one can make you feel inferior without your consent." You are not a "UFO nut" who can be dismissed or laughed at. Have no fear. That wind you feel at your back is the truth. That others do not yet feel it says more about them than you.

Although ending UFO secrecy is inevitable, the kind of Disclosure that comes with it still must be decided. Ditto in regards to how we all handle the new reality. To get the best possible outcome:

- We must be willing to discuss this topic patiently and rationally with people who do not yet share our understanding.
- We must increase personal knowledge of the topic, in order to become clear and persuasive.

We need to bring our game up. This means that more is not always better. More misspelled, angry rants littered with unfounded assumptions and leaps of faith do not help. They only provide the secret-keepers, and the rank-and-file of citizens, with the ammunition they need to dismiss us as amateurish. The crazier we sound, the lower our public credibility. As in public speaking, so too in public writing: learn your facts, avoid hyperbole, and lower your voice.

This is so, even if the final answers to this mystery are more bizarre, more shattering, than anything we have even suggested in this book. The reason is simple: you cannot lead unless you have followers. Those around you, who know nothing of this topic, nothing of its profound implications, cannot always so easily dive into its depths. One step at a time is the surest way to keep other heads nodding, one step at a time in a logical, defensible sequence.

Of course, it is perfectly normal to speculate. It is even smart to do so, providing you distinguish between what you know and what you think you know, and providing you remind others of this difference. No one has every answer, and no one will expect you to have them all, either. Be comfortable with uncertainty.

Now is the time to begin the transition from an Internet collected group of "conspiracy theorists" to a potent political force of openness and honesty. We need to elevate our standards and take inspiration from political movements of the past. The civil rights movement may be the best example of any. No political group can ever act perfectly, nor will we always agree with our leaders, nor they with themselves. Martin Luther King Jr. and Malcolm X did not see eye-to-eye on tactics, but they both knew there was a mountain to climb.

If the UFO/ET reality is about a powerful signal that is obscured by the distortion of noise, it is time to focus on the signal. Even in writing this book, we were mindful that we needed to present an argument in a sequence that would not alienate readers needing to understand the basics before appreciating the nuances. As an example, it is important that people understand and accept that at least some UFOs are physical, structured craft from somewhere that is not here. They must become comfortable with that basic understanding before they can appreciate Zeti-Reticuli, Nordics, abductions, and other challenging concepts.

We have to stop talking only to ourselves. Although it is nice to meet with other like-minded individuals in meetings and conferences and even virtually, this is not where the battle will be won. Posting on our own websites will not force the hand of the secret-keepers. We need to move beyond our circles into the circles of others. Talk to people who do not believe or know what you know. Persuade them. Spend less time with those who agree with you, more with those who disagree.

The battle for UFO Disclosure comes from millions and millions of individual conversations, individually and in groups, with people who simply do not believe. It involves speaking to our friends, family, and colleagues in a calm and rational way. This often involves substantial bravery. After more than 60 years of denial and ridicule, it is always easier to keep quiet about this, especially in polite company. The antidote to ridicule is knowledge.

This involves work. Read more. Think more critically. Remember that you are an activist in a wholly new kind of political movement. So many years ago, during the Vietnam War, the images that motivated change were on the news every night. In our movement, the images and facts are not on the news. Quite the opposite. We seek to force acknowledgement of a reality that has long been hushed up and swept away. We must explain that we are not waiting for radio telescopes to confirm other life in the universe. We are waiting for the rest of the world to wake up and see that which has been placed before them, but which most have refused to see.

Do not ask politicians if they believe in UFOs. In today's climate, their only appropriate answer to that question will be to dodge it. Instead ask them to their faces, during campaigns, if they support full disclosure of UFO related material. Ask them if they know anyone who has ever seen a UFO. Ask them if they believe we are alone in the universe. They can answer these questions without getting branded by their opponents, and it helps us build a consensus.

Particularly important to remember is that most of the people involved in secrecy have their own friends and neighbors. They live in nice homes, get married, have children, maybe even go to soccer games. But they also lead a double life in which they carry this incredible secret around with them, every day. Anyone you meet in government, aerospace, technology and the military—particularly those in private industry as contractors—is a potential candidate for being one of them, or knowing someone who is. Speak your mind to these people about the need to end the secrecy.

Be the change you want to see. You know this is real. Go about your daily life and make sure you let others know that you know. Change the dynamic one person at a time.

Then, one day, when the mass sighting or the physical evidence or the deathbed confession pushes the issue to the top of international agenda, the secret-keepers will look around and realize that we already know, and they will finally come clean.

It can happen. It starts with you.

Our Last Thought

The journey we have taken to write this book has been life-altering. We have been forced to consider things that others have danced over lightly in previous books, or even ignored altogether. We have had to look inside our own souls to try seeing the souls of our fellow humans, even those of the Others.

The Others are the great wildcard in this game. They have always had it in their power to disclose themselves, yet they decline to do so. Will the fact that we have disclosed them to ourselves change their thinking? Perhaps in such a scenario, Disclosure will be the active ingredient in creating whatever comes next.

Will knowing that Others are lurking in our own neighborhood create the "oneness of man" that so many have speculated about? Will former adversaries suddenly reconcile? North and South Korea? Israel and the Arabs? India and Pakistan? The United States and its list of terrorists? Multinational corporations and their competitors, to say nothing of the rest of the world?

Probably not, to say the least. Disclosure may, however, focus our attention in new ways that can benefit us and lead to resolution of thorny problems.

A study such as this, which seeks to peer into a volatile future, can never be complete. This is especially so, as it is the first of its kind. Many will disagree with various of our conclusions. We have simply done our best to advance the cause of ending secrecy and beginning Disclosure. Others will follow and draw different conclusions. Only when Disclosure is a reality will we truly know how it will unfold.

The world will change with this knowledge, of that there can be no doubt. Merely contemplating this reality changes a person, but actually seeing it may be almost too much to bear. We shall see.

The only thing we can know for certain is that no one has the right to hold such a deep knowledge from the rest of us, no matter what it is, no matter how it might change us. The policy of denial, the policy of lies, does not propel us forward. It only holds humanity hostage.

We are ready to be told. It is time for truth to turn the page.

Even after that happens, it will take at least a quarter-century before our changed world dynamic becomes something of a routine to live with. Then, finally, we as a species will perhaps embrace the idea that we have company in the universe, that some of these Others are long-term visitors. Of course, by that time, we may be visiting strange new worlds ourselves. We may then become "Others" to other intelligent species, and hide our presence from them as was done to us.

Soon, we shall tell ourselves the truth. The day is coming when we shall look toward the stars and see ourselves looking back.

Vignette #9:

Text Message

✧✦✧

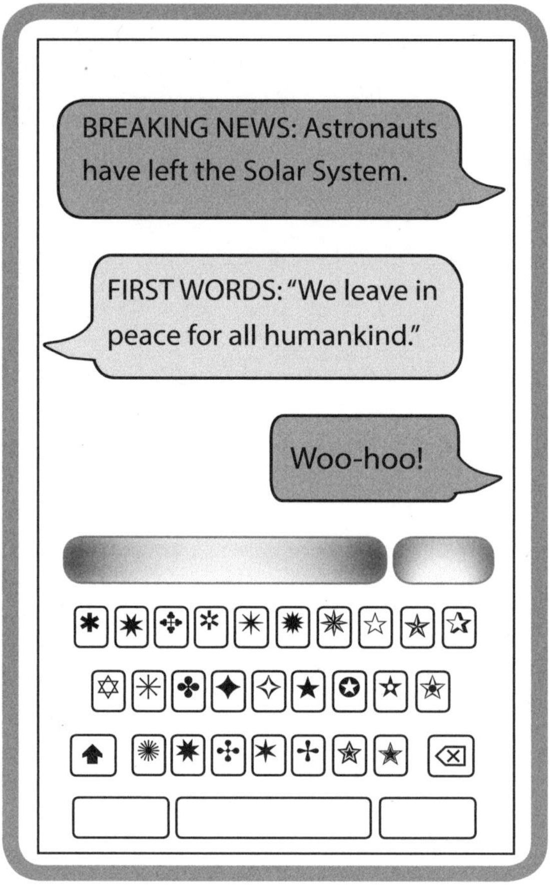
BREAKING NEWS: Astronauts have left the Solar System.
FIRST WORDS: "We leave in peace for all humankind."
Woo-hoo!

✧

Notes

Chapter 2

1. "Proposed Studies on the Implications of Peaceful Space Activities for Human Affairs," a.k.a. "The Brookings Report." Submitted April 18, 1961 to the Committee on Science and Astronautics of the United States House of Representatives.
2. "Air Force Order on 'Saucers' Cited," *New York Times*, February 28, 1960.
3. Carey, Thomas J. and Donald R. Schmitt. *Witness to Roswell.* Revised and Expanded Edition, Career Press, 2009.
4. Rowe, Frankie. Interview with the authors. International Roswell UFO Museum, July 2, 2010.
5. Friedman, Stanton T. *Top Secret/Majic, Operation Majestic-12 and the United States Government's UFO Cover-up*. Marlowe and Company, 1996.
6. See Menzel, Donald H. *Flying Saucers: Myth, Truth, History*. Cambridge: Harvard University Press, 1953; with Lyle G. Boyd. *The World of Flying Saucers: A Scientific Examination of a Major Myth of the Space Age*. Doubleday, 1963; and with Ernest H. Taves. *The UFO Enigma: The Definitive Explanation of the UFO Phenomenon*. Garden City, N.Y.: Doubleday, 1977.
7. Friedman, *Top Secret/Majic*, p. 30–31.

8. Bernstein, Carl. "The CIA and the Media," *Rolling Stone*, October 20, 1977. *www.carlbernstein.com/magazine_cia_and_media.php*. See also Hansen, Terry. *The Missing Times: News Media Complicity in the UFO Cover-up*. Xlibris, 2000.
9. Stonor Saunders, Frances. *The Cultural Cold War: The CIA and the World of Arts and Letters*. The New Press, 2001.
10. Winks, Robin. *Cloak & Gown: Scholars in the Secret War, 1939–1961.* William Morrow, 1987. See also Hulnick, Arthur S. "CIA's Relations with Academia: Symbiosis Not Psychosis" in *International Journal of Intelligence and Counter Intelligence*, V1, N4 1986 , p. 41–50. See also Gibbs, David N. "Academics and Spies: The Silence that Roars." *Los Angeles Times*, 28 January 2001.
11. Klass, Philip J. *UFOs: Identified*. Random House, 1968; *UFOs Explained*. Random House, 1974; *UFOs: The Public Deceived*. Prometheus Books, 1983; *UFO Abductions: A Dangerous Game*. Prometheus Books, 1989; *The Real Roswell Crashed-Saucer Coverup*. Prometheus Books, 1997.
12. Kean, Leslie. *UFOs: Generals, Pilots and Government Officials Go On the Record*. Crown, 2010.
13. Cox, Billy, "Did Cronkite get 'snookered'?" *Herald–Tribune*, July 21, 2009.
14. Saunders, David R. *UFOs? Yes! Where the Condon Committee Went Wrong.* World Pub. Co. 1969. p. 129, 194.
15. Dolan, Richard M. *UFOs and the National Security State: Chronology of a Cover–Up, 1941–1973*. Hampton Roads, 2002. p. 66.
16. A history of these documents, and the debates generated by them, is contained in Dolan, Richard M. *UFOs and the National Security State, Volume Two: The Cover–Up Exposed, 1973–1991.* Keyhole Publishing Co., 2009.
17. *UFOs and Defense: What Should We Prepare For?* An Independent Report on UFOs written by the French Association COMETA. This report details the results of a study by the Institute of Higher Studies for National Defense. This paper originally appeared in a special issue of the magazine *VSD* published in France in July 1999.
18. 1997, U.S. Senate Document 105–2, "Report of the Commission on Protecting and Reducing Government Secrecy."

19. Testimony before the House Appropriations Committee: Fiscal Year 2002 Defense Budget Request As Delivered by Secretary of Defense Donald H. Rumsfeld, Chairman of the Joint Chiefs of Staff General Hugh Shelton,, Rayburn House Office Building, Washington, DC, Monday, July 16, 2001. *www.defense.gov/speeches/speech.aspx?speechid=408*
20. Gilmore, Gerry J., "Zakheim Seeks To Corral, Reconcile 'Lost' Spending," American Forces Press Service, Feb. 20, 2002, *www.defense.gov/news/newsarticle.aspx?id=43927*. See also "Statement of the Honorable Tina W. Jonas, Under Secretary of Defense (Comptroller), Senate Armed Services Committee, Subcommittee on Readiness and Management Support," November 18, 2004, *http://armed–services.senate.gov/statemnt/2004/November/Jonas%20 11–18–04.pdf*
21. Sweetman, Bill. "In Search of the Pentagon's Billion Dollar Hidden Budgets: How the US Keeps Its R&D Spending Under Wraps." *Janes International Defence Reporter*, January 5, 2000.
22. Priest, Dana and Arkin, William M. "Top Secret America. A hidden world, growing beyond control," in 3 Parts. *Washington Post*, July 19–21, 2010. *http://projects.washingtonpost.com/top–secret–america/*
23. Confidential source. Interview with the authors.
24. Confidential source. Interview with the authors.
25. Cameron, Grant. *The Presidential UFO Website*, *http://www.presidentialufo.com/nixon1.htm*
26. Ford, Gerald R. Letter to George A. Filer, 17 March 1998. See *www.presidentialufo.com/gerald–ford/92–the–ford–ufo–letter*
27. Cameron, Grant. "Presidents and Crashed Flying Saucers." *The Presidential UFO Website*. *www.presidentialufo.com/articles–a–papers/192–presidents–and–crashed–flying–saucers*
28. Dolan, *The Cover-Up Exposed,* p. 138.
29. Following this startling statement, Reagan backed away and spoke symbolically. "What could be more alien to the universal aspirations of our peoples than war and the threat of war?"
30. Dolan, *The Cover-Up Exposed,* p. 34–35, 276.
31. Dolan, *The Cover-Up Exposed,* p. 439, 565–568.
32. Hubbell, Webster. *Friends in High Places.* William Morrow & Co, 1997.

33. Cameron, Grant, "Dick Cheney" at *www.presidentialufo.com/george-w-bush/183-dick-cheney*. The questioning of Dick Cheney took place during Cheney's appearance on the Washington D.C. Public Radio Station WAMU on April 11, 2001. Dick Cheney spoke from the White House.
34. The White House. "Searching for ET, But No Evidence Yet," November 4, 2011.
35. "Rothschilds & Rockefellers, Trillionaires of the World," by New World Order (pseud.) Dec 2, 2007, *www.indybay.org/newsitems/2007/12/02/18464823.php*. See also Sir Anthony, James & Diletosso, Jim, "More From The Archives" DVD Presentation, *www.ufocongressstore.com/*
36. Confidential source. Interview with the authors.

Chapter 3

1. Keyhoe, Donald. *The Flying Saucers Are Real.* Fawcett, 1950. p. 63.
2. See, for example, Rux, Bruce. *Hollywood Vs. the Aliens: The Motion Picture Industry's Participation in UFO Disinformation.* Frog, Ltd. Books, 1990.
3. Harrison, Albert, PhD and Kelleher, Colm A., Ph.D., NIDS, "The Day After Contact: Forecasting Reactions to Extraterrestrial Life," 1999. *www.ufoevidence.org/documents/doc853.htm*
4. "Churchill and Eisenhower 'agreed to cover up RAF plane's UFO encounter during WWII', secret files reveal." *Daily Mail* (UK), August 5, 2010. *www.dailymail.co.uk/*
5. See, for instance, W Joseph Campbell. "The Halloween Myth of the War of the Worlds Panic." *BBC* (UK), October 29, 2011. *www.bbc.co.uk/news/magazine/*
6. Jung, Carl. Letter to Major Donald Keyhoe, 1954.
7. Condon, Dr. Edward U. *Scientific Study of Unidentified Flying Objects.* Bantam Books, 1969. p. 407.
8. Zabel, Bryce. "Sixty Years On: The McMinnville UFO Photos." *www.afterdisclosure.com/2010/05/mcminnville-60-years-on.html*
9. Kean, *UFOs On the Record.*
10. Davis, Evan. "The Truth Is Not Out There." *BBC Today*, August 11, 2010. *http://news.bbc.co.uk/today/hi/today/newsid_8901000/8901936.stm.*

11. Corn, David. "Where are all the UFO Photos?" August 20, 2010. *http://www.politicsdaily.com/2010/08/20/where–are–all–the–ufo–photos/*
12. Hough, Andrew. "WikiLeaks: new diplomatic cables contain UFO details, Julian Assange says" *The Telegraph*, December 3, 2010.
13. Mitchell, Edgar. Interview with Lisa Bonnice. *http://ufos.about.com/od/governmentconspiracyufos/a/edgarmitchell.htm*
14. Carey & Schmitt, p. 285–286.
15. Chassin, L. M. Preface to Michel, Aime. *Flying Saucers and the Straight–Line Mystery* Criterion Books, 1958.
16. Hill–Norton, Admiral Lord, interview July 2000 with James Fox. *www.topsecrettestimony.com/*
17. Bourret, Jean–Claude. *La nourvell vague des soucoups volantes.* Paris: editions france–empire, 1975. See also Berliner, Don, et.al. *UFO Briefing Document.* Dell, 2000. p. 174.
18. Benitez, J. J. *La Gaceta del Norte.* Bilbao, Spain, June 27, 1976. See also Benitez, J. J. "Release of Further Official Spanish Documents on UFOs," trans. by Gordon Creighton, *Flying Saucer Review*, March–April 1979.
19. Good, Timothy. *Above Top Secret: The Worldwide UFO Cover-Up.* William Morrow & Co., 1987. p. 430.
20. Hellyer, Paul. Statement made at the Toronto Exopolitical Conference, September 25, 2005.
21. Marquard, Alexander. "Russian Governor Tells Tale of Alien Abduction, President asked to Investigate." ABC News, May 5, 2010.
22. Statement made to authors.
23. Benitez, J. J. "Release of Further Official Spanish Documents on UFOs," trans. by Gordon Creighton, *Flying Saucer Review*, March–April 1979.
24. "UFOs on Air Defense Radars," *Rabochaya Tribuna*, Moscow, 4/19/90. English translation by the U.S. Foreign Broadcast Information Service (FBIS). See also Dolan, *The Cover-Up Exposed,* p. 516–520.

Chapter 4

1. Sanderson, Ivan T. *Uninvited Visitors: A Biologist Looks At UFOs* Cowles Education Corporation, 1967.2. These are Epsilon Eridani,

Tau Ceti, Sigma Draconis, Delta Pavonis, 82 Eridani, Beta Hydri, Zeta Tucanae, Beta Canum Venaticorum (Chara), Gliese 67, Gliese 853, 18 Scorpii, 51 Pegasi.

3. "Many, Perhaps Most, Nearby Sun–Like Stars May Form Rocky Planets." February 17, 2008. *www.spitzer.caltech.edu/Media/releases/ssc2008–05/release.shtml*
4. The TV series, *Dark Skies*, had as a central point that the alien "Hive" expected to reach "Singularity" before or shortly after the Millennium.
5. Zyga, Lisa. "Physicists Calculate Number of Parallel Universes." *PhysOrg*, 16 October 2009. Deutsch, David. *David Deutsch's Many Worlds.* Frontiers, 1998. Tegmark, Max. "Parallel Universes," in *Science and Ultimate Reality: From Quantum to Cosmos, honoring John Wheeler's 90th birthday*. J.D. Barrow, P.C.W. Davies, & C.L. Harper, eds. Cambridge University Press, 2003. Kaku, Michio. *Parallel Worlds: The Science of Alternative Universes and Our Future in the Cosmos*. London: Allen Lane 2004.
6. Keel, John. *UFOs: Operation Trojan Horse.* Manor Books, 1970.
7. Zabel, Bryce. Writer, Co-Producer, Wilshire Court Productions. Its premise was that Majestic-12 used a known alien abductee as bait for an operation that used America's SDI program to shoot down an alien craft ("Operation: Forced Encounter").
8. Greer, Stephen, MD. "Disclosure Project Briefing Document," April 2001.
9. Michaud, Michael. *Contact with Alien Civilizations: Our Hopes and Fears about Encountering Extraterrestrials.* Springer, 2006.
10. Leake, Jonathan. "Don't talk to aliens, warns Stephen Hawking." The Sunday *Times*, April 25, 2010.
11. Dolan, *The Cover-Up Exposed,* p. 181. See also Huneeus, J. Antonio, "A Chilean overview," *MUFON UFO Journal*, 6/86.
12. White, Vince. "A Planetary Prison Break: A Proposal for Empowerment and Freedom." April 28, 2009.
13. Oberth, Hermann. "Flying Saucers Come from a Distant World." *The American Weekly*, October 24, 1954.
14. Leir, Dr. Roger K., DPM. *The Aliens and the Scalpel. Scientific Proof of Extraterrestrial Implants in Humans*. Foreword by Whitley Strieber. New Millennium Library, 1998.

15. Jacobs, David M., Ph.D. *The Threat. The Secret Agenda: What the Aliens Really Want...and How They Plan to Get It.* Simon & Schuster, 1997.
16. Anon. The Black Box. alt.alien.visitors, September 1, 2000
17. "M'Arthur Greets Mayor of Naples." *New York Times*, October 8, 1955. See also "General MacArthur's Thayer Award Speech—Duty, Honor, Country" (1962) *http://www.au.af.mil/au/awc/awcgate/au-24/au24-352mac.htm* and *http://www.snopes.com/quotes/macarthur.asp*. Incidentally, MacArthur's two separate statements are often incorrectly conflated as though he made one definitive statement on the subject, which he never did. MacArthur also never made his most famous alleged statement on the subject, "the nations of the world will have to unite, for the next war will be an interplanetary war."
18. Strieber, Whitley. "The Danger of Disclosure," May 6, 2010. *www.unknowncountry.com/*
19. Harrison, Albert A. PhD. *After Contact: The Human Response to Extraterrestrial Life.* New York, NY: Plenum Press, 1997. p. 237.
20. Hopkins, Budd and Rainey, Carol. *Sight Unseen: Science, UFO Invisibility and Transgenic Beings*. Atria Books, 2003.
21. Incidentally, it appears that the majority of remote viewers for the intelligence community had some encounter or another with what appeared to be extraterrestrials, many of whom seemed to be aware that they were being "viewed."
22. Swann, Ingo. *Penetration: The Question of Extraterrestrial and Human Telepathy.* Ingo Swann Books, 1998.
23. Feschino, Frank. *Shoot them Down!* Lulu Enterprises, 2007.
24. "JASSM Cruise Missile of the Future," *Future Weapon Technology*, Feb. 29, 2008.
25. Pae, Peter. "Northrop Advance Brings Era Of The Laser Gun Closer." *Los Angeles Times*, March 19, 2009. See also Rincon, Paul. "Record power for military laser," *BBC News*, 22 February 2007.
26. Jean, Grace V. "Navy Aiming for Laser Weapons at Sea," August 2010. *www.nationaldefensemagazine.org/archive/2010/August/Pages/NavyAimingforLaserWeaponsatSea.aspx*
27. Dolan, *The Cover–Up Exposed,* p. 457–461.
28. Jeff Challender's website can be accessed at *http://keyholepublishing.com/projectprove/index-2.html*

29. Regehr, Ronald. *How to Build a $100 Million UFO Detector.* Self published, 1998.
30. Guo Ji–wei, Xue–sen Yang. "Ultramicro, nonlethal, and reversible: looking ahead to military biotechnology." *Military Review*, July–August, 2005.

Chapter 5

1. Jung, Carl. *Flying Saucer Review.* Vol. 1, No. 2, 1955.
2. Keyhoe, Donald. *The Flying Saucers are Real.* Fawcett, 1950, p. 180.
3. Admiral Lord Hill–Norton, Interview with James Fox, July 2000. *www.topsecrettestimony.com/*
4. Cooper, Gordon. Interview with J. L. Ferrando, in "Major Gordon Cooper, USA Astronaut, and UFOs." *www.ufoevidence.org/news/article157.htm*
5. Bassett, Stephen. September 29, 2007. *www.bibliotecapleyades.net/exopolitica/esp_exopolitics_ZZZZZ.htm*
6. Schiff, Steven. Remarks on CBS radio's *The Gil Gross Show*, February 1994. *www.ufoinfo.com/filer/1998/ff9847.shtml*
7. Confidential source, discussion with the authors.
8. Yergin, Daniel. *The Prize: The Epic Quest for Oil, Money, and Power.* Free Press; New edition 2008. p. 770.
9. Price Waterhouse Coopers. "The Economic Impacts of the Oil and Natural Gas Industry on the U.S. Economy: Employment, Labor Income And Value Added." Prepared for the American Petroleum Institute, September 8, 2009. The percentages are comparable in other nations around the world.
10. *Aviation Report*, 7 September 1954. *Aviation Report*, 12 October 1954. *Aviation Report*, 9 December 1955. "Electro-gravitics Systems: An examination of electrostatic motion, dynamic counterbary and barycentric control" in *Aviation Studies* (International) Ltd. 1956. "The Gravitics Situation," Gravity Rand Ltd. 1956. The latter two studies are included in Valone, Thomas, Ph.D. (ed.). *Electrogravitic Systems: Reports on a New Propulsion Methology.* Integrity Research Institute, Washington, DC 20005.
11. Porter, Hilary. "Fly at Your Own Risk." *www.beamsinvestigations.org/hilary–porter.html*
12. "Apollo 14 astronaut claims aliens have made contact—but it has been covered up for 60 years." *Daily Mail*, July 24, 2008.

13. "Aliens Are Monitoring Our Nukes, Worry Ex-Air Force Officers." FoxNews.com, September 23, 2010. "Former Air Force officers discuss UFO sightings." King, Ledyard, *Air Force Times* (Gannett), September 27, 2010. Kelly, John. "UFO visits to nuclear facilities? Hmmmm." *Washington Post*, September 27, 2010. For CNN's TV coverage of September 27, 2010, see "Clips Of Military Men Talking About UFO Encounters At National Press Club Today," Youtube.com.
14. Beaton, Jessica. CNNGo.com, "UFO Shuts Down Hangzhou Airport," *www.cnngo.com/shanghai/life/ufo–shuts–down–hangzhou–airport–904924#ixzz0tPanKsnv*
15. Bernstein, Carl. "The CIA and the Media: How Americas Most Powerful News Media Worked Hand in Glove with the Central Intelligence Agency and Why the Church Committee Covered It Up," *Rolling Stone*, October 20, 1977. For a good start on contemporary intelligence community news manipulation, see the excellent website of Mario Profaca at *http://mprofaca.cro.net/*.

Chapter 6

1. Sallan, Bruce. *A Dad's Point of View. www.brucesallan.com*
2. Baiata, Maurizio. "Colonel claims he briefed Bobby Kennedy on UFOs." *Open Minds*, June 24, 2010. *www.openminds.tv/col–briefed–kennedy–on–ufos/*
3. Rush, Chris. *www.chrisrushcomedy.com/*

Chapter 7

1. Russell, Bertrand. *Religion and Science.* Home University Library, 1935.
2. Davies, Paul. *Are We Alone?* London: Penguin, 1995.
3. Alexander, Victoria. "Extraterrestrial Life and Religion: The Alexander UFO Religious Crisis Survey." In *UFO Religions*, edited by James R. Lewis. Prometheus Books, 2003. p. 359–370.
4. "UFOs & Extraterrestrial Life: Americans' Beliefs and Personal Experiences," prepared for the Sci Fi Channel by Roper Poll, 2002. *www.scifi.com/ufo/roper/03.html*
5. Peters, Ted and Froehlig, Julie. *The Peters ETI Religious Crisis Survey*. Pacific Lutheran Theological Seminary and the Center for Theology and the Natural Science at the Graduate Theological Union. Berkeley, CA, 2010.

6. Harris, Paola Leopizzi. *Connecting the Dots…Making Sense of the UFO Phenomenon.* Wild Flower Press, 2003. p. 42–47.
7. Consolmagno, Guy. *Intelligent Life in the Universe? Catholic belief and the search for extraterrestrial intelligent life.* Catholic Truth Society, 2005.
8. "Vatican: It's OK for Catholics to Believe in Aliens." Fox News, Tuesday, May 13, 2008. *www.foxnews.com/story/0,2933,355400,00.html*
9. Huppke, Rex W. "Enthusiasts say 'Amen' as Vatican allows alien belief." *Chicago Tribune*, May 16, 2008. *http://articles.chicagotribune.com/2008-05-16/news/0805151082_1_vatican-observatory-alien-intelligent-life*
10. Genesis, 6:1
11. Heiser, Dr. Michael. "Frequently Asked Questions," *www.michaelsheiser.com/FAQ.htm#q2*
12. For more on this idea, see *www.alienresistance.org/*
13. Luck, Coleman. Private correspondence with the authors, August 3, 2010.
14. Eph. 6:12
15. Eph. 2:2
16. 2 Thes 2:9
17. Matthew 24:24
18. "They are spirits of demons performing miraculous signs, and they go out to the kings of the whole world, to gather them for the battle on the great day of God Almighty." Revelation 16:14 New International Version.
19. *Book of Mormon.* Book of Moses, Chapter 1, v. 33–40.
20. For a good statement of this aspect of the Mormon belief, see Steimle, Joshua. "Do Mormons believe they get their own planet after they die?" *www.mormondna.org/mormon-beliefs/mormons-planet-die.html*
21. *Holy Qu'ran*, 9th U.S. Edition. Tahrike Tarsile Qu'ran, Inc. Elmhurst, NY, 2002. *Encyclopaedia of Islam*. Ahmed, Mufti M. Mukarram. Anmol Publications Pvt., Ltd., New Delhi, 2005. p. 406.
22. *Holy Qu'ran.* Ash-Shura 42:29, in Ahmad, Mirza Tahir, *Revelation, Rationality, Knowledge & Truth*. Islam International Publications. Illustrated edition, 1998.

23. Yusuf, Ali, Abdullah. *The Qu'ran: Text, Translation and Commentary.* Ad-Dar Al-`Arabiah, Beirut, 1938. p. 1314.
24. "Security, and Prosperity Committee on Science, Committee on Scientific Communication and National Security, National Research Council." *Beyond 'Fortress America': National Security Controls on Science and Technology in a Globalized World.* National Academies Press, 2009. Another study published in 2009 estimates that possibly half—and possibly more than half of all U.S. government documents are classified. Which means that, for an American citizen, half of his or her government's history is an official secret. This situation is likely to be similar in many other countries. See Paglen, Trevor. *Blank Spots on the Map: The Dark Geography of the Pentagon's Secret World.* Dutton Adult, 2009.
25. The most influential book regarding the Mars anomaly thesis is Hoagland, Richard C. *The Monuments of Mars: A City on the Edge of Forever.* 5th Edition. Foreword by Richard Grossinger. Frog Books, 2002.
26. Friedman, Stanton. "An Open Letter to Dr. Carl Sagan." *MUFON UFO Journal*, May 1989.
27. Rees, Lord Martin. "Life and the Cosmos." Lecture delivered at the University of Melbourne, Australia, March 30, 2010. *http://live.unimelb.edu.au/episode/derek–denton–lecture–life–and–cosmos–lord–reed–ludlow*
28. Bryner, Jeanna. What Drives Evolution? 16 August 2007. *www.livescience.com/strangenews/070816_gm_evolution.html*
29. "The Bloom Box: An Energy Breakthrough?" *CBS News*, Feb. 18, 2010. *www.cbsnews.com/stories/2010/02/18/60minutes/main6221135.shtml*
30. Although this may soon change. See Cowel, Alan. "Solar–Powered Plane Flies for 26 Hours." *New York Times*, July 8, 2010. *www.nytimes.com/2010/07/09/world/europe/09plane.html*
31. Macdonald, Gregor. The Myth of Energy Breakthroughs, March 9, 2010. *http://gregor.us/nuclear/the–myth–of–energy–breakthroughs/*
32. Varchaver, Nicholas. "Is nanotech ready for its close–up?" *Fortune Magazine*, May 17, 2004. *http://money.cnn.com/magazines/fortune/fortune_archive/2004/05/17/369606/index.htm*

33. "What is Nanotechnology?" Center for Responsible Nanotechnology. *www.crnano.org/whatis.htm*
34. Collins, Dr. Francis. "Why this scientist believes in God." *CNN*, April 6, 2007.

Chapter 8

1. Greer, Steven, *www.disclosureproject.org/congress.shtml*
2. See *www.exopoliticsinstitute.org/*
3. The White House. November 4, 2011. "Searching for ET, But No Evidence Yet."
4. See the links at the website of Exopolitics Denmark, one of the most active exopolitical groups. *www.exopolitics.dk/*
5. Bassett, Stephen. "PRG Mission Statement." *www.paradigmresearchgroup.org/mission.html*
6. Richard Sauder's three books dealing with these themes are *Hidden in Plain Sight: Beyond the X–Files.* Keyhole Publishing Co., 2010; *Underwater and Underground Bases.* Adventures Unlimited Press, 2001; and *Underground Bases and Tunnels: What is the Government Trying to Hide?* Adventures Unlimited Press, 1995.
7. The U.S. military has used small nuclear reactors in its submarines for years, and has expressed an interest in obtaining portable and "readily deployable" nuclear reactors. See Page, Lewis. "Nuclear synthi–jetfuel plants wanted for US Afghan bases." *Register-UK,* March 31, 2010.
8. Confidential source to the authors. [Note from the authors: much more is known about this story, which must be withheld due to the sensitive position of the source.]
9. Confidential source, interview with the authors.
10. Confidential source, interview with the authors.
11. Podesta, John. "Statement at the National Press Club," November 14, 2007. *www.youtube.com/watch?v=B_2YcFQbijg*
12. Australia's laws have long been the most restrictive, although enforcement has been spotty.
13. Risen, James and Lichtblau, Eric. "Bush Lets U.S. Spy on Callers Without Courts." *New York Times*, December 16, 2005. See also Lichtblau, Eric. "The Education of a 9/11 Reporter. The inside drama behind the Times' warrantless wiretapping story." *Slate*, March 26, 2008.

Glossary

abduction The forcible carrying away of a person.

academicians People who follow or promote traditional rules of art, science, or philosophy; a member of a society for literature, art, or science.

ad-hoc Made or done without purpose or planning.

agnostic A person who does not have a belief either for or against the existence of a supreme being.

altruism Helping others unselfishly.

amnesty Pardon or forgiveness for a crime.

anathema A person or thing that is strongly disliked.

antediluvian Very old-fashioned; old.

clandestine Something done in secret.

collateral damage Injury or death to uninvolved people or their property during a fight, such as military action.

confabulation An informal discussion.

conspiracy A secret plan by a group of people.

crackpot A strange or crazy person.

cryptographer A specialist in deciphering and enciphering messages.

debunk To prove the falsehood of a belief or theory.

declassification Making previously secret information available to the public.

decrypted Decoded.

Deep Throat An anonymous source of secret information, originally the code name used for the source in the Watergate scandal.

edict An official order given by a person in authority.

electrogravitics A theoretical science, not endorsed by most in the scientific community, that tries to find a connection between gravity and electricity.

en masse A French term meaning as a whole.

erstwhile Past; formerly.

Eureka An expression of excitement after a discovery, first said to be used by Archimedes after he discovered a method for determining the purity of gold.

exobiologists Biologists who study and speculate about life outside earth and the effects of extraterrestrial environments on living things.

extratemporals Time-traveling humans.

foo fighters A term used by Allied pilots during World War II to describe strange phenomena, including UFOs, in the skies over Europe and the Pacific.

Full Monty A British slang phrase meaning showing or telling everything; a 1997 British film where a group of men perform without clothing.

gendarmerie A group of French police officers

hubris A foolishly high level of pride or confidence.

Mach A scale that measures the ratio of the speed of an object relative to the speed of sound, named for physicist Ernst Mach.

nomenclature The systematic naming or process of designation for something.

obfuscate To confuse.

Prime Directive A guiding principle of behavior based on the fictional Star Trek universe that prohibits Starfleet personnel from interfering with the natural development of alien civilizations.

propagandist False or exaggerated statements spread to help a political cause or agenda.

prosaic Dull or unimaginative.

raison d'etre A French term meaning reason for being.

scalar A type of radio wave that creates a Longitudinal Wave Interference. If two Scalar Waves meet, the result is a miniature atomic explosion without the harmful radiation.

sea change A major change.

smear An untrue story about a person told with the intent to injure that person's reputation.

spooks Undercover agents; spies.

subpoenaed Given a written order that commands the recipient to appear in court.

ufology The study of UFO phenomenon.

For More Information

Fund for UFO Research (FUFOR)
P.O. Box 7501
Alexandria, VA 22307
fufor@ufoscience.org
Website: www.ufoscience.org
FUFOR is a conservative site that provides resources for people doing serious research into the UFO phenomena.

J. Allen Hynek Center for UFO Studies (CUFOS)
P.O. Box 31335
Chicago, IL 60631
773-271-3611
Website: www.cufos.org
Hynek, a former chairman of the astronomy department at Northwestern University and a consultant on Project Blue Book, founded this group to research and do field investigations of UFO phenomena.

Mutual UFO Network (MUFON)
3822 Campus Drive Suite 201
Newport Beach, CA 92660

949-476-8366

Website: www.mufon.com

This is the largest civilian UFO organization, with chapters in every U.S. state. Its mission is purely investigative, to collect and analyze UFO data with the goal of understanding the UFO phenomenon.

National UFO Reporting Center (NUFORC)

P.O. Box 700

Davenport, WA 99122

director@ufocenter.com

Website: www.nuforc.org

A one-man operation, NUFORC allows people to report UFO sightings via phone or internet and has been in operation since 1974.

The Center for the Study of Extraterrestrial Intelligence (CSETI)

P.O. Box 265

Crozet, VA 22932-0265

773-271-3611

Website: www.ufoinfo.com

This international group of scientists, academics, and investigators collect and examine UFO phenomenon. They maintain one of the world's largest collections of original UFO data.

UFO*BC

5821 122 Street

Surrey, B.C.

V3X 3L5 Canada

contactus@ufobc.ca

Website: www.ufobc.ca

A non-profit society in British Columbia, Canada, UFO*BC's goal is to gather and investigate UFO sightings in British Columbia and the Yukon. They also gather data on other unexplained phenomena such as ghosts and sasquatch.

For Further Reading

Birnes, William J. *The Everything UFO Book: An Investigation of Sightings, Cover-Ups, and the Quest for Extraterrestrial Life*. Avon, MA: Adams Media, 2012.

Carey, Thomas, and Donald Schmitt. *Inside the Real Area 51: The Secret History of Wright Patterson*. Pompton Plains, NJ: New Page Books, 2013.

Friedman, Stanton T. *UFOs: Real or Imagined?* New York, NY: Rosen Publishing, 2012.

Friedman, Stanton T., and Kathleen Marden. *Captured! The Betty and Barney Hill UFO Experience: The True Story of the World's First Documented Alien Abduction.* Pompton Plains, NJ: New Page Books, 2007.

Good, Timothy. *Earth: An Alien Enterprise: The Shocking Truth Behind the Greatest Cover-Up in Human History*. London: Pegasus Books, 2013.

Halls, Kelly Milner. *Alien Investigation: Searching for the Truth About UFOs and Aliens*. Minneapolis, MN: Millbrook Press, 2012.

Hawkins, John. *Aliens and UFOs*. New York, NY: Rosen Publishing, 2012.

Kean, Leslie. *UFOs: Generals, Pilots, and Government Officials Go on the Record*. New York, NY: Three Rivers Press, 2011.

Pye, Michael, and Kirsten Dalley. *Encounters With UFOs and Extraterrestrial Life*. New York, NY: Rosen Publishing, 2013.

Index

About the Authors

Bryce Zabel has created five primetime network series and worked on a dozen TV writing staffs. A winner of the Writers Guild of America screenwriting award, he has written for nearly all major networks and studios and collaborated with producers like Steven Spielberg. His credits range from TV's *Lois and Clark* and *Dark Skies* to box-office successes *Atlantis* and *Mortal Kombat*. Zabel was the first writer elected chairman/CEO of the Academy of Television Arts & Sciences since Rod Serling. He also reported news as an on-air CNN correspondent. Zabel lives in Los Angeles, California.

Richard M. Dolan is the author of the ground-breaking historical series, *UFOs and the National Security State*, acclaimed as the finest history series of the UFO phenomenon available in any language on the subject of military encounters and government secrecy. Dolan has also published articles, spoken at conferences around the world, and appeared on numerous TV specials as an on-air expert. Prior to his interest in UFOs, Dolan was a finalist for a Rhodes Scholarship, studying U.S. Cold War strategy, Soviet history and culture, and international diplomacy. Dolan lives in Rochester, New York.